O9-BUA-237

Crimes *of* Justice

Also by David C. Anderson

Children of Special Value: Interracial Adoption in America

CRIMES
of
JUSTICE

IMPROVING THE POLICE,
THE COURTS, THE PRISONS

David C. Anderson

𝕿𝖎𝖒𝖊𝖘 BOOKS

Grateful acknowledgment is made to the following for
permission to reprint previously published material:
Brooklyn Paper Publications, Inc.: Excerpts from "Police"
column in *The Park Slope Paper*, week of November 30 to
December 6, 1985 © Brooklyn Paper Publications Inc. Reprinted by permission.
Straight Arrow Publishers, Inc.: Excerpts from "Obit" by Steve
Gettinger from *Rolling Stone*, February 2, 1984. All rights
reserved. Reprinted by permission.

Library of Congress Cataloging-in-Publication Data
Anderson, David C.
Crimes of justice.
Bibliography: p.
Includes index.
1. Criminal justice, Administration of—United States.
I. Title.
HV9950.A53   1988   364'.973   87-40581
ISBN 0-8129-1607-7

Manufactured in the United States of America
9 8 7 6 5 4 3 2
First Edition
Book Design: Jessica Shatan

This book is dedicated to
my mother, Virginia,
and the memory of
my father, Joseph.

ACKNOWLEDGMENTS

Numerous people deserve thanks: Max Frankel and Jack Rosenthal of *The New York Times* consistently encouraged my interest in criminal justice while helping me to grow as a journalist. Peter Matson, my agent, and Jonathan Segal, my editor at Times Books, offered unwavering enthusiasm. Andrew von Hirsch, Herbert Sturz, Herman Goldstein, Michael Serrill, and Michael Smith found time to read portions of the manuscript and made valuable suggestions. Steve MacDonald offered long-term friendship, advice, and, not least, the use of a fine cast-off computer. Mary, Michael, Sarah, and Thomas Anderson tolerated my sustained distraction with unexpected understanding. Betsy Burke Gilmore contributed more to the making of this book than she may ever know.

Crimes *of* Justice

1

A HARD QUESTION *to* LOVE

HOMICIDE ON THIRD AVE

A 25-year-old Park Slope man was shot dead last Thursday at about 7 p.m. while working in an establishment on Fifth Street and Third Avenue, reported detectives of the 78th Precinct.

According to detectives, the deceased was identified as Peter Masciotta of Fifth Avenue. He was allegedly shot by a .32 caliber pistol, police said. The motive is unknown.

Police said they will most likely rule out a robbery

motive, but they would not elaborate. Suspects are being sought.

CAUGHT

At 3 a.m. Monday, November 18, 78th Precinct police officers Louis Savelli and James Tierney arrested two 21-year-old men from Far Rockaway who were in the midst of burglarizing an apartment building on Sixth Avenue between Fifth and Sixth Streets.

The cops spotted the thieves while driving by the residence. They arrested them without incident and found them in possession of a purse, watch, stereo, calculator, tape player, and a VCR.

PURSE RECOVERED

The 78th Precinct reported that an unidentified man recovered a 36-year-old Park Slope woman's purse after she fell victim to a purse snatching at 7:45 a.m. November 15.

The woman was walking up Garfield Place toward Eighth Avenue when an unidentified man grabbed her purse and fled toward Prospect Park. The thief was pursued by a passerby, who recovered the purse on Prospect Park West and returned it to the victim with its contents intact.

CHAIN SNATCHED

At 7:45 p.m. on November 17, a 21-year-old Park Slope man fell victim to a chain snatching in the Fourth Avenue and Ninth Street subway station.

Two men in their late teens, both over six feet tall and weighing approximately 160 pounds, approached the victim with a big stick while he was waiting for a train, police said. They snatched the victim's chain and ran off to parts unknown.

CHOKED

A 31-year-old man was arrested on November 19 at 8:30 a.m. after he choked a security guard who tried to arrest him for shoplifting at the Fifth Avenue Key Food store.

The store's manager summoned 78th Precinct police after he observed the security guard being choked in the Key Food parking lot. The man was arrested on robbery and assault charges.

ROBBED IN SCHOOL

On November 18 at 8:20 a.m. a 15-year-old student was robbed in the Slope's John Jay High School.

The student told police that while walking down a school hallway a five-foot-ten-inch youth, approximately 17 years old, ripped two chains off his neck and punched him in the eye. The chains were valued at $50.

SUPER ROBBED

At 10:15 p.m. on November 17 the superintendent of a building on Eighth Avenue between President and Carroll streets was robbed after he discovered a man breaking into the money holders of the washers and dryers in the building's basement.

The super told police that a six-foot-two-inch man, approximately 180 pounds and 30 years old, turned on him after being discovered breaking into the machines. The man was carrying what the super believed was a fake gun, but the victim complied with the thief and gave him all of his money, which amounted to $28.

CHILD'S COAT TAKEN

At 12:20 p.m. on November 15 a 12-year-old Park Slope girl was robbed of her sheepskin coat on the corner of Fifth Avenue and Seventh Street.

Police said the girl was approached by three other girls, all between 16 and 17 years old, who demanded that she give them her coat or else they would beat her up. The girl complied, and the thieves fled toward Sixth Avenue.

—"Police" column in THE PARK SLOPE
PAPER, *a neighborhood weekly, for the*
week of November 30 to December 6, 1985

*T*he turn-of-the-century developers who created Park
Slope, a neighborhood of Victorian-style brownstones along
the western edge of Prospect Park in Brooklyn, were attempting to reproduce Manhattan elegance in New York
City's bedroom borough. For much of the twentieth century, however, Park Slope was self-consciously, if not
proudly, blue-collar. By the 1940s, its main business street,
Seventh Avenue, was home to plumbers and roofers, dry
cleaners and shoe repairmen. Bars were places where Irish
and Italian workers from the docks, down the hill to the
west, or the Brooklyn Navy Yard, an easy bus or subway
ride to the north, sipped gin or Rheingold, the local brew,
after work. Then they went home to the brownstones,
where parquet had been covered over with linoleum and
the fine detail work of ornamental woodworkers, plasterers,
and tilesetters had been blurred or obliterated by coat upon
coat of paint.

But jobs on the docks and in the Navy Yard began
disappearing in the fifties. As children of the Irish and
Italian workers grew up, they began to move away, to
other parts of the city or to Long Island, Westchester, and
New Jersey. A community of the lower middle class gave
way to welfare families and the working poor. Park Slope
declined, then hit bottom.

In the mid-sixties, Park Slope suddenly became the beneficiary of cultural revolution. Among young New Yorkers, it became fashionable to disparage a move to the suburbs as an act of betrayal. Escalating housing prices in Westchester and Long Island reinforced the idealism. Dozens, then hundreds of young families discovered Park Slope. They began buying up the old brownstones, vowing to restore the character and grace their builders had envisioned so many years ago, and to reestablish a stable family neighborhood. They spoke of themselves as pioneers, committing their lives to opening a sort of social frontier. But their pioneering also turned out to be a wonderfully lucrative investment.

Park Slope was only twenty minutes from Wall Street and half an hour from midtown Manhattan via several subway lines. A Victorian house on a quiet, leafy street, its gas lamp glowing a soft welcome beside the stoop on a summer night, its lovingly restored interior bearing witness to the good taste and commitment of its occupants, perhaps even a steak grilling fragrantly over charcoal in the garden out back—this was by many measures a better place to live than some sterile suburb. The meadows, lake, and woods of Prospect Park, weedy and unkempt as they had become, still could comfort oppressed urban souls in the ways the park's renowned designers, Frederick Law Olmsted and Calvert Vaux, had intended. Park Slope was even blessed with a decent elementary school.

So many young New Yorkers decided to move to Park Slope in the sixties and seventies that it became a national symbol of gentrification. As a result, the urban pioneers made millions. In the early seventies, one might purchase a house for $30,000 and invest another $30,000 in the renovation. Today it could sell for $500,000 or more. By the 1980s, with most brownstones renovated years before, real estate developers were buying up old warehouses, factories, and hospitals—anything remotely habitable—in order to turn them into co-ops and condominiums.

Seventh Avenue, meanwhile, had become a street of boutiques and galleries, a place to buy coffees from all over the world, fine pottery, running shoes, exotic cheeses. Residents still gathered in bars after work, but they were young stockbrokers and lawyers back from jobs in Manhattan, they shunned gin for white wine, and the beers they sipped were imported.

In the spring of 1969, my wife and I and our baby daughter became a part of this renaissance of real estate, which would become the backdrop for our young adult years of marriage and parenthood. In time, as our daughter and her three siblings—city kids, for better and worse— began to approach young adulthood themselves, we, too, could sit down at the kitchen table and figure, on a napkin or the back of a Con Edison bill, that we were rich.

The value of our house had appreciated so greatly in the years we had been building a life in Park Slope that our capital gain exceeded all the salary we had earned in eighteen years of going to work.

This prosperity, however, came at an unusual price,

over and above the investment risk and renovation work. It was not a price one thought about all that much or figured into the calculations of capital gain and net worth. But it was still very real. To survive in the Slope long enough to prosper, one had to learn to live with an aggravating level of crime and fear.

The crime and fear in Park Slope were hardly as great as in some other parts of the city. Yet the risks of burglary, armed robbery, auto theft, and even rape and murder were high enough to force changes in a person's habits. It was an annoying preoccupation that never went away—to escape it, one had to leave Park Slope. And if one thought about it long enough, the preoccupation turned to outrage.

———

My wife liked the idea of listening to music while she drove to work, so for Christmas one year I bought her a stereo radio and tape deck for her Volkswagen Rabbit. It sounded great and looked high-tech. My wife was thrilled— until she began to think about the temptation the stereo would present to the thieves who every night worked their way up and down the lines of cars parked along the streets of Park Slope. For a while, we halfheartedly tried to hide or disguise the radio with plastic bags or other objects. But we both realized that it was only a matter of time.

Time was up in February. Emerging from the house on a sparkling winter morning, I found the Rabbit's right front vent window shattered. It was especially upsetting because the car was parked right in front of our house, though the thief couldn't have known that it was. He, or she, was a clumsy amateur who had demolished most of the dashboard in order to remove the stereo. The more accomplished thieves, the police observed as they took our report, know how to steal a radio with surgical precision.

The heavy damage justified a comforting insurance payment. When the dashboard was repaired, however, my wife instructed the garage to install as cheap and ugly-looking a used radio as it could find. Within weeks the replacement radio's reception deteriorated to the point that it was only marginally listenable. She did not bother to get it fixed.

Exhausted from work one steaming summer evening, I nodded and dozed on the subway. Jerked awake at a stop, I sensed that I was no longer anonymous. Across the car, four pairs of eyes bored in on me with predatory determination. The oldest boy couldn't have been more than fifteen; the youngest was about ten. Their cold focus made clear their intent. My nodding had marked me as drunk, sick, or otherwise vulnerable.

The train rolled on. The eyes never wavered. I was awake now, but unsure what to do. Returning their stare might only encourage whatever they intended. Yet avoiding it seemed like a form of surrender.

At Grand Army Plaza, I rose to get off the train. The four rose and followed me out. As I walked down the platform, they surrounded me, laughing to each other, cursing my age and whiteness. They stuck with me up the steps and past the token booth, then suddenly spread out. Two headed for the exits to the street, while two hung behind. Momentarily relieved, I approached my stairway. Turning into it, I suddenly was face-to-face with the fifteen-year-old. One of the others fell in behind me. For a moment we stared at each other, the snake and the rat. As I started up the steps, he extended an arm to block my way.

What seized me then was either cowardice or good sense. "No way!" I yelled, and turned back to the token booth, pushing aside the younger boy behind me. At the booth I demanded that the clerks call the police. Other passengers stopped and stared. The four, having lost any advantage, melted away up the station's stairs. As the crowd from the next train passed through, I joined a group and made my exit. On the street I could see my stalkers standing together, half a block away. As I passed, they smirked at me, making clear that they would be back.

───

We were pleased when my oldest daughter was admitted to one of the better magnet high schools in Brooklyn. But she was not pleased at having to board a subway train by 6:30 each morning in order to make her first class at 8:00 in distant Coney Island. Some days, I would get up early and walk her to the station, treating her to a warm bagel from a shop along the way. But as winter came, the mornings grew darker and colder. It was my privilege as a parent to sleep in.

Or so I thought. Arriving home one night, I sensed the tension in the kitchen. Dinner proceeded quietly. Afterward my wife told me the story. Going to school in the dark that morning, our daughter had been surrounded by a group of older boys. One produced a knife and held it to her throat. They demanded that she go with them. Petrified, she neither struggled nor screamed. But before they could take her away, a man dressed for business and headed for the subway called out to her.

"Hi! How are you?" he said.

My daughter had never seen him before. She said nothing. Her abductors, however, were suddenly nervous.

"You know each other?" asked the knife wielder, lowering his weapon.

"We're neighbors," called the man cheerfully. As all eyes shifted to my daughter, she nodded.

That ended it. The boys dashed away. My daughter, shaken, accepted the anonymous Samaritan's offer to walk her the rest of the way to the train.

No Samaritan was on hand to help my wife the night she found herself surrounded by a similar group while walking to the bus stop from her nursing job at a hospital in nearby Fort Greene. They too had a knife, but were not interested in abduction. The blade they flashed expertly severed the strap on her purse. They tore it from her shoulder, knocked her to the ground, then ran off. I received the call at work and headed for home. She seemed well recovered by the time I arrived, my oldest son having comforted her manfully enough. Fortunately, there was little actual loss. The fall had bruised her only slightly, and the purse had contained little of practical value—for some reason before leaving the hospital she had transferred her wallet and keys to her coat pocket. It wasn't until a few days later that we realized the purse had contained some gold earrings that had been a cherished present. But their value was uncertain. When I talked of the police, my wife implored me not to call them. The last thing she needed was to relive the event. With so little to claim for insurance, I did not insist.

We should consider ourselves lucky, I suppose, that these were our only real brushes with crime. Our victimizations with crime were better material for dinner-party conversation than devastating drama. Yet the acceptable losses and the near misses were unnerving, especially since they occurred in such a malevolent context. Greater violence, or the potential for it, pervaded the neighborhood. Each week a community newspaper carried a police-blotter summary that made clear how commonly our neighbors were being held up at gunpoint, losing money, watches, gold chains, and other jewelry to teenage muggers, having their apartments burglarized and their cars stolen. For weeks one year the neighborhood was titillated by reports of the "green sneakers rapist," so called for the distinctive footwear that began recurring in successive victim's descriptions.

Just four doors down from our house, an intruder stran-
gled to death an elderly woman who had made the mistake
of staying at home in the morning, when burglars were
most active. At the local public high school, a disaster
compared with the fine elementary school (and therefore
routinely cursed by middle-class parents saddled with hefty
private-school tuition payments), idleness and crime had
long ago helped to stamp out any possibility of education.
Deans and police shaking down the student body harvested
drugs, knives, handguns, once even a sawed-off shotgun.
It was upsetting, but not surprising, to hear how a tenth-
grader named Charles Guica died in the schoolyard. The
fight was apparently over drugs. Charles was said to have
produced an ice pick, the other youngster a gun. Shots
were fired, and Charles ran toward the school, collapsed,
and died. A crowd of students chased the gunman up the
street until he jumped into a white Lincoln Continental
and sped off.

Why did we continue to live in such a place?

To an extent we did so simply because we still were
able to cope. The level of crime in Park Slope had not
risen so high as to banish all optimism. Bright streetlights
offered some measure of protection against muggers and
purse snatchers. Break-ins could be foiled with heavy locks
and window gates. And despite our stereo experience, there
was no reason not to enjoy music in the car. All one needed
to do was to buy the kind of receiver/tape deck that slips
in and out of a drawer in the dashboard. On parking, one
removes it and locks it in the trunk or carries it home.

Coping with crime was a way of defending our commitment to the city. As the joke says, a conservative is a liberal who has been mugged. Though we came to know and fear mugging, we balked at relinquishing our hold on liberalism, or on Park Slope. Beyond our rapidly increasing capital gains, there was much to love in the neighborhood and in the rest of Brooklyn. For the sake of it, we also coped with the decaying school and transit systems. Crime was another factor in the equation, tolerable so long as it did not seem too unbalancing.

As time went on, however, it was hard to escape the feeling that such tolerance was actually a cop-out, a way of denying the crime problem rather than confronting it. What about the places in the city where coping was not so possible? What about the neighborhoods where whole streets were taken over by drug dealers, so that anyone not involved in the trade felt real—and reasonable—terror when venturing out of the house? What about the places where teenaged gangs had seized effective power over whole communities? Or those where prostitutes and their customers not only made their deals but consummated them in the open, on the stoops or in the doorways of decent folks, while children watched? While none of those things went on in the Slope, they were going on constantly in neighborhoods uncomfortably close by.

Didn't such an evident failure of crime control reflect a breakdown of the social contract far more basic than any involved with the transit system, or even the schools? Didn't it demand a clearer, more forthright response than just coping?

These questions zoomed into painful focus on December 22, 1984, when a white man named Bernhard Goetz pulled a gun and shot down four young blacks he feared were about to rob him on a subway train. The shooting was not so surprising as the popular outpouring of congratulation and support for it. For a time in New York, to ask questions about the intent of the four who had approached Goetz, the degree to which they had threatened, the possibility that the situation might have been handled without gunplay—to ask the questions, in other words, that a society based on law would be obliged to ask—was to sound like a wimp. Hearing the story produced a rush of gratification in anyone who had felt threatened on the subway, had a daughter menaced, a wife mugged, a car stereo stolen. Goetz had realized the fantasies of all who ever wanted to fight back, and there were millions of us. While we tried to cope, he went ahead and pulled the trigger. For once, the presumed predators turned out to be the victims. In the grip of such satisfying real-life theater, who could bother with questions of the facts or the law of self-defense?

It felt good, certainly, to savor such feelings as more details about Goetz were revealed. He led a quiet, law-abiding life, it was said, residing in a small Manhattan apartment and working as an electronics engineer. He had begun to carry a gun after he had been mugged on the subway and then watched the courts let his assailant escape without sanction. When one of the four who made the mistake of clowning around with him that day on the subway asked him for $5, he was reported to have risen, drawn his gun, said, "I have five dollars for each of you," and fired.

As time passed, second thoughts began to intrude. Goetz's

behavior seemed most gratifying to those on the political right. Too much concern for criminals now cripples criminal justice, they argued. Let the Goetz case put the authorities on notice—if they aren't tougher about enforcing the law, more potential victims are going to try enforcing it themselves.

"What exactly was Goetz supposed to do?" asked Patrick Buchanan, the newspaper columnist who would soon join President Reagan's White House staff. "No state can take away from a man his inalienable and inherent right to defend his person, property, and family from an aggressor."

No slouch at finding inventive arguments to defend radical positions, Buchanan compared the lot of the New York City subway rider with that of "Jews in the early years of Hitler's regime. They could be hassled, humiliated, cuffed around, beaten up, their shops vandalized and ransacked, in the certain knowledge that their predators would go unpunished. In Germany, the thugs enjoyed the benediction of the state; in New York, they enjoy its impotence."

He ended by suggesting that lawmen be authorized to shoot criminals on sight. He acknowledged that "this would totally violate our concept of criminal justice. . . . But the roar of approval for Bernhard Goetz should already be read as a people's verdict, a democratic vote of no confidence in the system. Perhaps it is time to stop trying to reform the criminal justice system and to begin talking about its replacement."

Yet the issues raised by the Goetz case, and by extension the whole criminal justice problem, are hardly so simple. The four who approached Goetz on the subway were black teenagers with short histories of schooling and employment, longer ones of trouble with the law. Their alienation would lead them at least to plundering quarters from video games, an activity they claimed to be headed for when they encountered Goetz. Whether they also intended to rob him isn't clear. All four were wounded; one, Darrel Cabey, wound up brain-damaged and permanently paralyzed.

In the immediate wake of the shootings, Kenneth Clark, the distinguished black psychologist and educator, was one of the first to speak against the tide of support for Goetz. "This incident cannot be understood in isolation," he wrote. Fear of the mugger, he said, doesn't eliminate the question of what produces alienation and antisocial behavior.

"A painfully disturbing answer to this core question is that 'mugged communities,' 'mugged neighborhoods,' and, probably most important, 'mugged schools' spawn urban 'muggers.' "

Celebrating do-it-yourself justice, Clark wrote, can only escalate the confrontation. "There is no question that society must be protected from those who assault, rob, or otherwise violate others. These forms of lawless behavior should be punished. But they cannot be punished constructively by the lawlessness of another individual. Frustration, fear, and outrage afflict both the rejected and the 'respectables.' "

Nearly a year later, as the first anniversary of the Goetz shooting approached, a woman named Lea Evans Ash published an essay reflecting on her own victimization. While standing on a subway platform with her ten-month-old baby in a stroller, she had been attacked by three teenagers, who kicked her in the back. For more than twelve years, she suffered with paralysis and pain caused by the spinal injury. There was an explanation of sorts for the attack. The boys, all black, had just come from the funeral of a black child said to have been shot down in cold blood by a police officer. She had gotten in the way of three who were seeking retaliation.

For a time, she wrote, such an explanation only left her more bewildered and outraged. But the Goetz shootings, which resulted in severe spinal injury to Darrel Cabey, forced her to confront awful questions.

"He [Goetz] was hell-bent on retaliation. Did he achieve it? Some people cheered him as a hero. Was he?

"Would the same people who cheered him as a hero for taking matters into his own hands also cheer the three boys who attacked me? After all, they apparently felt justified in seeking retaliation. Who, I ask you, was more evil? Mr. Goetz? The boys he shot? The boys who attacked me? The policeman who allegedly shot the child in Brooklyn?

Concluding, she quoted Rilke: " 'Be patient toward all that is unsolved in your heart. Try to love the questions themselves.' I don't love the questions of evil but I live with them. I try to be patient toward myself. Perhaps that is finally the deepest source and the greatest power of self respect: learning to live with questions that have no answers."

The criminal justice question truly tortures the conscience. It is as glib to say that the rights and feelings of the victim must always prevail as it is to focus exclusively on the rights and feelings of the criminal whose deviance may spring from his own sense of victimization. The question is how to find a decent balance where the stakes— fear, pain, loss of freedom, death—are not to be taken lightly.

It is not a question that is easy to love.

2

The FACTS CRUMBLE

"We cover crime very well, but we cover the police department very badly," said [reporter] John Katzenbach about police press coverage in Miami. "It's extremely rare that you see a really incisive behind-the-scenes look at how the department is being run or what impact it has on community life." Added Thomas Crosby, a ten-year veteran at the *Washington Star* who now covers criminal justice: "If I had to characterize in one word our coverage of the police in Washington, I would say it's shoddy. Neither the *Washington Post* or the *Star* are very consistent in their coverage of police issues."

Harvard professor and criminologist James Q. Wilson [said], "The press isn't in the business to tell the public how our major institutions work; their basic interest is relating unusual events of public significance." As a result, says Wilson, "the press usually offers a very vague and largely inaccurate view of day-to-day police life."

—*Michael Kiernan, "Police vs. the Press: 'There's Always Tension,' "* Police Magazine, *July 1979*

*R*obert Leuci and the other detectives who served in the Special Investigating Unit, an elite narcotics squad of the New York City Police Department, were proficient cops, but many of them were also crooks.

Their mission was to pursue the biggest drug traffickers using the most sophisticated undercover techniques. And they were often amazingly successful.

"SIU detectives did not bother with junkies," writes Robert Daley in *Prince of the City*, "and they came in contact with thugs only by accident—if they happened, for instance, to witness a crime on the way home. Their prisoners usually were expensively dressed and often somewhat glamorous, being Frenchmen or Turks or South Americans, or high-ranking New York mafiosi."

One supposed secret of the SIU's success was its ability to function on its own, thereby minimizing the chances of detection by its prey. The unit, Daley writes, "was virtually unsupervised. . . . Some SIU detectives did not go near [their] office for months at a time, not even on payday—they would send someone in to pick up their checks. . . . They were rated on results only. All they had to do was to keep making big cases, big seizures of heroin. . . . They had citywide jurisdiction. They chose their own targets and roamed New York at will."

Their arrogance bred an alienation and the detective's special brand of contempt for the laws they were supposedly helping to enforce. To make cases, the SIU detectives would pay off informants in seized narcotics. They would divide up the cash from big busts among themselves. They were the envy of the department partly because of their elite status and freedom to operate, but also because they always seemed to have so much money.

Members of the SIU so loathed the drug dealers they pursued that they eventually "began to dispense their own justice. . . . They would take whatever money the dope dealer had, order him on the next plane to South America, and applaud themselves for accomplishing what no court seemed able to accomplish, a heavy fine followed by instant deportation."

It was Detective Leuci who finally brought down the SIU by deciding to unburden his conscience to a prosecutor. As a result, fifty-two of the seventy SIU detectives were indicted and the SIU was disbanded.

That was a victory for justice, certainly, and yet it left a small, if pointed, legacy of doubt. "There came a time," Daley writes, "when Assistant U.S. Attorney Rudolph Giuliani, trying to put together a major narcotics investigation with new narcotics detectives assigned to him, realized that they were all inept. They couldn't tail a suspect without getting made. . . . A great detective, Giuliani thought, should be a man of imagination and fearlessness. A man with a sense of adventure, a man not limited by procedure. . . . he asked himself in despair: Where have all the detectives gone? The answer that came back to him was this one: I put them all in jail."

———

Ivan Mendoza was arrested in 1983 for the murder of an old woman, Lena Cronenberger, who lived in his apartment house in New York City. She had been found in her apartment, stabbed to death with a carving knife and fork. Ivan went voluntarily to the police station and submitted to interrogation without calling a lawyer. Detectives later said that they got Ivan talking about camping and hiking and other outdoor activities he said he liked, and that eventually he confessed. Then a detective asked him if he had anything else on his conscience. Ivan said, "Well, yes, there was that Oriental woman around the corner."

He apparently was referring to Louise Kong, who had been found stabbed to death with a screwdriver about a year before.

The prosecutor had his doubts. Confessions were the heart of each murder case. No other evidence linked Ivan to either crime. Furthermore, after talking to a lawyer, Ivan had begun to talk about how a detective had forced the confessions by playing Russian roulette with him, pointing a revolver at his head, spinning the cylinder, and threatening to pull the trigger. New York appeals courts had lately been touchy on matters of confession. Even if convicted by a trial jury, Ivan might be freed by the appeals court if it decided the confession was coerced, or if it found some other problems with the trial.

That wasn't all. Even if he could get the confession admitted properly, there would be a serious problem with trying Ivan for the killing of Ms. Kong. Rules of evidence would prohibit any mention of the Cronenberger case at the Kong trial. The jury could be told only that Ivan was interrogated for three hours about something else, then suddenly confessed to killing Ms. Kong. It wouldn't be hard for a defense attorney to plant a lot of doubt in the jury's mind about the confession, and that's all he'd need for an acquittal.

So the prosecutor decided to play it safe. Instead of pressing for a trial, he offered to take guilty pleas to both murders if Ivan would accept two five-year prison terms, to run concurrently.

Ivan refused. He was enjoying all the attention and was "hot to trot," the assistant district attorney said, with his story about Russian roulette. So he went on trial for killing Mrs. Cronenberger.

That was his mistake. Ivan made a poor witness, and the jurors didn't buy a word of his Russian-roulette story. They deliberated for only a couple of hours before finding him guilty, and the judge gave him nine years, the maximum allowable, since Ivan had been a juvenile at the time the crime was committed.

Now what to do about the case of Ms. Kong? Again, the prosecutor decided to play it safe. If he could get Ivan to plead guilty to killing her as part of a bargain for a specific sentence, the plea would be recorded in open court. Ivan would swear that he was making an admission freely and voluntarily. It might stand up on appeal even if the conviction in the Cronenberger case was thrown out. In effect, the plea bargain for killing Ms. Kong would become a kind of insurance policy against reversal on the conviction in the Cronenberger case.

Ivan, chastened by the jury's unwillingness to believe his story in the first case, now readily accepted the prosecutor's offer of five years concurrent time.

That produced a flurry of criticism from politicians and editorialists in the city. Unsympathetic to the prosecutor's worries about Ivan's confessions, they denounced the court for letting Ivan get away with two murders for the price of one.

Was that what had happened? Or had the prosecutor in fact played his hand in the most responsible way, in order to ensure that a murderer who deserved to go to prison would stay there for at least five years?

Jack Henry Abbott gained notoriety as a person who spent most of his adolescence and adulthood in reform schools and prisons, then wrote a book about prison life that attracted the attention of leading publishers and literary figures like Norman Mailer. With their sponsorship, Abbott finally was paroled from prison in Utah, but shortly after his release, he murdered a waiter outside a restaurant in lower Manhattan. He was convicted of that crime and sent back to prison in New York.

The fuller story is worth closer examination. Shortly before his release, Abbott had been locked up not in Utah, but at the tough federal penitentiary at Marion, Illinois. And though many spoke of his having somehow been rehabilitated through literature, the wardens and guards at Marion considered him a disciplinary problem and had confined him to the prison's "control section." While there, Abbott would say, he was savagely beaten by guards retaliating against inmates after someone hurled a tray of food. After the beating, Abbott began to fear for his life.

He therefore became an informer. In a 116-page statement, he named leaders of a prison work strike and accused his former lawyers of smuggling drugs into the penitentiary. This cooperation was followed by his transfer to Utah, where the authorities stood ready to grant him parole from a previous sentence.

The cynicism on all sides was breathtaking. In his book, Abbott had written with special venom about the depravity of inmates who would inform on other inmates. Now he had become such an informer himself. But the more pointed question goes to the Marion prison officials. Had they made a deal for parole only to get his testimony about inmate leaders and lawyers? Or were they also glad to rid themselves of a troublesome inmate? Abbott, they must have known, was a pathologically dangerous man, hardly a good candidate for release to the streets. They also knew that he was more than likely to be so released on his return to Utah. And if the Utah officials approved the release, nobody at Marion would be immediately blamed for what might happen.

———

Criminal justice is rarely what it seems. The official handling of Leuci, Mendoza, and Abbott makes clear how commonly men and women acting in the name of the law exercise enormous discretion over matters whose profound moral complexities they may or may not grasp.

Must cops be allowed to enrich themselves on seized drugs in order to produce the big arrests that conceivably could make a difference in the level of drug abuse? When is plea bargaining an effective way to keep a dangerous person off the streets and when does it simply reveal a prosecutor's timidity or laziness? And what is the real price paid for the purchase of information about a troubled prison from a troubled inmate when the currency is his release to the streets?

The combination of such official discretion and moral challenge sometimes fosters brilliance, sometimes deadly folly. Most of all it fosters an almost furtive sense of privacy. The sort of dealings detailed in these three cases go on every day, in cases large and small, yet only rarely do they come to public light.

For that, the news media bear much of the blame. The criminals who inspire the most fear and therefore define crime as a public issue are the relatively anonymous muggers, burglars, and auto thieves who plague the lives of city residents. Just the knowledge of their recent activity is enough to inflict anxiety on the person who would venture out after 10:00 p.m. to buy a newspaper or a carton of milk. Their presence is felt by every homeowner who lays out money for expensive locks and window gates, every car owner who writes a check for an exorbitant insurance premium. Awareness of street crime feeds a simmering sense of outrage. It forces the better political leaders into hiding and the worst into demagoguery.

Only rarely, however, do the morning paper and the nightly television news devote much in the way of resources to educating the public about who street criminals are, what motivates them, and how criminal justice agencies deal with them. Routine crimes aren't newsworthy. It takes a Jean Harris, who shot to death her lover, the prominent physician Dr. Herman Tarnower, or a Claus Von Bulow, who stood trial and was acquitted of trying to murder his wealthy wife, to trigger automatic and lavish coverage.

Yet the resident of Brooklyn or St. Louis or Chicago who wants to go out after 10:00 p.m. doesn't have to worry about being attacked by people like Mrs. Harris or Mr. Von Bulow. It is not because of them that insurance companies raise premiums and locksmiths get rich in city neighborhoods.

Why are there so few stories that explore the real sources of community fear?

One obvious answer is simply that journalism has always appreciated the entertainment value of crime news. The stories of Mrs. Harris and Mr. Von Bulow are real-life soap operas. Why shouldn't they get a lot of media attention as long as people want to hear about them?

A less obvious reason for the superficiality of crime coverage is that it remains an intake assignment for new reporters. Ambitious young journalists don't look forward to making a career following the police or the lower courts any more than ambitious young lawyers aspire to low-level criminal defense. The young reporter assigned to the police beat simply wants to do well enough with it to please editors and get promoted. The Peter Principle applies with great force: Once a reporter of any talent learns enough to chronicle criminal justice with a degree of savvy, he is likely to be moved up to coverage of something else.

If media coverage is unsatisfying, scholarship is even less so. Though studies of the criminal mind and personality have gone on for many decades, only recently have researchers begun to measure more politically germane matters, like how much crime actually occurs, and how different police patrol strategies or prison programs might affect it.

Such research rarely provides clear answers. It typically demonstrates what does not work rather than what does, and reveals how easily the apparently hard facts of criminal justice may crumble apart under relatively slight scrutiny. For an example one need look no further than the fundamental question of how much crime occurs and whether it has been increasing or decreasing.

The Federal Bureau of Investigation regularly publishes crime statistics based on reports to police of the "index" crimes—murder and nonnegligent manslaughter, forcible rape, robbery, aggravated assault, burglary, larceny theft, auto theft, and (more recently) arson. These statistics showed big increases through the sixties and seventies. For several years, annual updates of the reports generated alarming headlines. Then in 1981 the increases slowed down and the headlines proclaimed an easing of the crime wave.

To any honest student of crime statistics, the headlines look wildly irresponsible. Since 1973, the Bureau of Justice Statistics and the Bureau of the Census have been trying to measure the level of crime in a different way, with the National Crime Survey. Every six months it canvasses a national sample of about 50,000 homes, asking if members of the household (about 100,000 people) have been victims of crime in the past six months. These victimization surveys immediately confirmed a startling fact: A huge amount of crime goes unreported—as much as or more than is reported. In 1986, for example, when the FBI counted 13.2 million reports of crime, the victimization survey calculated that 34.1 million occurred.

The two measures aren't directly comparable. Among other differences, the victimization survey does not include homicides (20,613 in 1986), for the simple reason that the victim isn't available to interview. And the FBI compilation does not include the simple assaults (2.8 million in 1986) recorded by the National Crime Survey.

Each survey, furthermore, is subject to question on its own. The amount of reported crime may vary with the level of police presence in a community and public attitudes toward police. The victimization surveys are based on self-reporting, hardly the most reliable way to gather information. Not all victims' memories serve them well when the census interviewers call. Better-educated, more articulate victims are likely to report crime more readily than others. And all victims are more inclined to report assaults and other crimes at the hands of strangers than those that occur between neighbors or relatives. Such problems of methodology, however, only suggest that the actual level of unreported crime is even higher than the surveys indicate.

As startling as the amount of crime revealed by the victimization surveys was what they implied about the trend. While the crime reports marched steadily upward in the seventies, the amount of crime indicated by the victimization surveys remained remarkably constant from year to year. Between 1973 and 1980, for example, the FBI's count of reported crimes rose 53 percent, from 8.7 million to 13.3 million. In that same period, the number of crimes estimated on the basis of the victimization surveys was much larger—35.3 million in 1973 and 40.3 million in 1980. Yet the increase was only 14.2 percent. When the crime figures are measured per 100,000 persons, in order to account for population growth, the discrepancy is even greater. Between 1973 and 1980, the number of reported robberies per 100,000 rose from 183.1 to 243.5. Yet according to the victimization survey, the number of robbery victims per 100,000 actually *fell* in those years, from 690 to 656.

Explanations of the difference abound, and some make good sense. Why, for example, did reports to police of rapes increase from 24.5 per 100,000 women to 36.4 per 100,000 women in those years when acknowledging victimization declined from 181 to 157 per 100,000? Most likely because those years also saw rising feminist consciousness that encouraged rape victims to come forward and report the crime rather than hushing it up. As a result, police administrators and hospital emergency staffs grew more sensitive to the feelings of rape victims and developed new procedures that made it easier for them to report. The increase in reports of rape therefore ought to be considered evidence of progress in law enforcement, not failure.

And what might explain the increase in reports of burglary from 1,222.5 per 100,000 to 1,668.2 per 100,000 in a period when the estimate of households victimized sank from 9,267 per 100,000 to 8,426 per 100,000? Probably nothing more mysterious than the spread of crime insurance among city dwellers, who found that to make a claim for reimbursement one must first report a burglary to the police.

A variation on the insurance motive may have inflated auto-theft reports. This was because of the growth of "chop shops"—garages that purchase stolen cars in order to dismantle them and sell the parts. A driver who was tired of an old car could turn it over to a middleman for $100 or

$200, report it stolen, and collect the insurance reimbursement. The middleman would sell the car to the chop shop, which could make a big profit on the sale of individual parts. Everyone made money at the expense of insurers and their premium payers. In 1984, the New York City police and the FBI mounted a sting operation to arrest middlemen and close down chop shops, an effort that generated heavy media coverage. As a result, reports of auto theft dropped by 20 percent. The stepped-up enforcement certainly reduced crime, but it was the white-collar crime of insurance fraud, not the more threatening street crime of auto theft.

Such explanations do not account for all the discrepancy between the two kinds of crime figures, however, and it would be a mistake to conclude on the basis of the victimization surveys that crime was actually falling when it appeared to be rising. It is unlikely that many homicides, not included in the victimization surveys, go unreported, so it's reasonable to take at face value the FBI figures for reported murder and nonnegligent manslaughter. Between 1973 and 1980 they increased from 9.4 per 100,000 to 10.2 per 100,000. That increase of 8.5 percent indicates some increase in violence, though well below the 42 percent increase for all reported index crimes.

It is also instructive to take a longer view of the whole question. In a fascinating essay on the history of crime rates, Ted Robert Gurr, a political scientist, points out that urban America has had to cope with three great crime waves, as indicated by homicide rates. The first occurred from the late 1850s to the 1870s. The second began in 1900 and lasted until the early 1930s. The third began

about 1965 and may or may not have peaked in 1980—
it is too early to tell whether the leveling off of murder
rates since then marked the beginning of a sustained decline. The two twentieth-century crime waves, the evidence suggests, were due mostly to increases in killings
among blacks.

What caused such breakdowns of order? Economic
changes? Migrations from Europe to America, or from the
Southern states to the North and the West Coast? Wars
that legitimized violence and gave generations of young
men direct exposure to it? A combination of such events,
some or all of which occurred in the three periods? No
one can say for sure, but the analysis does make possible
one conclusion: The effectiveness of the criminal justice
system is only one factor, and probably not the most important.

That fact of life is rarely confronted, for doing so hope-
lessly complicates the debate over what to do about crime.
The fearful public, or at least its political leaders, finds it
easiest to hold criminal justice officials fully responsible
for the level of crime. Yet doing so puts the officials in
an impossible position. Coping with it, they exercise their
discretion, quietly, and for better and worse.

3

"AMERICA
can
CONTROL CRIME
if it
WILL"

We are cruelly afflicted with crime because we have
failed to care for ourselves and for our character. We are
guilty of immense neglect. Neglect, not permissiveness,
is the culprit. Do not blame the precious little true freedom that the individual can squeeze out of mass society
for the sins of generations of selfish neglect. It was from
too little love and help, not too much liberty, that the
child across the street ran with the gang. We—his family,
friends, neighbors, school, church—all watched him for
years, and no one was truly surprised when, just back
from the reformatory again, he was arrested for mur-

dering a store clerk while committing armed robbery. What can his mother—an alcoholic, unemployed, husbandless with four children—do for him? What can a fifth-grade ghetto schoolteacher, barely able to maintain classroom order among forty students, do to help such a youngster? Can we hope to create a just society and assure domestic tranquillity by reacting in anger with force? We will assure violence if government acts only to keep the poor in their place.

—*Ramsey Clark,* Crime in America, *1970*

Since [the Law Enforcement Assistance Administration's] establishment, crime rates—especially for violent crime—have continued to soar (except for a brief and unexplained period in 1972). Last year alone, reported crimes went up 18 percent, the largest increase since the Federal Bureau of Investigation (FBI) began collecting statistics almost 50 years ago. Meanwhile, all the manifest ills of the criminal justice system persist. State and local criminal justice systems remain as fragmented as ever. The courts are still overloaded; jails are still crowded; prosecutorial offices are generally underfunded; and sentencing and parole procedures and decisions remain arbitrary and uncoordinated. Nor do we know any more about the causes of crime than we did before LEAA came into being.

It would be naive to blame LEAA for not solving these problems. . . . It is both unrealistic and unfair to expect an agency whose budget represents only 5 percent of all state and local expenditures on law enforcement to have a significant impact on the crime statistics. But LEAA certainly is responsible for the confusion that its own rhetoric has generated regarding its purpose.

—*Law Enforcement:* The Federal Role,
*Report of the Twentieth Century Fund Task
Force on the Law Enforcement Assistance
Administration, 1976*

You are a 50-year-old woman living alone. You are asleep one night when suddenly you awaken to find a man standing over you with a knife at your throat. As you start to scream, he beats and cuts you. He then rapes you. While you watch helplessly, he searches the house, taking your jewelry, other valuables, and money. He smashes furniture and windows in a display of senseless violence. His rampage ended, he rips out the telephone line, threatens you again, and disappears into the night.

At least, you have survived. Terrified, you rush to the first lighted house on the block. While you wait for the police, you pray that your attacker was bluffing when he said he'd return if you called them. Finally, what you expect to be help arrives.

The police ask questions, take notes, dust for fingerprints, make photographs. When you tell them you were raped, they take you to the hospital. Bleeding from cuts, your front teeth knocked out, bruised and in pain, you are told that your wounds are superficial, that rape itself is not considered an injury. Awaiting treatment, you sit

39

alone for hours, suffering the stares of curious passers-by. . . .

An officer says you must go through this process, then the hospital sends you a bill for the examination that the investigators insisted upon. . . . Finally, you get home somehow, in a cab you paid for and wearing a hospital gown because they took your clothes as evidence. . . .

You didn't realize when you gave the police your name and address that it would be given to the press and to the defendant through police reports. . . . You're astonished to discover that your attacker has been arrested, yet while in custody he has free and unmonitored access to a phone. He can threaten you from jail. . . . At least you can be assured that the man who attacked you is in custody, or so you think. No one tells you when he is released on his promise to come to court. . . . You learn only by accident that he's at large; this discovery comes when you turn a corner and confront him. . . . Now nowhere is safe. He watches you from the bus. Will he come back in the night? . . .

The phone rings and the police want you to come to a line-up. It may be 1:00 a.m. or in the middle of your work day, but you have to go; the suspect and his lawyer are waiting. It will not be the last time you are forced to conform your life to their convenience. . . .

—*President's Task Force on Victims of Crime*, Final Report, *December 1982*

ONE

*T*he roots of confusion stretch back twenty years and more to the time when groups like the Southern Christian Leadership Conference and the Student Nonviolent Coordinating Committee took their campaign for racial justice into the streets, riots inflamed urban ghettos, rebellious students took over college administration buildings, women's skirts got very short while men's hair got very long, young white radicals played with bombs while young black radicals postured with guns, marijuana and some harder drugs moved up from lower-class depravity to middle-class recreation, and young men filled with fear and passion burned draft cards and American flags to protest America's involvement in the war in Vietnam.

Those years of tumultuous challenge to authority may ultimately be remembered in terms of demographics—the baby boomers' postadolescent acting out. At the time, however, America seemed to pass through an epic moral struggle. The young, the minorities, all who claimed alienation, joined in denouncing the corruption of a society that appeared too tolerant of poverty, racism, pollution, dehumanizing corporate life, and a war that consumed tens of thousands of lives and billions of dollars for purposes no one could make clear.

Defenders of the "establishment," meanwhile, would claim moral superiority of their own, over disrespect for authority and law, permissiveness and denial of global responsibility.

Television, coming into its own as an instant communicator of news, fanned and distorted the debate. If the issues, in hindsight, seem almost quaint, the events were deadly.

In 1964, racial disturbances flared in black neighborhoods of New York City; northern New Jersey; Rochester, New York; Dixmoor, Illinois; and Philadelphia. The following year the Watts ghetto in Los Angeles erupted in a riot that raged out of control for six days. Thirty-four people died, 875 suffered injuries, nearly 4,000 were arrested, and the property damage totaled $40 million. A Congressional committee would count twenty-one riots in 1966 and seventy-five more in 1967, including two in Newark and Detroit on the scale of Watts. By the end of that year, the death toll for all such urban riots in the sixties exceeded two hundred. In the spring of 1968, the assassination of Martin Luther King produced another round of rioting in 125 cities, including Washington and Chicago. It was followed within weeks by the assassination of Robert Kennedy as he campaigned for the presidency.

Black militants made a fetish of guns; too often, police seemed eager to return lethal fire. The ultramilitant Students for a Democratic Society fragmented into smaller groups that apparently hoped to spark general revolution with terrorist bombings. In May 1970, national guardsmen were called to the campus of Kent State University in Ohio after students began protesting the extension of the Vietnam War to Cambodia and the ROTC building burned to the ground. Guardsmen opened fire on students after an antiwar rally, killing four and wounding eleven.

Street crime, emerging as a national issue after years as a strictly local responsibility, inevitably got mixed up with the broader cultural, racial, and political warfare. Those who assailed racism and the inequity of American society saw them, plausibly enough, as an explanation for criminal behavior. Too often, however, that respectable idea would be twisted to the point of justifying robbery and rape.

Eldridge Cleaver, a black California prison inmate, wrote with some pride of his career as a rapist in his best-selling book, *Soul on Ice.*

"Rape was an insurrectionary act. It delighted me that I was defying and trampling upon the white man's law, upon his system of values, and that I was defiling his women—and this point, I believe, was the most satisfying to me because I was very resentful over the historical fact of how the white man has used the black woman. I felt I was getting revenge. From the site of the act of rape, consternation spreads outwardly in concentric circles. I wanted to send waves of consternation throughout the white race."

Another California inmate, George Jackson, introduced the popular compilation of his prison letters, *Soledad Brother*, with the assertion that "all my life I've done exactly what I wanted to do just when I wanted, no more, perhaps less sometimes, but never any more, which explains why I had to be jailed."

His imprisonment on relatively minor charges would last for a decade as his term was extended for disciplinary violations. He professed himself to be an admirer of Cleaver and the Black Muslim leader Malcolm X, and he pursued Marxist studies. Held at California's troubled Soledad prison, he and two other inmates would be charged with the murder of a white guard. As the radical community promoted the defense of the "Soledad Brothers," Jackson's younger sibling Jonathan mounted an armed raid on the Marin County courthouse, capturing a judge and some jurors to hold as hostages for George's release. Both the judge and Jonathan Jackson died in the ensuing gunplay with police. George Jackson, now transferred to San Quentin, died shortly thereafter in a shootout with guards who insisted that he and other inmates had captured and killed three guards and two inmates, apparently as part of an escape attempt. These dramatic events heightened the issues of racism and oppression to the point that they could obscure any question of the "martyred" Jackson's criminality.

The urban street criminal shared with the ghetto rioter and the civil rights demonstrator a common adversary: the white-dominated machinery of criminal justice. Why not share in the claims of oppression as well? Middle-class white radicals were more interested in protesting the Vietnam War, economic inequality, and vaguer failings of America than in finding political vindication for criminal activity, with which they had slight experience. But they expressed sympathy for the portrayal of street crime as revolution and reinforced it with their own ridicule of police and the courts. Campus takeovers and demonstrations against the war often led to confrontations with the police, and before long, arrest, especially if accompanied by gassing or beating, became a matter of pride. The growing middle-class fascination with recreational drug use meant more contempt for laws on the books and efforts to enforce them.

The volatile quality of such politics made it understandable, perhaps, that Democratic officialdom in Washington hesitated to dismiss much of the radical foolishness for what it was, especially the foolishness about street crime. In 1970, Ramsey Clark, who had been Lyndon Johnson's Attorney General, strained to accommodate the alienation he saw around him. In a book called *Crime in America*, Clark argued passionately for a view of crime that fitted neatly the new radicals' portrait of America as a society in a prerevolutionary state: To speak of stronger law enforcement, to assert the moral value of punishing wrongdoers whatever had led them to do wrong, was to deny the real problem and prop up a corrupt establishment.

The only meaningful response to crime, Clark declared, was to solve the problems of "slums, racism, ignorance and violence, of corruption and impotence to fulfill rights, of poverty and unemployment and idleness, of generations of malnutrition, of congenital brain damage and prenatal neglect, of sickness and disease, of pollution, of decrepit, dirty, ugly, unsafe, overcrowded housing, of alcoholism and narcotics addiction, of avarice, anxiety, fear, hatred, hopelessness and injustice."

However numerous and profoundly rooted such human problems might be, Clark insisted that ridding America of them, and therefore of crime, was simply a matter of goodwill. All that needed to happen was for enough Americans to care.

In his passion for that idea, Clark equated stronger law enforcement with "repression" and seemed almost contemptuous of those whose feelings of fear and victimization made them support it. "There is no conflict between liberty and safety," he stated baldly. "We will have both, or neither. You cannot purchase security at the price of freedom, because freedom is essential to human dignity and crime flows from acts that demean the individual. We can enlarge both liberty and safety if we turn from repressiveness, recognize the causes of crime and move constructively."

Not all would take such rhetoric seriously, but no Democratic leader of the time felt he could ignore the attitudes behind it.

Such was the developing background as criminal justice entered national politics with the presidential campaign of 1964. The credit—some might later prefer to call it blame—for that event goes to Barry Goldwater, the proudly right-wing Republican senator from Arizona. Goldwater sought to link the fears generated by urban riots, the militance of civil rights activism, and common street crime. At the Republican convention, he vowed to make "the abuse of law and order" a major campaign issue. He asserted that during the Kennedy and Johnson presidencies, crime had increased "five times faster than the population." He also attacked those who would take the freedom to protest injustice to the point of "lawlessness, violence, and hurt of his fellow man or damage of his property." Repeatedly, he vowed to make the streets safe for women and children. When Adlai Stevenson, Johnson's ambassador to the United Nations, praised those who were willing to go to prison for the sake of their ideals, Goldwater leaped to link civil disobedience with common crime: "Perhaps we are destined to see in this law-loving land, people running for office not on their stainless records, but on their prison records." It was all part of general moral decay, Goldwater suggested, tolerated, if not encouraged, by Democratic administrations. Elegant social theorizing, Goldwater charged, so transfixed liberal Democrats that they now would grant criminals more sympathy than either their victims or the police. Their attitudes also legitimized political militance to the point of lawbreaking, he added, and undercut the authority of local officials faced with riots.

Goldwater lost the election but won his point. The campaign left Johnson with a plain challenge to do something at the federal level to address a crime problem now more bound up than ever with the larger debate over authority, racism, and repression.

"It was clear that the fall campaign of 1964 had sharpened the voters' mood of frustration and that presidential leadership of the 'war against crime' was expected," recalls Gerald Caplan, who served in the Johnson administration and would go on to head the National Institute of Law Enforcement under President Nixon. The campaign had impressed upon the nation that from 1940 to 1965 the crime rate doubled and that it had increased five times faster than population growth since 1958. (In hindsight, the meaning of such numbers is hardly clear, since there were no victimization studies to provide a better perspective.) Goldwater's views about crime were not responsible for his resounding defeat. In winning by a landslide, Johnson won the responsibility for doing something about crime.

But what was he to do? "There was no preexisting theory of federal assistance to refer to and no federal experts waiting to be called to duty," Caplan points out. And an information drought severely hampered the task of developing new policies. "Little was known about the effectiveness of the primary institutions of crime control—police, prosecution, courts, and corrections. . . ." One of Johnson's first acts, therefore, was to appoint a National Crime Commission, whose task would be to "deepen our understanding of the causes of crime and of how our society should respond to the challenge of our present levels of crime." It would be the first of a number of such groups appointed in response to the rising violence of the era.

The commission was chaired by Johnson's then Attorney General, Nicholas DeB. Katzenbach, and directed by James Vorenberg of the Harvard Law School. Its nineteen members included such pillars of the liberal establishment as Kingman Brewster, president of Yale, and Robert Wagner, former mayor of New York City. Eventually, the commission's staff would number more than forty, and more than two hundred consultants and advisers would be called upon to help.

The result, a 308-page report and nine additional volumes that delved into the report's various topics in greater detail, was by any measure extraordinary. Its strength was its encyclopedic effort to link each aspect of criminal justice with all the others, and even to broader questions of education, housing, and poverty. Some would later look back on its greatest statement as a chart, spread across two pages, that depicted the progress of criminal cases from first contact with the police to final disposition. It made clear that the system worked inefficiently, with many cases leaking out along the way. It also made clear, however, that for better or worse, the system *is* a system, with the success or failure of any single agency powerfully influencing the effectiveness of those around it. In the insular world of criminal justice, where police and prosecutors, for example, might pride themselves on their hostility to each other, that alone was an enormous contribution.

The report also offered more than two hundred recommendations for reform, ranging from better salaries for police to strengthening slum schools to the licensing of handguns. This broad scope would become a source of criticism. Which of the scores of ideas were most important? Where should government agencies begin their efforts to reform the system and fight crime?

James Q. Wilson, the Harvard political scientist who would become the academic darling of conservatives for his tough-minded writings about crime, found the report troubling. "The lay reader might respond, 'Yes, of course, but what do we do tomorrow morning that will reduce the chance of my wife having her purse snatched by some punk on the way to the supermarket?' Not much, it appears."

He and other critics had a point. And in hindsight, the report also deserves some criticism for raising false hopes, to the extent that it could not resist rhetorical bows to the broader Great Society optimism. "Warring on poverty, inadequate housing, and unemployment is warring on crime," the report stated. "A civil rights law is a law against crime. Money for schools is money against crime." The ringing final paragraph read: "Controlling crime in America is an endeavor that will be slow and hard and costly. But America can control crime if it will." Too often, too soon, it would be quoted with derision.

Yet to dwell on excess optimism is petty, given the larger substance of the study. And its diffuseness, while indeed frustrating to practical politicians, was also a mark of integrity. For in fact there were no obvious measures that might quickly and dramatically reduce crime.

Lyndon Johnson announced the second part of his response to crime in his 1967 State of the Union address. He would ask Congress for a spending program, and a big one: $50 million in the first year and $300 million in the next for categorical grants to states and localities. The idea of this Safe Streets and Crime Control Act would be to finance reforms and innovations in all parts of the system.

The spending proposal grew out of the National Crime Commission's report, which at one point endorsed the idea of spending several hundred million dollars annually for a decade to reform criminal justice. Yet the commission had hardly made obvious that money could work such a miracle. Its exhaustive report had portrayed a criminal justice system that suffered from insularity, lethargy, and poor coordination among agencies. Many of its recommendations—"stress ability in making promotions" of police, for example—were matters of basic management. Hindsight makes it easy to argue that ladling out huge sums to such agencies was to invite careless spending.

Even if such wisdom had been available at the time, however, it is unlikely that it would have made a difference, for the legislation would be shaped mostly by politics. To senators and representatives, the Safe Streets Act was first and foremost a vast new pool of funds to be distributed. The issue was its control. Republicans didn't want to give mayors and other local officials, mostly Democrats, the power to apply directly to Washington for cash. They argued for block grants to state governments, more heavily Republican, which would set up their own planning agencies to hand out the money. The Republicans also objected to spending so much money on research and innovation. Let the cops have it to buy more equipment, build up their manpower, and thereby do a better job of catching crooks, they argued.

Democratic supporters of the President's bill hoped Johnson would lend his considerable talents of persuasion and horse trading to salvage the original concept. But perhaps because by then he had become distracted by growing controversy over his escalation of the Vietnam War, he hung back until it was too late. In June 1968, the bill passed with the Republican block grants and get-tough measures intact. In an election year, Johnson had no choice but to sign.

TWO

The law-and-order issue that seemed only an intriguing footnote to the 1964 election became a main text in 1968. That spring, the assassinations of Martin Luther King and Robert Kennedy had traumatized the country and moved the issue of violence and disorder to the top of the political agenda. Richard Nixon responded shrewdly to the radicals' careless legitimizing of street crime. Arguing for the linkage of crime, poverty, and racism could cut two ways, after all. Let the left use such an argument to excuse or even justify common crime. Nixon could play upon fear of it to excuse or even justify lack of sensitivity to the disadvantaged and the oppressed.

Goldwater, Nixon showed, had indeed been ahead of the times on the crime issue. Yet if the Arizonan's campaign had at least succeeded in awakening politicians to the problem, Nixon's failed miserably in educating about solutions. He and his running mate, Spiro Agnew, had enjoyed raising the hackles of civil libertarians with outrageous law-and-order rhetoric. Yet their calls for tougher laws and more powers for police, prosecutors, and judges actually promised no more effective crime control than did the rhetoric of Ramsey Clark. Nor had the Nixon team thought through what they would do about crime if they won the election.

Thomas and Tania Cronin and Michael Milakovich, in their history of recent crime policies, lament that the "candidates failed, for instance, to discuss the consequences of distributing massive amounts of federal funds to local police departments at a time when civil rights groups, antiwar protesters and college students were demonstrating against U.S. involvement in Vietnam. They failed to discuss reform ideas for police departments, where money would be most efficiently spent to make streets safe, the opportunity costs of spending money one way or the other, or the strengths and weaknesses of state and city governments administering the funds."

Nixon won the election, they assert, not because he offered sound policy but because he "played to these frustrations and fears and succeeded." That cynicism would not end with the campaign.

Having made such effective use of the law and order issue to win votes, President Nixon found himself a prisoner of it. He replaced Ramsey Clark with John Mitchell, his campaign manager and law partner, and a man who would thoroughly enjoy the role of hard-boiled crime fighter. But the administration would soon find that role-playing was the most they could hope to do.

Edward Jay Epstein, who studied the Nixon administration's attempts to exploit public fear of drug abuse, reported that on taking office, Nixon decided to make good on his anticrime campaign rhetoric by achieving a national reduction in burglaries and robberies. Savvier colleagues had to explain, gently, that such a strategy wasn't realistic, because most burglaries and robberies are state crimes. The federal government's power to control them is severely limited, and any new initiatives would inevitably require sharing political credit with state and city leaders. Nixon was dismayed. After the campaign he had just waged, he couldn't just turn the problem back to state and local government. He and his advisers settled on a strategy of "jawboning" crime: promoting symbolic responses at the federal level.

Yet the problem of naiveté remained. In fact, a measure of the Nixon adminstration's depth on the crime issue was the appointment of Egil Krogh, who served as an assistant to John Ehrlichman, to oversee federal law enforcement matters. Krogh was only twenty-nine years old. He had acquired a law degree and gotten a job in Ehrlichman's Seattle land-use law firm because Ehrlichman was a family friend. It was young Krogh's first job as an attorney, and he held it only a few months before joining Ehrlichman in Washington.

These were heady times. "I had been given the District of Columbia liaison responsibility in February 1969," Krogh, also known as Bud, told Epstein. "And I remember in a meeting with the president, he said, 'All right, Bud, I'd like you to stop crime in the District of Columbia.' And I said, 'Yes,' I would do that. So I called the mayor, Walter Washington, and asked him to stop crime, and he paused for a moment and said, 'Okay,' and that was about it."

Nixon and Mitchell would also pursue the jawboning with legislation—notably the District of Columbia Crime Control Bill, which Mitchell touted as a model for other cities. It included a "no-knock" provision, which relaxed limits on the power of police to enter a residence unannounced. It also gave the District "preventive detention"—power to hold suspects without bail because of their potential dangerousness if released, rather than only to assure their appearance at trial. The administration would also send up bills on organized crime and drug enforcement.

The more significant event of the Nixon era was simply that the river of LEAA money swelled to a mighty flood. By 1971, it reached $529 million. It paid for college classes for police, computer systems for the courts, new jails and prisons, organizing of neighborhoods to resist crime, establishing new "standards and goals" for criminal justice agencies, and a blizzard of research papers. All this developed without any larger rhyme or reason, and the potential for embarrassment loomed as crime statistics showed little improvement and journalists began having fun with reports that, for example, Washington doled out $2.3 million for new patrol cars that police found too cramped. House oversight hearings in 1971 documented that money was haphazardly spent, or not spent at all. The impression was growing that LEAA was an enormous boondoggle, a pool of money created before its appropriate use was understood, an unseemly feast for politicians.

In Nixon's second term, the chances for a more rational approach to the crime problem grew even dimmer. The deepening Watergate scandal distracted Nixon from the war on crime along with all other regular business and eroded his credibility on law and order. In June 1973, he would feel forced to fire John Ehrlichman and H. R. Haldeman, stalwarts of his White House staff. Richard Kleindienst, who had succeeded John Mitchell as Attorney General, would resign. The following year, Haldeman, Ehrlichman, and Mitchell would be indicted on charges arising from the Watergate burglary and cover-up, and the law-and-order President would be named an unindicted co-conspirator. That summer, as impeachment proceedings went forward, Nixon resigned.

The effect was incalculable on national attitudes about criminal justice. In embracing law and order, Nixon, as Goldwater had done before him, put the public in touch with deeply rooted feelings about the duty of government to stand up for society's most basic values. Such was the foundation of the social contract. Now the President, implicated in criminality himself, had opened a wound of betrayal that would not heal easily, or soon.

The LEAA, meanwhile, had acquired a life of its own. In 1975, it ladled out a phenomenal $895 million, the most it would spend in a single year. That kind of money created its own constituencies, rendering even more remote any hope of reforming the program's administration. Instead, the chickens of its prolonged confusion and mismanagement now began coming home to roost. For reasons no one now can explain, the national crime statistics had dipped in 1972, prompting the Nixon people to crow. "Crime in America was growing at an annual rate of more than 15 percent when Congress passed the Omnibus Crime Control and Safe Streets Act of 1968. Four years later the trend had been reversed and the nation recorded a 3 percent crime decrease—the first such reduction since 1955," proclaimed an LEAA-funded report in 1973.

But, alas, the following year the statistics resumed their

upward march, prompting LEAA officials to assert that the agency never should have been sold to the public as an engine of crime reduction.

Gerald Ford, assuming the presidency on Nixon's departure, restored a sense of honesty and straightforwardness to the White House. As a supporter of the hard-line Nixon-Mitchell D.C. crime bill, he shared Nixon's view of the criminal justice issue and might have restored public faith. But then he pardoned Nixon, throwing his own credibility into doubt. He would not survive in the presidency for more than the balance of Nixon's term.

Meanwhile, the General Accounting Office and the Office of Management and Budget launched attacks on LEAA. The agency, they charged, simply handed out money without assessing the effects, and it freely spent on projects that appeared to have little relationship to crime control. The agency fought back with "Project Scheherazade," an effort to identify 1,001 successful LEAA-funded projects. But Abt Associates, the consultant hired to conduct the search, could only come up with 650 of the 85,000 LEAA projects that could be said to have reduced crime or improved the workings of criminal justice cost-effectively and in ways that might be duplicated.

Though crime rates as then compiled remained as high as ever, crime figured little in the 1976 presidential campaign, in which Jimmy Carter defeated Ford. Disillusioned over Watergate and LEAA, which would eventually spend more than $7.5 billion to no certain purpose, the public no longer looked to Washington for responses to the crime problem. In office, Carter and his Attorney General, Griffin Bell, made clear that they felt LEAA had worn out its welcome. For a time they went along with Senator Kennedy's attempts to reorganize the agency and sustain the funding levels. But in his 1980 budget message, Carter finally abandoned the program, saying that local authorities were better positioned to fight street crime than the federal government.

The issue would not again command much more than lip service from the nation's political leadership. Defenders of LEAA would point to its funding of projects offering services to victims and to other constructive ideas that eventually caught on. But the overwhelming impression remained that criminal justice was a political witch, fascinating and then frustrating Washington, leaving it drained of billions and more befuddled than ever.

THREE

In the presidential campaign of 1980, Ronald Reagan would speak out on crime in terms that recalled Goldwater and Nixon, if somewhat mutedly. ("The criminal justice system has failed in large part because of lenient judges, inadequate punishment and unnecessarily slow and cumbersome court proceedings.") But Reagan came to office powerfully determined to reduce the federal government's role in all areas of American life. He had no trouble resisting the idea of greater federal involvement, and especially greater federal spending, for local crime fighting.

His first Attorney General, William French Smith, appointed a Task Force on Violent Crime, whose report, issued in August 1981, showed how far official thinking had evolved from the confident days when an earlier commission could assert that "America can control crime if it will."

"We are not convinced that a government, by the intervention of new programs or the management of existing institutions, can by itself recreate those familial and neighborhood conditions, those social opportunities, and those personal values that in all likelihood are the prerequisites of tranquil communities," the Reagan task force asserted. "We are mindful of the risks of assuming that the government can solve whatever problem it addresses." Its most substantive recommendation was for Washington to spend $2 billion to help states build prisons.

The President's response was to give a speech to a police chiefs' convention in New Orleans. He ignored the proposal for spending on prisons while drifting deeply into ideology: "It has occurred to me that the root causes of our other major domestic problems—the growth of government and the decay of the economy—can be traced to many of the same sources of the crime problem," the President said. "This is because the same utopian presumptions about human nature that hindered the swift administration of justice have also helped to fuel the expansion of government.

"The underlying premise in both cases was a belief that

there was nothing permanent or absolute about any man's nature—that he was a product of his material environment, and that by changing that environment—with government as the chief vehicle of change through educational, health, housing, and other programs—we could permanently change man and usher in a great new era.

"The solution to the crime problem will not be found in the social worker's files, the psychiatrist's notes, or the bureaucrat's budget; it's a problem of the human heart, and it's there we must look for an answer. . . . Men are basically good but prone to evil and society has a right to be protected from them. Only our deep moral values and strong social institutions can hold back that jungle and restrain the darker impulses of human nature."

Here was the crime issue fitted to the age-old liberal-conservative debate over the nature of man. While the police chiefs cheered such oratory, it offered no more real comfort to the fearful city dweller than Ramsey Clark's calls for more social programs. The conservative philosophy, in fact, seemed to accept that crime is inevitable. How on earth could government, especially conservative government, hope to alter a problem of the human heart? What beyond such rhetoric might in fact produce deeper moral values and stronger social institutions? The President, true to his colors, seemed to be saying that it shouldn't. The cynical, however, could argue that the President didn't deserve that much credit: The speech, they suggested, was no more than an elaborate effort to get comfortably around the commission's call for spending $2 billion on prisons.

The following year, Reagan vented similar rhetoric, along with similar aversion to spending, on drug enforcement. In January, he named Vice-President George Bush to head a law enforcement task force that would assemble teams from several federal law enforcement agencies and the military to challenge the wide-open drug trafficking in south Florida. It was to be the model for twelve drug enforcement units deployed around the country.

By October, in the midst of midterm elections, Reagan declared the south Florida operation a success and called for a "major initiative that I believe can mark a turning point in the battle against crime." This was to be the expansion of the task-force concept to the twelve regions. If it was a battle, however, it was one in which the warriors were as mindful of thrift as victory. During the year of planning for the initiative, administration officials struggled to find ways drugs might be fought effectively without any need for new spending—by, for example, cadging surveillance planes, Coast Guard cutters, and helicopters that were scheduled for training exercises.

The "major initiative" would require $160 million to $200 million a year, money finally freed up by juggling other law enforcement accounts. Once the task forces were established, however, the rhetoric quickly faded from public consciousness. Soon enough, it was clear that no "turning point in the battle against crime" had been reached. The General Accounting Office found in 1984 that the best efforts of law enforcement to track smugglers' ships and planes, sniff out drug-laced shipments in port warehouses, and collar couriers arriving by land, sea, and air had managed to interdict only about 16 percent of marijuana shipments and less than 10 percent of the heroin and cocaine pouring into the United States.

The drug issue would be roused again in 1986 with a storm of media publicity about drug abuse. Just why all the coverage occurred when it did isn't fully clear—some surveys showed levels of drug abuse stable or even beginning to decline. The emergence of "crack," a cheap, smokable form of cocaine, may have been a big factor, along with the lack of other issues in that year's Congressional elections. The summer of "drug crisis," however, produced a hastily drawn anti-drug-abuse act that authorized $1.7 billion in new spending, mostly for domestic drug-law enforcement and better patrolling of the Mexican border.

The President and the First Lady participated actively in the campaign, vowing all-out war to achieve the goal of a "drug-free society." After the election, however, the administration made clear that it had again been willing to invest more in talk than in money. The President's new budget proposed to cut $913 million out of the drug bill.

Another of President Reagan's contributions to criminal justice appeared to involve just as much show business, but perhaps more useful show business. It was another task force, on victims of crime.

Nothing more obviously contributes to the political force of the crime issue than the trauma of the crime victim, which may convulse whole communities with anger and fear. Yet for years criminal justice officials seemed studiously ignorant of the victim's feelings.

Modern criminal justice makes pursuit and punishment of wrongdoers a duty of the state, relieving the injured parties of the right to obtain private satisfaction. Too often, especially in the big overworked urban court bureaucracies, that leaves those victimized by criminals likely to be victimized again by the system.

Victims of crime in the hands of police and courts are cogently compared with victims of disease in the hands of physicians. The doctors may focus most urgently on conquering the disease and consider the victim's feelings interesting only to the extent they can help with that fight. A patient's dignity and peace of mind are to be respected more because his mental attitude might make treatments more effective than because of any concern for his feelings.

So also do the law enforcers tread lightly on a traumatized victim's feelings only if the trauma seems to limit the victim's ability to provide evidence or inhibit his performance as a witness. Otherwise, no indignity may be allowed to slow an investigation. The rape victim shouldn't follow her natural inclination to bathe after the attack—she might wash away crucial evidence. Instead, she should present herself to doctors who will violate her body once again in search of her assailant's blood, semen, and hair. And she must submit to detailed questioning about an event she wants desperately to put out of her mind.

Even when the crime is less traumatic, victims still have plenty of grounds for complaint: required attendance at court sessions that may be postponed after a long day of lost wages and frustrated waiting; procedures that seem designed to deprive them of information about the status of the case; rules that require the police to hold their property as evidence for the months it may take for a case to be resolved.

The President's task force offered recommendations

ranging from the sweeping (federal funding of state programs to compensate crime victims) to the mundane (providing separate waiting areas in courthouses for crime victims and defendants). It endorsed the ideas that victims are entitled to be informed about the status of their cases as they progress through the system, and to more opportunities to express their feelings to sentencing judges and parole boards. The report was flawed and to an extent demeaned by the inclusion of traditional right-wing demands for preventive detention of arrested suspects, an end to the exclusionary rule, and other verses of the Goldwater-Nixon-Reagan crime scriptures. Criminals don't choose their victims on the basis of their ideology, the report's critics could argue, with reason. Why should support for victims' rights necessarily be linked to so clear a political orientation on crime?

This report led to no more practical results than that of the Attorney General's task force. To the extent that it publicized the growing victims' rights movement and granted it a heavy new dose of legitimacy, however, it was the more important document.

The Reagan years made clear how deep was the federal government's failure, after twenty years of heavy spending, research, and experiment, to follow through effectively on the warnings sounded by the old Johnson commissions on crime and violence. The criminologist Elliott Currie, who served on the staff of the 1968 Commission on Causes and Prevention of Violence, recently recalled the alarming scenario that group had painted of the future should "effective public action" to address crime and violence not occur within "a few years."

The safety of central business districts would be guaranteed only in the daytime, because crowds of workers and shoppers would inhibit street crime. At night, business areas would be abandoned as decent folk took refuge in "fortified cells"—apartments secured with locks and window bars, high rises protected by doormen and elaborate security technology. The report predicted a boom in surveillance devices for private homes, a new army of private security guards to supplement public police forces, and underground parking garages. Armed guards, it warned, would patrol schools and other public places, poor neighborhoods would become "places of terror," beyond the control of police at night, and the affluent would commute between the relative safety of suburbs and the relative safety of the downtown daytime workplace on "sanitized corridors"—expressways—through the no-man's-land of unsafe neighborhoods.

"When the commission's *Final Report* was released in late 1969, this scenario was one of the things that interested the media and the public most strongly," Currie writes. "I can remember, in fact, thinking at the time that it was a usefully overwrought portrait—one that exaggerated the terrors before us considerably, but did so deliberately, in the wholly justifiable cause of spurring public action against the roots of urban violence.

"But the 'few years' have passed, and what most strikes me today about the commission's scenario is that, with some exceptions, it came true to such an extent that we now simply take most of it for granted."

4

"WE HAVE MADE
OUR SOCIETY
and
WE MUST LIVE
with it"

I am struck by how keen and sure are people's awareness of their own problems and interests (thus, public
opinion was well ahead of political opinion in calling
attention to the rising problem of crime), how insightful
is the public understanding of the cause of crime (the
average person locates the principal cause right where
criminologists, after much puzzling, have suggested it might
be—in attitudes formed by family and peer group), and
how uncertain and dubious are many of the public's fa-
vorite remedies for crime (more police, tougher laws,
better criminal rehabilitation). It is the duty of the states-

man to try to take the confident instincts and immediate knowledge of the public and convert them, by persuasion and inducement, into reasonable policy proposals. American statesmen have not done that job very well when it comes to crime, nor have many of us who are supposed to advise them on how to do it given them very good advice.

—James Q. Wilson, Thinking About Crime, *1975*

*F*rom the elevated hopes of the Johnson years through the era of heavy LEAA spending to the more passive and parsimonious approach of the Reagan administration, the recent history of the crime issue traces the gradual deflation of policy, the defeat of easy certainties, and the triumph of confusion. For the most part, the lavish expenditure of public money and rhetoric wound up teaching us how much we don't know about crime control.

Academia proved just as disappointing as politics when it came to making sense of crime. In 1978, after six years of study supported by the Ford Foundation, the author Charles Silberman published a richly researched, thoughtful book titled *Criminal Violence, Criminal Justice*. Its searching history of violence in America ended with a courageous chapter that confronted the subject of race and crime, a topic previously considered unmentionable, at least in liberal company.

Blacks, Silberman pointed out, are responsible for a disproportionate share of violent crime, and he argued persuasively that the violence was a logical consequence of blacks' experience in America. "For most of their history in this country, in fact, blacks were victims, not initiators, of violence," he asserts. The book also provided rigorous discussions of policing, adult and juvenile courts, and corrections. Yet for all its weight, its conclusions are muted and tentative.

Silberman's insightful journey through the black experience only leads him back to platitudes about inequality. "[Black] involvement in street crime drops sharply as blacks move into the middle class," he writes, but he provides no new ideas for hastening that movement. And as if anticipating the catcalls from critics of the frustrated Great Society, he concludes on a hesitant note: "It would be disingenuous to contend that an end to racial inequality will guarantee domestic tranquillity." He quotes Herbert Wechsler, an authority on criminal law, to the effect that social reform is desirable even if it doesn't reduce crime.

After his discussions of the parts of the criminal justice system, Silberman offers a final chapter even less satisfying to anyone looking for practical advice. Returning to the idea that much crime results from the breakdown of community institutions that had historically stabilized poor neighborhoods, he asks, "[Can] 'the mores' . . . be strengthened to the point where laws are effective? The answer is yes."

It is yes, that is, to the extent that one can put faith in the optimistic rhetoric of the sociologist Robert K. Merton, who said, "More is learned from the single success than from the multiple failures. A single success proves it can be done. . . . Whatever is, is possible."

What, then, is possible? In East Palo Alto, California, a panel of teenagers and adults arranges community service assignments for youngsters who get in trouble with the law. In Park Slope, Brooklyn, a community residence run by nuns for troubled youth has become the base for other kinds of community social work. In the La Playa section of Ponce, Puerto Rico, a delinquency prevention project has also become a center of community organizing.

Silberman's telling of these apparent success stories makes stimulating reading, but in what sense are they answers? By his own account, the East Palo Alto program remained very much an experiment whose full impact was a matter of speculation. As he observed it, he was struck by the fact that its main benefits might have more to do with the development of leadership talent among the volunteers who staff the panels than in any effects on the criminality of the community's youth. The Park Slope program—anomalous to the extent that Park Slope is not a particularly disorganized or impoverished community—seemed heavily dependent on the "extraordinary energy and charismatic presence" of the nuns who had started it, and who resigned shortly before Silberman wrote about them. As for the Ponce project, though it apparently contributed to the resurgence of community and a corresponding decline in crime in La Playa, Silberman is quick to acknowledge that similar "success would be hard to come by in the harsher, more violent black and Hispanic ghettos of Chicago, Philadelphia, New York and a hundred other cities."

Silberman concludes his book with an unwitting echo of the Johnson crime commission, which had asserted a decade earlier that "America can control crime if it will." "We are not likely to enjoy the domestic tranquillity for which the Republic was founded until we become truly one society," Silberman writes. "The question is no longer what to do, but whether we have the will to do it." Anyone trying to figure out what to do, however, would find it hard to agree.

Seven years later, in 1985, the sociologist Elliott Currie ventured forth to defend the same territory. In *Confronting Crime: An American Challenge*, he attacks the "conservative model" of crime control based on punishing the impulses to deviance that are a fundamental part of human nature. He objects to the argument that crime can be curtailed if only liberals, with their concern for social justice and civil liberties, would stop inhibiting forthright punishment of criminals.

"In a world of dramatic national variations in criminal violence [the conservative argument] blames crime on an invariant human nature. In a society that ranks among the most punitive in the developed world, it blames crime on the leniency of the justice system. In a country noted for its harsh response to social deviation, it blames crime on attitudes of tolerance run wild."

Currie then follows up with a rigorous case for the futility of relying on imprisonment to control crime. Between 1970 and 1984, he points out, the state and federal prison population more than doubled to 454,000. Yet crime rates continued to increase during that time. It is by no means certain that sending even more criminals to prison would reverse the rising tide of crime, but assume for the sake of argument that it might be reduced by 20 to 25 percent by tripling the current population. With the cost of constructing maximum-security facilities running to $100,000 per cell, and with operating costs between $15,000 and $20,000 per year, the effort to reduce crime through imprisonment would cost $70 billion for construction and another $14 billion per year to operate. The $70 billion, he observes, is more than twice the amount necessary to raise all the poor families in America above the poverty line. And the $14 billion per year could provide a million youngsters with jobs paying $7 per hour.

As such calculations suggest, Currie's own proposal for crime control is based on a hearty dose of old-fashioned Great Society thinking. Crime is caused by the American economy's failure to provide job opportunities, by social inequality, and by the collapse of the family, he argues. He calls for enactment of a lengthy menu of social programs to help teenage mothers, expand job training and opportunities, and provide moral and financial support to struggling families.

"Taking this road will not be easy, for it means not only interfering with the prerogatives of those who benefit from our current social and economic arrangements, but also challenging some of the deepest cultural and political tendencies of contemporary American life. . . . The cultural roots of American crime must be sought in the . . . spread throughout so much of our social and economic life of a distorted emphasis on the values of the economic marketplace at the expense of all others."

To end crime, in other words, all we need to do is radically redesign the American economy and the way we think about it. The fearful are not likely to find much comfort in that idea, nor in its implicit corollary: that so long as we refuse to conduct such a revolution, we deserve all the crime that we suffer.

The spectacle of such straining on the left, however, was no cause for smugness on the right. In the mid-seventies, scholars like Ernest Van den Haag and James Q. Wilson could write scornfully about the wrongheadedness of looking to control crime by attacking poverty and other social ills, while arguing with confidence for increasing the certainty of punishment. Doing so, they pointed out, would add to the potential costs of crime, thereby altering the risk-benefit calculation the potential criminal would make. By the 1980s, however, Wilson would acknowledge that the certainty of punishment and other hard-line approaches could no more substantively or reliably control crime than the social engineering he so disparaged.

In his 1975 book *Thinking About Crime*, Wilson offered

wonderfully intelligent meditations on criminal justice that showed a healthy irreverence for the Great Society thinking that had seemed to dominate the intellectual debate even in the Nixon era. One important Wilson theme was an impatience with the old liberal desire to eliminate the "causes" of crime. "Social problems—that is to say, problems occasioned by human behavior rather than mechanical processes—are almost invariably 'caused' by factors that cannot be changed easily or at all. . . . If we regard any crime-prevention or crime-reduction program as defective because it does not address the 'root causes' of crime, then we shall commit ourselves to futile acts that frustrate the citizen while they ignore the criminal."

Criminals, Wilson argues, must be assumed to be at least rational enough to make self-interested calculations about the gains and risks of committing crimes. To deter crime, society needs to maximize the risks, and it ought not to be ashamed of policies designed to punish wrongdoers with certainty. "One may deter a criminal by increasing the costs or reducing the benefits of crime, but that strategy does not deal with the 'causes' of criminality, and hence does not go to the 'root' of the problem."

He points to the work of economists who show that increasing the certainty of a punishment does appear to have some effect on criminal behavior. "A serious policy-oriented analysis of crime . . . would place heavy emphasis on manipulation of objective conditions, not necessarily because of a belief that the 'causes of crime' are thereby being eradicated, but because behavior is easier to change than attitudes."

At the end of the book, he restates this idea with some confidence. "Wicked people exist. Nothing avails except to set them apart from innocent people. And many people, neither wicked nor innocent but watchful, dissembling, and calculating of their opportunities, ponder our reaction to wickedness as a cue to what they might profitably do."

Ten years later, Wilson published a revised edition of *Thinking About Crime* that showed much less confidence. "We know more in 1983 than we knew in 1975," Wilson writes in the introduction to the revision. "As a result, this book . . . tells a more complicated story than did the first edition—there are more qualifications, exceptions and uncertainties. . . ."

In a new chapter, he elaborates on the idea that criminal behavior may be affected by altering either the risks of doing wrong or the rewards for doing right. Much new research and Wilson's own thinking lead, in the end, to a new tenuousness. "It is possible to lower the crime rate by increasing the certainty of sanctions, but inducing the criminal justice system to make those changes is difficult, especially if committing the offense confers substantial benefits on the perpetrator, if apprehending and punishing the offender does not provide substantial rewards to members of the criminal justice system, or if the crime itself lacks the strong moral condemnation of society."

In another new chapter, Wilson tries to take the debate, and the uncertainty, a step farther. His essay "Crime and American Culture" traces the development of informal social controls—family structure, moral teachings—through American history and concludes that modern American society remains at odds with itself. Though we consider the level of crime in our society too high, we continue to value an "individualistic ethos." "The factors that most directly influence crime—family structure, moral development, the level of personal freedom—are the very things that we cannot easily change or for persuasive reasons do not wish to change."

This reflects, Wilson suggests, a profound evolution of American life. "We have become a nation that takes democracy to mean maximum self-expression," which is all well and good for "reasonable, decent people." But "in the hands of persons of weak character, with a taste for risk and an impatience for gratification, that ethos is a license to steal and mug."

Are there practical implications to such an insight? In the end, Wilson shrugs: "We have made our society and we must live with it."

Wilson's most recent book, coauthored with a Harvard psychologist, Richard Herrnstein, probes even more deeply into new territory. After a massive review of research, Herrnstein and Wilson conclude that there is good reason for thinking "constitutional" factors—prenatal care, IQ, sex, and so forth—are associated with a predisposition to criminal behavior. And there is also much reason to believe that whether or not a person with such a predisposition actually commits crimes depends heavily on his immediate family. The most meaningful crime policy, they suggest, might involve finding ways to make families more effective at instilling the basics of character, morality, and self-control.

These samplings from the work of Silberman, Currie, and Wilson hardly encompass all that has been written about criminal justice in the years since 1964. To study the three, however, is to gain a reliably comprehensive sense of the intellectual search for answers, for their predispositions range across the political spectrum—Currie leaning to the left, Silberman more toward the middle, and Wilson to the right—and all three based their books on extensive reviews of the existing scholarship.

What is most remarkable, in the end, is how much their answers fail to satisfy. Their best advice on how to control crime can be summarized in one cumbersome sentence:

Drastically reform the American economy and culture to reduce the underclass (Currie); hope that reduced crime will result from experiments with innovative ways to organize poor communities (Silberman); work with families to improve the quality of parenting in the early years of childhood (Wilson).

In other words, the impatient question Wilson hurled at President Johnson's crime commission—"What do we do tomorrow that will reduce the chance of my wife having her purse snatched by some punk on the way to the supermarket?"—remains unanswered. Indeed, it is only barely disturbed by twenty years of outrage and effort.

It is time to admit that the question has no meaningful answer. Impolitic as it might seem, such an admission at least permits the immediate recovery of intellectual respect. Even in concept, setting out to reduce crime was never as logical as it might have appeared. As the earlier discussion of crime rates suggests, to this day no one knows for sure how much crime actually afflicts American society, or to what extent it has been increasing. Nor has it ever been clear just what makes it rise or fall. In that sense the crime problem serves as a giant Rorschach test into which the American people read their fears and frustrations. Over the years crime has variously been blamed on the poverty that denies expectations and the affluence that raises them, on the permissiveness that erodes social institutions and the authoritarianism that makes them oppressive, on indulgent parenting and child abuse.

Some take refuge from all such speculations in demographics: Street crime is overwhelmingly the pastime of teenage boys and young men; at times when society is overrun by them, so will it be overrun by crime. There may be merit to that point, but it suggests that the only hope for crime control is birth control, an answer that offers little immediate satisfaction. Others make much of America's huge appetite for drugs and its historic fascination with firearms, especially handguns. But such discussions inevitably turn into hopeless chicken-and-egg debates. Does the spread of drugs and guns cause crime, or does crime cause the spread of drugs and guns?

The most notable aspect of all such ponderings is how rapidly they move beyond the concerns of the criminal justice system. They expose the uncomfortable point that criminal justice remains a primitive device. Trying to control crime is something like trying to fine-tune the economy. Police, courts, and prisons exert only uncertain and imprecise influence; changing them may affect levels of crime only marginally.

That idea, rarely confronted, still seems widely and

profoundly understood. Certainly it would have to be acknowledged by President Reagan, who says crime is a
problem of the human heart, and also by Ramsey Clark,
who says it arises from society's "generations of selfish
neglect."

There is much evidence that the public accepts it as
well. A 1981 *Newsweek* poll found people evenly divided
when asked, "How much confidence do you have in the
police to protect you from violent crime?" Forty-nine percent had "a great deal" or "quite a bit" of confidence, while
50 percent had "not very much" or "none at all." Beginning in 1967, the Louis Harris survey asked people whether
they "feel that our system of law enforcement works to
really discourage people from committing crimes, or don't
you feel that it discourages them that much?" The number
who believe law enforcement doesn't discourage crime rose
steadily from 56 percent in 1967 to nearly 79 percent in
1982, the last time the question was asked. The number
who believe law enforcement does discourage crime shrank
from 25 percent to about 16 percent.

Yet in 1981, a majority of the public also said the job
being done by local law enforcement was "excellent" or
"pretty good." The public also accepts the idea that forces
outside criminal justice cause crime. In a 1981 Gallup
poll, 69 percent cited such nonsystemic factors as unemployment (37 percent), breakdown of family and social
values (19 percent), and drugs (13 percent) as responsible
for increasing crime, while only 33 percent cited lenient
courts (20 percent) and inadequate punishment (13 percent).

After the Goetz incident, the New York police feared a rash of similar self-defense violence, but it never materialized. Most New Yorkers, it appeared, already were handling their fears in other ways and didn't need Goetz to tell them what to do.

But if how to control crime is the wrong question, then what is the right question? What is the purpose of criminal justice if it is not to control crime?

The answer isn't obscure. A society's response to its wrongdoers has always involved much more than practical issues. Such a response also sends powerful signals about values. We expect our police to pursue or deter criminals, but also to respect individual rights. We expect the courts to weigh guilt and impose punishment, but to do so in a deliberate fashion, according to carefully devised procedures. We expect prisons to confine and punish, but to do so according to a basic standard of decency.

If the years of confusion over criminal justice haven't enhanced its ability to control crime, neither has it enhanced its ability to meet such expectations, to send the right messages. That disappointment at least presents a way to make sense of the criminal justice problem: Instead of measuring the success of criminal justice in terms of crime control, leaving it hostage to the imponderables of crime rates, measure it by the messages it sends.

In those terms, real improvements might indeed be born of money, intellect, imagination, and, yes, goodwill.

5

The
FUNNEL

Herminio is twenty-eight years old, and for the past six years, he says, he's been addicted to heroin.

"How big was your habit?"

"Oh, I did seventy to a hundred and fifty dollars a day."

"How did you come up with that kind of money?"

"I was a master car thief. It was my line of work. I'd take orders for parts—tires, radios, sometimes the whole car. Then I'd go out at night and get what I needed. I could make the hundred and fifty with four radios."

"And you did that for six years."

"Oh, sure."

"Were you ever arrested?"

"Only twice."

"What for?"

"One, it was for possession. I was on my way to a shooting gallery. I had my bag of dope and my works. I was picked up in a sweep."

"And the other time?"

"They caught me inside a car."

"And what happened?"

"Well, the first time I just walked. I had two hundred dollars in my pocket from the previous night's work. So I paid my bail and walked. The second time I did have to do a short bit. They kept me seven days on Riker's Island and then let me go."

"But in six years of stealing cars, those were the only times you ever got caught?"

"That's right. They called me 'The Phantom.' "

—Interview with a recent enrollee in the methadone maintenance treatment program at New York City's Beth Israel Hospital

*I*n the case of Bernhard Goetz, too little attention was paid to a young man named Fred Clarke.

It was because of Fred Clarke that Goetz had begun to carry a gun. In 1981, when Clarke was sixteen, he was arrested after an incident that Goetz would describe as a mugging attempt. Goetz was riding on the subway in Manhattan with some expensive electronic equipment. It was only by chance that an off-duty housing police officer intervened to arrest Clarke, who was said to have beaten Goetz severely enough to injure him. But Clarke protested to the officer that Goetz had provoked him, and when the case reached the police station, both parties were issued desk appearance tickets and released. Clarke failed to appear on the return date.

The arrest was not entirely meaningless, however: A short time later, Clarke was arrested in Brooklyn on charges of attempted robbery. When the computers spit out the Manhattan arrest, the prosecutors were moved to extract a plea of guilty to misdemeanor charges, and Clarke was given six months in jail.

Two years later, Clarke was arrested for two robberies, one in Manhattan and one in Brooklyn. Now the courts got serious; Clarke was convicted and sentenced to three to nine years.

Some criminal justice officials will defend the handling of the Clarke case: The increase in severity of punishment from nothing to a jail term to serious prison time shows an ability to deliver measured justice and focus corrections resources on the more serious offenders.

Other New Yorkers have reason to look on the career of Fred Clarke with alarm: He was allegedly allowed to commit an attempted mugging, an attempted robbery, and two robberies before he was punished with serious prison time. And only Fred Clarke knows how many other crimes he might have attempted or committed in that time that never came to the attention of the authorities.

No wonder Bernhard Goetz decided to carry a gun.

▬▬▬

One way to visualize the messages criminal justice sends is to think of a funnel. At the top a broad flood of crimes challenges and mobilizes the police, courts, and correctional system. At the bottom is the apparent result of all their labors: a relative trickle of convicted felons actually sent to prison.

Statistics for New York City in a recent year (1986) are typical. Police took 550,000 reports of felonies, crimes serious enough to merit punishment of more than a year in prison. Assuming the victimization surveys are correct about the percentage of victims who call the police, the reports imply a million or more felonies actually committed. There is the first great narrowing of the funnel: Half or more of all crimes do not even engage the criminal justice system.

The next narrowing of the funnel occurs with the police. Of the million felonies committed and 550,000 reported, only 124,000 resulted in arrest on a felony charge. The 20 percent–plus figure for arrests has remained relatively constant over the years.

The neck of the funnel closes further as prosecutors and judges exercise their discretion. Only 35,000 of the 124,000 arrests led to an indictment on a felony charge. After that, slight narrowing occurs as some defendants are acquitted— the 35,000 indictments produced 27,500 felony convictions. The final constriction occurs at sentencing. Of the 27,500 convicted, only 16,755 were sent to jail or prison.

Such figures are not quite as alarming as they might seem, since substantial percentages of felonies are committed among friends and acquaintances. This is particularly true for assaults. Some 41 percent of black male assault victims say they knew their assailant. The figure for whites is 33 percent. For black women, the figure is 66 percent, reflecting the extent to which assaults of females arise from domestic strife. (The figure for white women is 55 percent.)

Yet a crime committed by a friend or relation is still a crime. And the figures for other felonies do not afford even such perverse comfort. Fully 85 percent of white male robbery victims and 91 percent of black male robbery victims, for example, report being robbed by strangers. (The figures for white women are 75 percent and for black women 76 percent.) The funnel figures, therefore, mislead only slightly in documenting the vague general sense that criminal justice does little to control crime. To the extent that imprisonment for a year or more constitutes American society's most credible punishment, the arithmetic of the funnel squelches any expectation that most criminals will be punished. The 16,755 sent to prison amount to a tiny 1.7 percent of the million felonies originally committed. The chances of committing a crime and getting off without serious punishment are more than sixty to one.

Such a disadvantage can't be easily or cheaply overcome. Suppose New York were to decide to double the number sent to prison in a year to 33,500. Achieving such a goal would require revolutionary upheaval in the court system as judges and prosecutors and defense attorneys altered ways of thinking and acting they have followed for decades. And it would require immense public expenditures to build the prison space. For the sake of prison cells, legislators would have to approve unpopular tax increases or diversion of money from such fundamentals as public schools, public health, and mass transit.

Yet even if society were willing to pay that price, the result would only be to increase the percentage of felonies punished by imprisonment from 1.7 percent to 3.4 percent. The chances of committing a crime and getting off without serious punishment would have been reduced—from about sixty to one to about thirty to one.

Over the years, the message about the limits of crime control has fed mightily upon itself. This is apparent from a closer look at the first narrowing of the funnel, the difference between crimes committed and crimes reported. A recent National Institute of Justice study suggests that the 50 percent reporting rate assumed for the New York statistics may be quite high. Researchers examining the National Crime Survey figures for 1983 found that of the 37,115,000 crimes that took place, only 12,880,000, or 35 percent, were reported to the police. Predictably, the more violent crimes and those involving the largest losses of property were reported more frequently. Yet even such serious felonies as rape and robbery were reported at rates of 48 percent and 52 percent, respectively. The most frequently reported crimes were auto theft (69 percent) and aggravated assault (58 percent).

Why don't more victims report crimes? To a great extent it is because the victims feel they can't be bothered. More than 60 percent who suffered crimes of theft like purse snatching and pocket picking said they didn't report either because they didn't feel the crime was important enough (30 percent), because they felt nothing could be done about the crime since there was no proof or no way to identify the criminal (17 percent), because the property would be hard to recover (5 percent), or because they didn't discover the crime until long after it had happened (7 percent). The numbers were similar for household crimes like burglary and larceny. Victims of violent crimes shared the reluctant attitude. Twenty-two percent didn't report robberies or assaults because they did not think them important enough to report, and another 28 percent considered such crimes personal matters to be settled without involving the law.

The National Institute of Justice study betrayed some dismay at such findings. Reporting crime, the study observes, is an "essential dimension of citizen involvement in the criminal justice system." It points out that "in calling the police, victims and others introduce themselves to the criminal justice system. . . . If criminal incidents are not made known to the police, they are likely to remain outside of, or hidden from, the system which has been established to deter wrongdoing." Yet the idea that reporting crime amounts to an obligation of good citizenship seems lost on most of the victimized public. Only 35 percent of those who did report crimes said they did so for such reasons.

So the topmost section of the funnel, the difference between crimes committed and crimes reported, reveals the public's alienation from the official criminal justice process. To an extent, that alienation may be deeply rooted in an American culture that has encouraged self-reliance and a mistrust of government. But it also surely reflects some degree of resignation to the fact that cooperating with the authorities will likely be too frustrating, time-consuming, or pointless to be worth even minimal effort. The National Institute of Justice researchers are right to see that as a reason for concern.

Altering that message, somehow revaluing the criminal justice process in the eyes of victims and potential victims—thereby automatically altering the message for criminals and potential criminals as well—would do much to cool the fevered politics of law and order. But how to accomplish such a thing—especially when the chances of substantially improving the crime-control figures seem so slight?

A general answer lies in shifting the whole system's attention to the crimes and criminals that remain outside the funnel. That chances remain slight for controlling such criminal activity ought not to permit simply giving up on it. As the victim studies suggest, to do that is to reinforce the wrong message. Is it possible to think in terms of improving the message in ways that don't need to be ratified in the crime-rate figures? How would police go about meaningfully addressing those criminals whose crimes are never reported, and those who are never arrested for crimes that are reported? How would courts make it clearer that society does care about the offenses of the hundreds of thousands who are arrested but escape serious punishment even though their guilt is obvious or even admitted?

The search for answers could even extend beyond the funnel, to those who do wind up in prison. The funnel, after all, is the conscious artifact of a mind-set shared by the public, much of the press, and political leaders along with the managers of criminal justice. It considers punishment in the form of a prison term to be the ultimate goal. Yet only the most savagely violent criminals go to prison for so long that society can rest easy about their causing more trouble. Most are released after only a few years. How could the practical interest in encouraging their good behavior after release balance the legitimate need to punish their wrongdoing?

To find answers to such questions, one must learn to look upon the process of criminal justice as important on its own, whatever one makes of its results.

6

COPS
and
COMMUNITIES

"See that building down there? People are selling drugs out of there. At least that's what the neighbors tell me. I've asked them to watch the building, note license numbers of cars stopping by. Before long we'll be able to go in and close it down. Before that, though, there's a special problem. One of the customers drives up each day in a school bus. I've asked a person who lives on the block to watch for it and get me the number of the bus. I'm going to try to bust that guy with the goods on him. If I can't do that, then I'm going to find out who his boss is and go and have a talk with him, try to get him fired. I don't want a junkie driving school kids around on my post."

—*Interview with a community patrol officer
in Sunset Park, Brooklyn*

ONE

*I*n the autumn of 1964, my wife and I entered a program of the United States Peace Corps that would eventually take us to a place called La Colonia Quince de Setiembre, on the outskirts of San José, Costa Rica. We were twenty-one years old, and we had just graduated from college.

The designers of the Peace Corps had envisioned Americans volunteering their skills to provide developing Third World countries with midlevel managers and professionals deemed necessary for economic advancement. What the Peace Corps tended to get, however, was people like us: long on enthusiasm, idealism, and a desire for adventure, but short on any managerial or professional skill, not to mention experience of any sort save four years of liberal-arts college.

What could we possibly offer Costa Rica? Some of us

claimed training as schoolteachers and so were put to work instructing Costa Rican pupils in English as a second language. But most of us were like my wife and me: as eager to learn as to teach. What could we do?

The Peace Corps had a good answer. Along with solid doses of the Spanish language and Latin American history and culture, we were given several weeks of instruction in a kind of social work known as community development, a self-help therapy for neighborhoods.

It was the sixties, and an American government blundering into a war in Vietnam was hypersensitive to accusations of imperialism and disregard for the backward societies' need of their own nationalism and collective self-respect. Such cultural arrogance, it was said, was the international equivalent of "unconscious white racism" at home. The Peace Corps labored under the burden of reversing that perception, as a matter of honest policy, beyond image making. Community development played a central role.

The last thing we were to do, we were told, was to behave as if we were messengers of progress who knew what backward peoples needed to do in order to advance. Instead we would go to great lengths to demonstrate our respect for the culture of the "host country nationals"— "natives" was considered pejorative—and to help them do what they themselves felt was important for their own betterment. This was the fundamental precept of community development.

The process would follow a well-established pattern: general research, identification of problems, organizing to address them. The people of the community were to be involved from the beginning. No matter how clearly the Peace Corps volunteer might perceive needs they did not immediately recognize, no matter how impatient he might become with their slowness to see what was good for them, he dared not substitute preaching for quiet motivation, act as a savior rather than a coequal.

In practice this meant spending a good deal of time initially doing nothing but conversing with anyone in the neighborhood willing to talk. There was no shortage of informants in a community where many were unemployed and where visiting remained a basic recreation: women at home with their kids, men drinking in a bar, the group of teenagers kicking a soccer ball around. Inevitably, one discovered that the problems that seemed most obvious to an outsider remained low on the list for much of the community. Middle-class Americans arriving in a place like La Colonia Quince de Setiembre might be appalled by general filth and the malnutrition apparent in the swollen bellies and stick-thin limbs of too many soulful-looking children. It would not take many days of conversation, however, to learn that the people were more concerned with the lack of furniture for the shed that had been constructed for use as a school, or the intermittent running water that turned indoor toilets into a health menace and forced many to bathe and do laundry in the muddy river that meandered nearby.

One pursued the process by organizing community meetings, ideally along with a "counterpart"—a host-country national interested in accepting the responsibilities of leadership (in our case, the priest from the church up the road). The meetings would focus on the problems that had come up in conversation. If the volunteer had done his work well, he would have the meeting talking about school furniture and running water. Over time the people would be encouraged to say which problem they considered most important and to consider strategies for addressing it. A community board might be elected, representatives appointed to lobby with the education ministry and the water bureau. Their reports would provide the focus for the next meeting. Eventually, some relief might be achieved by the community's own efforts at helping itself. Older students would be organized to build desks and stools from lumber left over from construction of the school building. Men of the community would contribute days of work to help hasten the installation of a new water main.

The process was every bit as important as achieving the goal. It might be possible for a Peace Corps volunteer to talk the American Agency for International Development into giving the community money for school desks or an improved water system, resolving either problem in a matter of weeks. But this would have been considered failure. Give a man a fish, the adage said, and you feed him for a day; teach him how to catch fish himself, and you will feed him for a lifetime.

Why begin a discussion of American police with a description of community development in the Peace Corps? Because this relatively simple, easily taught process suggests an excellent answer to the question of how the police could improve their message.

TWO

The police forces established in American cities during the nineteenth century differed from the police of European countries in a fundamental respect: Americans, mistrusting central government, wanted the power to enforce the law under local control. Let the Irish have their constabulary, the Italians their carabinieri, the Spanish their Guardia Civil. Americans would have none of a federal police. Why hand the central government such a potent tool for the abuse of political freedom and other civil rights?

All that distinguished the early American police officer was his badge. He patrolled in civilian clothes and might carry a weapon only as a matter of personal style. It was not until the second half of the nineteenth century that the need for greater identifiability and persuasiveness on the street led to the introduction of uniforms and revolvers. By the turn of the century most urban police were so equipped, but the tradition of dispersed local administration continued strong.

Yet as agents of local government, American police suffered identity conflicts from the beginning. All understood that they were to maintain public order. But what did that mean? Robert M. Fogelson, in his excellent history of urban police, notes that in addition to pursuing criminals, "the police cleaned streets and inspected boilers in New York, distributed supplies to the poor in Baltimore, accommodated the homeless in Philadelphia, investigated vegetable markets in St. Louis, operated emergency ambulances in Boston."

The tradition of decentralization combined with the confusion over mission left the urban departments open to heavy political influence. By the turn of the century, Fogelson writes, many departments appeared to serve political machines before the general public. "The precincts rather than headquarters carried out most essential police functions; the captains or ward bosses rather than the chiefs or commissioners made most vital departmental decisions."

The waves of European immigration that were transforming American cities drove their politics. The police played a central role. They were charged with enforcing the WASP establishment's laws against drinking, gambling, and other vices. Yet under the control of local politicians linked to vice operations that thrived in the new ethnic neighborhoods, police tended to ignore that duty, at least as long as the offensive behavior remained confined to the immigrant communities. The political bosses solidified their control, often doling out sought-after positions on the police force in the same ethnic neighborhoods.

The same accommodation that reinforced ethnic politics fed cynicism and corruption that could weaken the police and victimize those same ethnic constituents. Political connection could outweigh all other qualifications for a police job. "Small wonder," Fogelson writes, "that within a few days many applicants grew several inches taller and years younger, learned to read and write and, like the pilgrims who traveled to holy places, recovered from serious and even chronic ailments. . . . One Kansas City patrolman had a wooden leg."

Meanwhile, abuses of the public were egregious. An 1894 commission investigating New York City police heard the story of Ceala Urchittel. "A Jewish widow with three children who ran a cigar store on the Lower East Side, she was blackmailed by a precinct detective who falsely accused her of keeping a disorderly house. Unable to raise the money, she was arrested, convicted and fined; as a result she lost her business, home, health, and children."

The corruption and abuse led repeatedly to commissions of inquiry and eventually to an initial period of reforms over the first three decades of this century. A second generation of reformers took over in the 1930s, and their legacy would continue a tradition of earnest examination and revision of police practice through the decades after World War II. The tension between the reformers and defenders of police business-as-usual would shape larger philosophical and practical debates over what the role of the police ought to be.

In the first era, the reformers, led by adherents of the Progressive movement, sought to break the hold of the political machines on city police departments. They campaigned for strictly administered civil service hiring to replace political-machine recruiting. They called upon central headquarters to establish a serious chain of command by which superior officers would rein in the freewheeling precinct captains. The reformers also sought to consolidate precincts and to turn over tasks that posed the greatest corruption hazards, like enforcement of vice laws, to special squads reporting to headquarters rather than precinct commanders.

They would focus the police role as exclusively as possible on crime prevention and emergency response, while relieving their officers of responsibilities for things like boiler inspection and street cleaning. They sought to upgrade recruiting and training, enforcing standards for intelligence, physical fitness, and character background.

The early reformers commonly called for such measures in the context of a military analogy. The public responded to the thought of police officers as a sort of army deployed against vast and determined forces of crime. And the idea well suited the Progressives' agenda for wresting control of basic police administration and recruiting from the ward bosses. A successful army, after all, needed central control by a strong chain of command, well-chosen and well-trained soldiers, and an objectively defined mission.

In the second era of reform, the leadership shifted from the civilian Progressive movement to the police administrators themselves. They would have to confront emerging racketeering and other organized crime, the rise of the drug trade, teenage gangs and other juvenile crime problems, and, eventually, rioting in urban ghettos, the expansion of modern drug trafficking, and the plague of chronic street crime.

The military model would survive to some extent: Politicians and police administrators alike would periodically vow "war on crime" or particular crime problems, like the drug trade, well into the sixties and seventies. But the police administrators who emerged as national leaders were more interested in the idea of policing as a profession. They carried forward the basic reform effort to separate the police from local politics. One distinguishing feature of a profession, after all, is that it is guided by its own standards and codes, which insulate it from the interference of outside interests. The professionals easily embraced the original reform agenda of a centralized chain of command over fewer precincts, limiting the police mission to crime prevention and control, and more objective recruiting based on higher standards and serious training. The professionals would also take great pride in police technology, beginning with the patrol car. O. W. Wilson, who served in Chicago and would become perhaps the most influential of American police chiefs, formulated the basic theory of motorized patrol in the 1930s. Police presence deterred crime, he argued, and the most efficient way to maximize deterrence was to maximize presence by fielding officers in cars that could rapidly cover large areas of the city. He also believed the rapid response time the cars made possible would produce more arrests and please the public. These ideas were enshrined as axioms of policing in the textbook *Police Administration*, which Wilson coauthored with R. C. McLaren. It would mold generations of American police managers.

The professional chiefs sought to emulate the estimable J. Edgar Hoover, whose Federal Bureau of Investigation seemed the paragon of professional law enforcement: its nationwide fingerprint files and crime laboratories could scientifically link criminals to crimes with sophisticated tests of firearms and bullets, blood, hair, paint, fibers, and other evidence. Eventually the professional chiefs would also develop 911 call-in networks and computerized systems for handling crime records, tracking cars on patrol, and simulating the face of a suspect from a victim's description.

And the professional chiefs would make much of scholarship and research. It would become *de rigueur* among urban police chiefs and their ambitious senior officers to acquire advanced degrees in fields like management and public administration. In the seventies, a few departments—in Multnomah County, Oregon, and San Jose, California, for example—even boasted chiefs who were doctors of philosophy. Such chiefs would display a healthy appetite for planning based on objective research rather than seat-of-the-pants judgments about crime problems. In the seventies, the heavy flow of Law Enforcement Assistance Administration money nourished such interest and spawned a generation of police managers with advanced grantsmanship skills. It also inspired more sophisticated academic interest in the police and crime as a part of urban life.

Fogelson points out that just as the military model suited the Progressives' need for a politically palatable way to justify administrative policies advancing their campaign against ward politics, the professional model served deeply felt needs of the enlightened police administrators. It fit their strong desire to upgrade the popular image of the police, long characterized by Keystone Kops movies and police-scandal headlines. And it was so neutral and unexceptionable an idea that it could become a focus for uniting police chiefs with otherwise sharply divergent views.

However appealing and useful the military and professional models might be, however, neither is especially appropriate. The military analogy breaks up quickly once one gets past uniforms, weapons, and titled ranks. A city's population of street criminals doesn't operate according to a coordinated battle plan, and city streets hardly resemble battlefields, or even the areas torn by modern guerrilla warfare. Police officers on patrol only rarely will operate according to well-coordinated tactics. For the most part they function with great autonomy, exercising enormous personal discretion in response to randomly assigned tasks. While centralized administration and obedience to orders are essential, they mostly have to do with supervision of a group of people engaged in fairly passive activity rather than motivation of a force mounting a concerted, aggressive attack.

As for the professional model, it simply strained credulity. The few months of training that the best police departments required for the preparation of new recruits could hardly compare with the years of study required of doctors and lawyers, or even teachers and accountants. Furthermore, it is unlikely that new officers approach police work with the idea of a commitment to a profession. In his study of police at work in eight cities, *Varieties of Police Behavior*, James Q. Wilson cautions against overqualifying the police. "The patrolman is neither a bureaucrat nor a professional, but a member of a craft. As with most crafts, his has no body of generalized, written knowledge nor a set of detailed prescriptions as to how to behave—it has, in short, neither theory nor rules. Learning in the craft is by apprenticeship, but on the job and not in the academy. The principal group from which the apprentice wins (or fails to win) respect are his colleagues on the job, not fellow members of a discipline or attentive supervisors." All the talk of standards and professional identity, in other words, remains somewhat wishful.

Perhaps more important than their applicability is the fact that neither the military nor the professional model could be shown to have much effect on crime. Fogelson refers to a speech Chief Francis O'Neill of Chicago gave to the International Association of Chiefs of Police in 1904. "He claimed that any police department deserved the public's wholehearted support if it faithfully carried out the following duties and nothing more: suppressing gambling only where known to the police, regulating saloons according to the law, wiping out vice only in communities that found it objectionable, and handling all criminals in an impartial and nonpolitical manner."

No chief who took himself seriously as a general engaged in war on crime could possibly profess to be satisfied with such limited goals; nor could a professional administrator determined to bring the latest management techniques to the struggle. Nor would public common sense have allowed him to do so even if he had been so inclined. The models for reform might in fact have been conceived mostly as ways to handle "all criminals in an impartial and nonpolitical manner." Yet they automatically added crime control to the police agenda. How to judge a military force if not by the degree to which it could be said to win battles? And how to judge professionalism if not by the degree to which an organization met what seemed to be an obvious goal?

And yet even down to the present, most experienced police in honesty would have to agree that their actual work made much more sense in Chief O'Neill's terms than in those of the reformers. From the earliest days, police work had always been more reactive than proactive. The reformers and their supporters in the mayor's office, the city council, and the press might talk of making war on criminals. Every patrolman knew that his ability to win many battles, or even to identify strategies that could have much effect, remained severely limited. Professional management might result in some new efficiencies, and technology might improve internal supervision and reduce response time. But patrol officers knew better than anyone what the professional managers' research would eventually confirm: Patrol does not necessarily deter crime.

One now famous study of police patrolling Kansas City, Missouri, for example, sought to assess the effectiveness of O. W. Wilson's standard patrol model: cruising around a beat in a patrol car. The researchers identified five groups of three beats each that shared similar populations and crime levels. In each group, police patrolled one beat in the traditional way, with a single car responding to calls and otherwise cruising randomly. In a second beat, more patrol cars were deployed to increase the sense of police presence. In the third, police cars responded to calls but did no random patrolling.

After a year, the results were provocative. So far as researchers could tell, the level of random patrolling and visible police presence made no substantial difference in levels of criminal activity, citizen fear, amount of reported crime, criminal victimization as reported in follow-up studies, or citizen satisfaction with the police. While researchers would caution that the finding ought not to be taken as proof that police are impotent in the face of crime, most would agree that it suggested a need to rethink the deployment of police.

Other research would challenge the commonsense belief in the importance of rapid response time. Not only did the victimization studies reveal the huge amount of unreported crimes for which there is no police response at all; other studies would show that victims typically wait several minutes before calling the police, thereby drastically diminishing the value of seconds shaved off the time between receipt of a call and arrival of police at the scene. Research would also challenge common assumptions about the role of the detective. A 1975 Rand Corporation study did for investigation what the Kansas City research did for patrol. "The single most important determinant of whether or not a case will be solved is the information the victim supplies to the immediately responding patrol officer," the study found. Much, in other words, is left to chance—the extent to which witnesses are willing to pass information along, the clumsiness or remorse of the criminal. "If information that uniquely identifies the perpetrator is not presented at the time the crime is reported, the perpetrator by and large will not be subsequently identified." Only a small percentage of crimes are ever subjected to serious investigation by detectives backed up by crime laboratories, fingerprint files, and computers.

When police order a ransacked apartment processed for fingerprints in the absence of a suspect, they do so mainly to help the distraught victim handle his or her feelings, not because fingerprints are likely to lead to an apprehension. A blind search of millions of fingerprints, conducted by hand, would take weeks and seems justifiable only in order to solve the most savage or otherwise outrageous crimes. In routine cases, fingerprints are of use mostly as corroborating evidence once an arrest is made on other grounds or a suspect is otherwise identified. Only very recently have programmers figured out how to use a computer to link a name with a fingerprint in a matter of minutes. When the new technology is introduced to a police department, it is hailed as a wonderful breakthrough that could actually bring the reality into line with the public myth for the first time.

Thus even for victims of violent crimes like purse snatchings and muggings, the routine is depressing: Call the police to get a dispatcher, who tries to determine if the perpetrator might still be around. Chances are he's not, so officers are assigned to come by later and take a report. Hours or even days after that, a detective may call to pursue the investigation, which consists of inviting you down to the precinct station to leaf through pages of photographs. You study page after page as the detective looks on wearily. He doesn't expect you to find anything, and neither do you, though the exercise may make you feel better in some slight way. Then for all practical purposes, the investigation stops. (Police in New York City's 90th Precinct once claimed some success in reducing robberies in part by using the books of photographs more effectively. They compiled special books containing photos of suspects charged with robbery and some other crimes who lived in the precinct, no matter where they had been arrested. The books would be taken to the homes of victims for their perusal, and since in this neighborhood many victims happened to be mothers of teenagers, the teenagers had a chance to examine the books themselves. As they recognized their friends, they would spread the word that the police were disseminating their photographs—news that apparently had some deterrent effect.)

Your case might be "cleared" if the mugger gets arrested for a subsequent crime and acknowledges having committed yours. In fact, huge numbers of cases are closed in just that fashion. Police departments are likely to make much of clearance rates based on dubious information—confessions of boastful criminals, or those who hope confessing to previous crimes, thereby helping police to improve clearance rates, will gain them more lenient treatment in court.

But if police don't behave like soldiers in a command structure or a professional elite, what do they actually do? A certain amount of the corruption and other misbehavior that motivated the reformers in the first place has continued through much of this century. It is all too evident today. Ward politicians may no longer control police departments as they did in the early 1900s. But police have remained vulnerable to groups linked to drug dealing, gambling, prostitution, and other organized vice. In the past two decades, major scandals involving police who take bribes, steal, or deal in drugs have shaken New York, Miami, even Los Angeles, where police enjoy a reputation for superior professionalism. The movie *Serpico* detailed the lonely heroism of an officer who refused to go along with a tradition of corruption that seemed to have eaten deeply into the most elemental routines of the police department. *Prince of the City* showed how highly proficient narcotics detectives, like chameleons, assumed the crooked values of the junkies and drug merchants they pursued. The Knapp Commission investigations of payoffs to New York City police in the 1970s in some ways echoed the historic investigations earlier in the century. They would lead to administrative reforms and the creation of an internal affairs unit based on a system of secret informers that made paranoia part of the routine for all New York City police. Yet some ten years later, the department again suffered through revelations about officers shaking down drug dealers and stealing on patrol.

Modern police may have achieved levels of selection, supervision, and discipline that make the old days of common brutality and other misconduct an ugly memory. But it is a memory that continues to haunt. Incidents of police brutality too often were the sparks that touched off the ghetto riots of the sixties. They would force searching national inquiries into police management and behavior. The last such riot, in 1980 in Miami, began when news spread that four white police officers had been acquitted of charges arising from the beating death of a black man. The question of when police should use deadly force simmered as an issue through the sixties, seventies, and eighties. In 1984 and 1985, New York City's police department reeled through a series of dismaying incidents, including a number of fatal police shootings. One victim was an aged, mentally disturbed woman who resisted eviction from a public housing project. In another case, police officers got drunk while on duty, drove their patrol car at high speed down Park Avenue, and ran down two pedestrians, killing one and severely injuring the other, then fled the scene.

During these years, students of police would examine with new assiduousness exactly how the honorable majority of police, along with the dishonorable minority, went about their jobs. Jonathan Rubinstein, a historian, gained the permission of the Philadelphia police to accompany officers on patrol. He enrolled in the police academy training program and then spent more than a year on the street with the police. His book *City Police*, published in 1973, makes clear that patrol remains a relatively formless activity, in which police officers hope to stay on top of crime by making a habit of suspicion and developing a sixth sense for trouble. Yet the precise quality of such skill remains elusive. "The rookie shares the widely held opinion that policemen have special skills to see things," Rubinstein writes. "If only he knew what those abilities were. At the academy he was encouraged to be suspicious of everything he sees. 'When you go on the street, you will develop a sense about these things,' one instructor said; another insisted that you develop 'a nose for trouble.' The mysterious skills hinted at by these phrases are not made explicit by the examples that the instructors offer—'Watch out for men sitting in cars around schools and playgrounds,' 'people walking late at night,' or 'people carrying large packages.' Always illustrations of heroics and cleverness from a dimming past when acuity paid off."

He also points out that police evaluate crimes according to a standard that appears at odds with the public interest. "For the policeman, the determining factor of any crime's importance is its setting. He defines the location of all crimes by the deceptively simple distinction between 'inside' and 'outside.' . . . Outside means any location a patrolman can be reasonably expected to see while on patrol. . . . Any outside crime is an affront to the patrolman's notion of himself as a guardian of his territory, an occurrence which suggests to his superiors that he was not doing his work properly." Allowing an inside crime, however, may be forgiven.

James Q. Wilson, in *Varieties of Police Behavior*, discerned three distinct patterns. The relatively primitive "watchman" approach entails using the law mainly as a way to maintain basic order as defined by the police themselves. Minor infractions are ignored so long as they don't prove too disruptive to the community. So, to some extent, are gambling, prostitution, and other vices. And officers feel free to apply the law to different groups in different ways. "Negroes are thought to want, and to deserve, less law enforcement because to the police their conduct suggests a low level of public and private morality, an unwillingness to cooperate with the police or offer information, and widespread criminality. . . . Motorists, unless a departmental administrator wants to 'make a record' by giving a few men the job of writing tickets, will often be left alone. . . . Private disputes—assaults among friends or family—are treated informally or ignored."

The watchman style Wilson observed appears quite similar to early approaches to policing described by Fogelson. Despite nearly a century of talk about reform, Wilson found that the watchman style persists to some extent with all police officers and that it remains the "operating code" in police departments of three of the eight cities he studied.

In two other cities, Wilson found the more advanced "legalistic" style in force. In these departments, police administrators sought to focus patrol activity on enforcing laws rather than maintaining order. The two functions often overlap, of course—much disruptive behavior is punishable by law. But the legalistic administrators were seeking to limit the individual discretion of officers by encouraging them to act according to the more objective standards encoded in law books. Thus "a legalistic department will issue traffic tickets at a high rate, detain and arrest a high proportion of juvenile offenders, act vigorously against illicit enterprises, and make a large number of misdemeanor arrests even when, as with petty larceny, the public order has not been breached." Such a department would not be likely to recognize different standards of enforcement for different groups like blacks and drunks. "Indeed, because such persons are more likely than certain others to commit crimes, the law will fall heavily on them and be experienced as 'harassment.' "

Police who follow the third style Wilson describes fall between the watchman and legalistic approaches. They "take seriously all requests for either law enforcement or order maintenance (unlike police with a watchman style) but are less likely to respond by making an arrest or otherwise imposing formal sanctions (unlike police with a legalistic style). The police intervene frequently but not formally." This approach, Wilson notes, often occurs in cities with a homogeneous middle class.

Herman Goldstein, a University of Wisconsin criminal justice professor who once served as an assistant to the legendary Chief O. W. Wilson, points to the multiplicity of problems police consider their responsibility, most of them having little to do with crime. Several studies, he notes, document that fewer than 20 percent of calls to police involve law enforcement. "The studies report the large number of hours devoted to handling accidents and illnesses, stray and injured animals, and intoxicated persons; dealing with family disturbances, fights among teenage gangs, and noisy gatherings; taking reports on damage to property, traffic accidents, missing persons, and lost and found property," Goldstein writes in *Policing a Free Society.* Especially in the inner city, Goldstein writes, police become a kind of catchall social agency of last resort, expected to cope with the ultimate effects of problems—poverty, family breakdown, unemployment, deteriorated schools— that overwhelm other city services. Despite a commitment to professionalism and crime control, modern police still are forced to act as a multiservice agency, functioning much as Fogelson described police activity in the nineteenth century. The police officer is often "called upon to serve as surrogate parent or other relative, and to fill in for social workers, housing inspectors, attorneys, physicians, and psychiatrists," Goldstein writes.

In 1983, David Couper, the chief of police in Madison, Wisconsin, published a brochure titled *How to Rate Your Local Police*. It reinforced Goldstein's observation and provided as blunt an assessment of the limits on police as has been heard since the days of Chief O'Neill. Chief Couper dismissed as meaningless such common measures of police performance as crime rates, numbers of arrests, the ratio of police on patrol to citizens, and response time. According to Couper, the size and makeup of a city's population have much more to do with its level of crime than anything the police can do. The ability to make an arrest often depends on factors beyond police control, like the promptness with which the victim reports the crime and the ability of witnesses to identify the criminal. The proper ratio of police to citizens depends greatly on the nature of a community and its crime problems. ("Shoplifting in Beverly Hills and ski larcenies in Aspen require dramatically different police responses than arson in the South Bronx or narcotics trafficking in Miami.") And response time remains a crude measure because victims normally wait several minutes before calling the police.

How then to rate police? Chief Couper argues that a law enforcement agency ought to be judged the way any other municipal agency is judged: by the quality of its leadership, the extent to which its policies are realistic and well considered, the effectiveness of its recruiting and preparation of its line officers, its ability to communicate with the public, and its overall integrity.

As such explorations reveal different realities of police work, they also expose the basis for profound public confusion. Police administrators, abetted by the media, typically promote a myth the public wants to believe: The police officer carries out a coherent mission designed to control crime. To the extent that he fails, the myth holds, it is because of laws that tie his hands by setting strict limits on his powers to search or interrogate, courts that squander his efforts by carelessly releasing the criminals he has pursued and arrested.

Yet despite modern technology and efforts to shape up management, patrol remains a relatively aimless activity, and investigation a haphazard one—those are the filthy secrets of police. Some even suggest that it would be irresponsible to publicize the idea that the police understanding of crime control remains so unclear. It may be asking too much of the public to appreciate sound management and integrity without any higher expectations of results.

Confusion over what the police can and cannot do, meanwhile, breeds cynicism all around. The citizen watches a police press conference in which grim-faced officers display pounds of heroin and cocaine, along with a fearsome arsenal of weapons seized in a raid. Yet sleazy young men continue to sell drugs openly in the park a few blocks away. The chief goes before the cameras with the district attorney to announce a sophisticated program that will use computers to identify "career criminals" and single them out for special surveillance and tough prosecution. This efficient focus of resources, the officials assert, is bound to make a dent in street crime. Yet months later, muggings and burglaries are as frequent as ever.

Officers in the lower patrol ranks, meanwhile, sense that their superiors are not about to disabuse the public of its expectations. In response, they hunker down in alienation. "If both legal mandates and public expectations are taken literally, and if the reality of the situation that the police confront is recognized, the demands on the police appear so contradictory that the police task is simply unworkable—an impossible mission," Goldstein writes.

From such stress springs the police subculture, "a formidable force . . . that determines the way in which much police business is handled. It is inclined to oppose strongly any proposed changes in policing that are seen as threatening the protective bond between officers."

Wilson observes that "the police organization develops its special ethos: defensiveness, a sense of not being supported by the community, and a distrust of outsiders. Most officers adjust to this by adopting the habit of 'minding your own business' and 'keeping your mouth shut.' The young patrolman is taught 'not to stick his neck out' and to 'keep his nose clean.' . . . The most important consequence of this state of affairs is that with respect to routine police matters, *the normal tendency of the police is to underenforce the law.*"

THREE

Continuing public confusion and police alienation in the seventies and eighties were accompanied by two other trends. One was the growth of the "underclass." The other was the economic crisis of municipal governments that in some large cities forced police to make severe choices.

In 1965, Daniel Patrick Moynihan, then a Labor Department official, wrote a report to President Johnson that described the breakdown of the black family in ghetto neighborhoods as an urgent national problem. For years it was impossible to address it, however, or even to talk in terms of doing so, because a chorus of black and white civil rights leaders denounced the analysis as racist. To focus on the troubled black family, the critics asserted, was to blame the victim. The crimes were the racism and greed of the white majority, which profited from a social order that kept blacks uneducated, unemployed, dependent, and disorganized. The challenge, they argued, was to correct the social order, not to force more discipline on struggling black families.

By the 1980s, however, Moynihan's point began to look unassailable, as leading black groups like the Urban League and the National Association for the Advancement of Colored People began proclaiming that the deterioration of family and community life in black urban neighborhoods had become too alarming to deny. Health and welfare officials watched with dismay as the black illegitimacy rate soared. In 1950, 17 percent of black babies were born to unmarried mothers. By the late seventies, the figure exceeded 50 percent. Today it may be as high as 60 percent, and it apparently continues to grow unchecked. Inner-city public school systems across the country were close to collapse, with high school dropout rates approaching 50 percent in some places. Unemployment rates for young blacks approached 60 percent. Many of those who showed up in the unemployment figures actually were hard at work in illicit underground businesses like prostitution, fencing stolen goods, and drug trafficking—especially drug trafficking. And blacks were said to commit serious crimes at rates ten times those for whites. In cities like Chicago and Los Angeles, whole areas seemed to have fallen under the effective control of outlaw gangs composed mostly of black or Hispanic teenagers and young adults.

The statistics traced the shape of the underclass. What had caused its new growth? Theories abound. To some extent, urban blacks' problems of dependency and family breakdown simply carried over from the life of poor blacks in the rural South and were intensified by big economic events in the seventies and eighties: oil shocks, inflation, severe recession, the Reagan administration's cuts in social welfare spending.

Nicholas Lemann attracted much attention in 1986 with an article advancing a more specific argument: The underclass grew more concentrated in America's urban ghettos during the seventies as a direct result of civil rights gains. As long as housing and job discrimination forced the more capable, self-reliant blacks to remain in the inner city, they would serve as leaders and role models, upholding education, hard work, disciplined family life, and community improvement. Then it became possible for these black "strivers" to move into the middle-class mainstream, and they did so in a big way. The ghettos more than ever were left to concentrations of the hopeless.

What followed the departure of the "black working and middle classes, who had been freed from housing discrimination by the civil-rights movement," Lemann writes, "was a kind of free fall into what sociologists call social disorganization." Far from being overcrowded today, he points out, inner-city neighborhoods have lost population. And as their populations declined, the statistics measuring crime, illegitimacy, and other signs of social breakdown rose sharply.

Whatever one makes of Lemann's analysis, the "free fall" remains undeniable, and among the other headaches it creates for managers of social policy, it forces a reexamination of what police should do. Another reexamination of sorts had already been forced upon many urban departments in the mid-seventies by fiscal necessity. Crises of municipal finance forced cutbacks in all municipal services, including police. In the decade between 1975 and 1985, police employees per 1,000 in communities across the country declined by 10 percent. In New York, layoffs and attrition reduced a department that had numbered 30,522 to 21,838. There and elsewhere, police managers responded with a conscious policy of "triage"—the remaining patrol strength would be focused where it seemingly would do the most good, responding to major felonies.

"The police now give highest priority to responding to violent crimes or in-progress calls for robbery, murder, sexual assault, assault with a deadly weapon, and burglary," writes James K. Stewart of the National Institute of Justice. "Other calls, such as 'cold' burglaries or larcenies, received a deferred response. Complaints of rowdy youths on the street corner, public drunkenness, abandoned cars, graffiti and loud parties also are relegated to low priority." Thus in Los Angeles between 1975 and 1985, the reported crime rate rose from 75 per 1,000 to 98 per 1,000, while the annual arrest rate of a police officer for serious crimes remained constant and declined for all crimes from 33 to 22.

In such cities, the courts would participate by paying little attention to defendants who did not face serious charges or had been arrested only a couple of times. These were years of enthusiasm for the career-criminal strategies— saving scarce resources for the worst offenders in order to maximize return on the criminal justice investment. In those terms, the triage policies tended to work: Most urban neighborhoods were not totally overrun by murderers, rapists, and armed robbers.

But in avoiding that result, triage produced another: virtual total neglect of lesser crimes and criminals. As police in the affected cities struggled to keep up with the major felons, the ones considered minor got a free ride. And in some cases, those who learned that they could commit crime without fear of serious police response were considered minor only by police administrators trying to make sense of manpower losses. It gradually dawned on the residents of such cities that whole categories of offenses were virtually decriminalized. These included auto thefts, the lower levels of drug dealing, burglaries when no one was home, and the lesser robberies, like purse snatchings, when there were no physical injuries and losses of property were small.

One obvious result of all this was an increased level of fear. The Gallup poll has for years asked a national sampling whether they feel fearful walking alone at night anywhere within a mile of their homes. In 1965, about 40 percent of urban Americans said yes. By 1982, the figure had increased to 57 percent in the largest cities.

Such fear would become a powerful, if perplexing, factor in urban politics. City officials might consider the neglect of lower crimes a tolerable way to manage austerity. But it remained a grinding preoccupation for the public. One felt the fear whenever one ventured out in the evening; one was reminded of the cost whenever one paid an automobile insurance premium. The fear could inhibit one's freedom in fundamental decisions about where to live, how to get to work, how to socialize.

The fear would create new costs and difficulties for businesses, large and small, that wanted to locate in the city. The factory owner invested heavily in electronic alarm systems and platoons of security guards, while the owner of the bodega bought a bulletproof vest and kept an illegal gun under the counter. The fear played a role in the collapse of public education. Middle-class parents willingly paid thousands in tuition to send children where their basic safety could be assured along with an education. Public-school teachers struggling to cope with the remaining students found themselves faced with appalling questions: How would the presence of armed police in school corridors affect the learning environment? Should undercover cops be allowed to pose as students in classrooms in order to make drug arrests? Should students carrying guns or knives to school be disarmed at the door—even if, as many claimed, such a rule would mean they would no longer come to school, since they considered their weapons essential to their survival on the street?

The fear also dealt body blows to the institutions and amenities that were the strength of neighborhoods. Church and civic groups might hesitate to schedule evening meetings or host social events. Young families and old folks avoided the parks they once had taken for granted as places for relaxation and socializing.

It was disturbing enough to watch fear and its effect on community become a dominant issue of city life. It was even more disturbing to realize how woefully unprepared urban police departments were to respond. Not only had they consciously decided for fiscal reasons to neglect the low-level criminality that fed such fear. The years of evolution guided by reforms had left them with an operating approach that allowed little room for fighting fear. Each neighborhood had its own sources of fear, best understood at the neighborhood level, yet police administrators, worried about political influence and corruption, had long sought to limit the autonomy of neighborhood precincts. Police managers aspiring to professionalism prized the radio patrol cars that reduced response time to minutes and seconds. Yet officers riding in cars were poorly positioned to get to know communities and their problems. Modern police administrators boasted of their ability to assess crime trends with computerized research, then direct patrol forces to respond where the need seemed greatest. Yet fear is often subjective. Those neighborhoods most blighted by anxiety over crime weren't necessarily those that statistics proved to be the most crime-ridden.

The problem of community fear and the police response to it were explored by James Q. Wilson and his Harvard colleague George Kelling in a controversial article first published in 1982. They referred to the "broken windows" theory of behavior long recognized by social psychologists: As long as an abandoned building appears clean and untouched, it will remain so, but once one broken window appears and remains unrepaired, more vandalism is sure to follow. "Window breaking does not necessarily occur on a large scale because some areas are inhabited by determined window-breakers whereas others are populated by window-lovers; rather, one broken window is the signal that no one cares, and so breaking more windows costs nothing."

So it is with whole neighborhoods, Wilson and Kelling argued. Once one kind of offensive behavior—rowdy teenagers gathering in an empty lot to drink beer and play loud radios—is tolerated, others are likely to follow: The sidewalk becomes littered, fights break out, drug dealers and prostitutes appear. Then begins a downward cycle as decent folks avoid the area, granting even more implied license to the lowlifes. Eventually businesses may close and stable families move away.

Such a quiet disaster might occur, Wilson and Kelling point out, even though no serious crime is ever committed. It is enough that lesser crimes and the spreading disorder inspire fear of it. Yet a police department set up to deal primarily with major felonies may offer little help. "Patrol cars arrive, an occasional arrest occurs, but crime continues and disorder is not abated," they write. "Citizens complain to the police chief, but he explains that his department is low on personnel and that the courts do not punish petty or first-time offenders. To the residents the police who arrive in squad cars are either ineffective or uncaring; to the police, the residents are animals who deserve each other. The citizens may soon stop calling the police, because 'they can't do anything.' "

Wilson and Kelling emphasize that maintaining order is the historical responsibility of police, antedating by decades their well-equipped, professionally managed efforts to pursue major felons. "From the earliest days of the nation, the police function was seen primarily as that of night watchman: to maintain order against the chief threats to order—fire, wild animals, and disreputable behavior." For years the investigation of major crimes was a job for private detectives and victims pursued their own cases in courts. Police detectives and state prosecutors are more recent inventions.

In *Varieties of Police Behavior*, Wilson had implied,

quite properly, that the "legalistic style" was an advance. Now he and Kelling would amend that thinking. It is a mistake, they argue, to assume that if police do a good job of enforcing the law, order will take care of itself. Law enforcement deals in specific responses to specific cases, while "the essence of the police role in maintaining order is to reinforce the informal control mechanisms of the community itself." The habits and procedures of law enforcement may even inhibit that goal, as, for example, police hesitate to run rowdy teenagers off a street corner for fear of violating their rights. The police were not always so inhibited. Once upon a time, Wilson and Kelling write, "young toughs were roughed up, people were arrested 'on suspicion' or for vagrancy, and prostitutes and petty thieves were routed. 'Rights' were something enjoyed by decent folk, and perhaps also by the serious professional criminal, who avoided violence and could afford a lawyer."

The attempt to reinforce the community's informal control mechanisms, therefore, poses a hard question, which Wilson and Kelling state succinctly: "Should police activity on the street be shaped in important ways, by the standards of the neighborhood rather than by the rules of the state?" The answer isn't obvious. The authors describe, too approvingly perhaps, how police in Chicago's Robert Taylor Homes, a public housing project where Nicholas Lemann did much of his reporting on the underclass, had managed to reassure residents fearful of gang intimidation. "What the police in fact do is to chase known gang members out of the project. In the words of one officer, 'We kick ass.' Project residents both know and approve of this."

Whatever its problems, the underclass remains properly sensitive to police abuse, as recent brutality controversies in several cities have made abundantly clear. No police department is likely to make "kicking ass" overt policy. Nor should it necessarily encourage such conduct informally. How then to meet a responsibility for maintaining order, especially at a time of straitened finances? Wilson and Kelling's proposals are halfhearted: Assign more officers to foot patrol as the budget allows, encourage citizens' groups to supplement police patrols, ask cops to take the bus or subway to work. Their conclusion, however, remains cogent: "Above all we must return to our long-abandoned view that the police ought to protect communities as well as individuals. Our crime statistics and victimization surveys measure individual losses, but they do not measure communal losses."

Critics of the broken-windows theory would argue, with some reason, that Wilson and Kelling romanticized the watchman-style patrolling of early police. Police patrol began in London in 1829 when Sir Robert Peel required officers to wear uniforms and to stick to assigned beats. The purpose, Carl Klockars points out, was not to maintain order or fight crime more effectively, but to reassure a wary public that police would not be used as spies for the crown. Peel's uniformed "bobbies" "would be confined to the street . . . would not be used as spies and would be clearly identifiable, so when people furnished information they would know it was a constable they were giving it to. . . ." In America the issue was not the possibility of spying so much as basic supervision. With local politicians in control of police hiring, the job of the superior officers was to make sure the ill-trained, dubiously qualified, and poorly motivated patrolmen did some sort of work instead of repairing to bars or brothels or going home to sleep. "Uniformed patrol allowed early police administrators to set an extraordinarily minimal standard for job performance: Be in uniform on your beat! In the earliest days of American policing compliance with this order could be checked by setting up 'straight beats' laid out so that a patrol sergeant could look down a long street to see whether or not his patrolman was where he was supposed to be."

Samuel Walker argues that America's nineteenth-century police did not enjoy the authority conferred by the trust of a cohesive community, but instead were major players in local political brawling and corruption. On the streets, their problem was the difficulty of getting the public to accept their authority, a difficulty that may have contributed to their brutality.

The broken-windows theory, Walker asserts, "turns in part on the question of purpose: what the police saw themselves doing. Historians have established that police officers had a few purposes. The first was to get and hold a job. The second was to exploit the possibilities for graft that the job offered. A third was to do as little actual patrol work as possible. A fourth involved surviving on the street, which meant establishing and maintaining authority in the face of hostility and overt challenges to that authority. Finally, officers apparently felt obliged to go through the motions of 'real' police work by arresting occasional miscreants. We do not find in this picture any conscious purpose of fighting crime or serving neighborhood needs."

Such perspective on the watchman idea is healthy, certainly, but in the end, the critics leave unchallenged the basic Wilson-Kelling point: In recent years the behavior that disrupts community life has increased. Controlling it remains an important responsibility of the police. The most cogent argument for that, Kelling points out in another context, is the considerable grass-roots activity that has developed in the absence of any official response. In an article titled "Neighborhoods and Police," Kelling points to the proliferation of neighborhood groups that set up their own patrols, organize to watch for suspicious visitors, escort the fearful on errands, improve street lighting and landscaping to inhibit crime, or simply lobby the local police for better service. In New York City such groups are called block associations and are organized for general block improvement, though 30 percent list crime as their primary concern. Similar groups are said to promote crime prevention and control in a host of other cities. Kelling explores the phenomenon in "Northeast City," where ninety-five groups meet regularly. Typically, fifty families in an area covering a few blocks support such a group, though membership of some may reach five hundred. Only a few receive any outside funding; the rest support their modest costs—whistles, walkie-talkies, a newsletter—by collecting dues or holding events like street fairs and bake sales. Only a dozen members may actually be active enough to attend meetings, but that is apparently sufficient to sustain some degree of effort. Kelling marvels at the democratic spirit evident on this level: "One group has attempted to

include in their anti-crime activities a 'bag lady' (a homeless woman who, for the most part, lives on the street)
who stays in their neighborhood. Invited by residents, she
attended a special neighborhood meeting on rape. Although
silent during most of the meeting, she surprised the group
with an account of being raped. Since then, members pay
special attention to her during patrol."

Shouldn't a police department seize on such a naturally
thriving movement, devoting major resources to nurturing
it and exploring its possibilities? Shouldn't such an effort
be considered as important as anything a police agency can
do? There is a powerful case for answering yes to both
questions. Yet in most police departments, relating to such
citizen groups is called "community relations" or "crime
prevention" and remains a secondary interest of police,
who believe their purpose is to arrest major felons. The
skills and activities involved, Kelling writes, "separate
crime prevention officers from the dominant view of their
organization and culture and place them, in the opinion
of many of their peers, in the 'empty holster crowd'—that
is, as not being 'real' cops."

The need to protect communities as well as individuals,
then, requires a radical adjustment of how police think of
themselves. A few departments have begun to experiment
with ways to do just that. Their experiences imply much
for the police message of the future.

FOUR

The idea that police need to pay more attention to communities is hardly new. It goes back at least to the sixties, when urban riots and rising street crime shook up much of conventional law enforcement wisdom. President Johnson's 1967 crime commission called for police to set up formal community relations units and neighborhood-based citizens'/police advisory committees. It also advanced the idea of "team policing"—turning over authority for the policing of a geographic area to a team of patrol officers and investigators who would get to know the neighborhood and focus on crime problems peculiar to it.

During the seventies, at least 128 cities were reported to have tried out some version of the idea. In Los Angeles, recently torn by the Watts riots, the outspoken, politically conservative Chief Ed Davis read Robert Ardrey's *The Territorial Imperative* and passionately promoted the idea of giving police officers responsibility for a piece of turf that they would grow to defend with the protective ferocity Ardrey had described. Davis's "basic car plan" required that a single car, staffed by the same crew of nine officers covering all shifts, patrol a given neighborhood. An officer with a new rank, "senior lead officer," would direct the basic car team. The teams were to meet monthly with groups of the residents they policed.

Chief Davis's plan inspired some griping in the ranks. David M. Kennedy, who chronicled the LAPD's experience with community policing, quotes one captain, now "an eloquent exponent of neighborhood policing," on his initial reaction: "I was in the locker room working out, and I heard two guys who were senior leads. One was talking to the other about how he needed cookies for his meeting, and he was really concerned about damnit, I can't find the cookies. And the other one needed a movie projector, and I looked at these two kids, good-looking and good cops, and I thought, oh my God, what have we done with our finest?"

Yet with the chief committed, Kennedy reports, the basic car plan would survive for several years and was even credited with reducing by 25 percent on some commands the "repressible crimes"—burglaries, robberies, and thefts from motor vehicles. It also impressed many police with the value of community contact. Kennedy reports the story of one Los Angeles officer troubled by a string of car thefts in a theater parking lot. He couldn't take the time to lie in wait for the thieves because he had to keep responding to radio calls. But he noticed an elderly couple who every night sat out on their porch across the street. He issued them a pair of binoculars and asked them to call him every time a thief entered the parking lot. The strategy worked. "He was kind of excited about it," a senior officer said of the patrol officer's story. "That's what team policing did. It moved them towards mobilizing the community," a process the patrol ranks had previously resisted.

Other team-policing experiments were even more ambitious in concept. Smaller cities like Holyoke, Massachusetts, and St. Petersburg, Florida, set up experimental police teams outfitted with special uniforms (the Holyoke officers patrolled in collegiate-looking blazers instead of military-cut tunics) and given broad responsibility. Those programs failed because they ignited conflicts within the department. Regular officers resented the publicity fuss being made over the teams, and top commanders grew nervous about permitting them too much autonomy. Much was made of a pilot program in Cincinnati, where teams were given broad authority for administering police activities in specific districts. Ultimately, the central command reasserted its control and the program faltered. "There was a great deal of nervousness at higher levels," one Cincinnati administrator explained at the time. He pointed out that it was one thing to decentralize authority, another to decentralize responsibility. "Management felt, if they screw it up at the team level, the chief and his staff just can't say, 'Well don't blame us,' especially in the area of police misconduct. It's a real conflict." Lawrence Sherman, a police researcher, declared that "if it's done right, team policing amounts to a major revolution [in a police department] and it's not surprising that many attempts at revolution fail."

In St. Louis, where police are subject to the guidance of a state-appointed board of police commissioners, a member of the board managed to sell her colleagues on the team-policing idea after a visit to Cincinnati. The chief didn't like the idea but had no choice. He therefore ordered a pilot program in the Seventh District, a center of urban decay that St. Louis officers considered a punishment assignment. "The chief hoped [team policing] would fall flat on its face," a St. Louis officer explained at the time.

The chief, however, did not count on Captain Gay Carroway, who decided to use team policing as a way to boost the morale of his downtrodden troops. In that he appeared to have succeeded. With team policing, the Seventh changed from the Siberia of St. Louis to a desirable assignment. The captain expanded training opportunities and gave patrol officers a greater voice in decision-making about everyday problems on their beats. The community responded to a host of social activities sponsored by the district: cookouts and breakfasts, Christmas parties, even a contest for high school beauty queen. Despite such response, team policing survived for only a few years in the Seventh before falling victim to the nervousness of top administrators.

Where team policing did not inflame department politics, however, it inevitably forced painful questions of resources. Every hour a team officer spent meeting with community groups or planning responses to problems of disorder was one he would not spend responding to the radio calls that poured forth as copiously as ever. For a time, departments experimenting with teams protected them from the fiscal pressure, but the years of municipal recession and retrenchment finally made team policing look like a luxury. The Los Angeles basic car plan, which survived longer than the other attempts, finally went belly-up in 1979, after Chief Davis had moved along to the state senate and California voters had started the political earthquake that would come to be known as the tax revolt.

Another round of interest in community policing developed around the 1982 publication of the Wilson-Kelling "broken windows" article. Police in several cities, including Boston, Newark, Detroit, Houston, and Minneapolis, reinstituted or expanded foot patrol and in a few places even opened storefront "substations" in an effort to bring patrol officers into closer contact with the public. Studies showed that such experiments could reduce fear, if not crime, and increase public satisfaction with police.

Shortly after taking over the department in January 1984, New York City Police Commissioner Benjamin Ward ordered "Operation Pressure Point," a massive street-level assault on the drug marketplace that had operated for years with impunity on the city's Lower East Side. The result was a clear win for the idea of protecting a whole neighborhood as well as the individuals who live in it.

By 1984, addicts all over the metropolitan area knew that for easy, relatively safe purchase of drugs, one went to the section of the Lower East Side called Alphabetville, for its avenues identified by letters of the alphabet rather than names or numbers. The place was an open scandal. "Drug buyers waited in orderly double lines," writes Mark A. R. Kleiman. "Stores and apartment buildings in the area were largely abandoned. Drug dealing appeared to have displaced virtually every other activity." It also had cast a pall of fear over a neighborhood that remained home to thousands of decent families. How could such a flagrant affront to the police and the citizenry have been allowed to develop?

Kleiman points out that "retail" drug enforcement commonly falls through the cracks of police management and strategy. If regular patrol officers were responsible for pursuing low-level drug traffic, they would have time for little else. The activity also poses a "corruption hazard"—even lower-level drug dealers have plenty of money with which to buy immunity from police harassment. Police departments therefore have turned drug enforcement over to special narcotics units. The narcotics specialists, however, have little interest in street sales, which too often don't even result in serious prosecution. They want big collars—arrests of major wholesalers and seizures of those impressive drug and weapons inventories that look good on the evening news.

Operation Pressure Point simply filled the gap, at least for one area of the city. A force of 135 patrol officers and twenty narcotics detectives descended on Alphabetville. At first they made sixty-five arrests per day. Before too long, as the continuing pressure caused the dealers to move away or at least to go indoors, arrests declined to fewer than twenty per day. The Pressure Point officers also wrote tickets and ordered tow-aways for illegally parked cars that appeared to belong to drug customers.

Kleiman argues the interesting case for the efficiency of retail enforcement. Pursuing the wholesalers reduces supply, but cannot hope to eliminate it altogether. Its main result is therefore to drive up the price of drugs, forcing some purchasers to spend more of their own money, others to commit more crime, and others to give up heroin altogether. Retail enforcement doesn't drive up the cost of drugs in money so much as in the time, trouble, and risk involved in completing the transaction. The net result may be that some addicts give up drugs even though the money price remains the same. On balance, that's a plus. "Decreased consumption with constant money price must mean fewer total dollars spent on heroin. A heroin-using thief facing increased search time and arrest risk in buying heroin has no such option. Stealing more doesn't help; his problem is not the need for more money, but the increased difficulty of turning money into heroin. Indeed, time spent stealing competes with time spent scoring junk." A reported increase of applicants for drug treatment programs in the area adds weight to such an analysis.

The campaign had even more obvious benefits. The open drug bazaar disappeared, and along with it much of the fear that had kept residents of the area from walking the streets. In the first eight months of 1986, Kleiman reports, homicides were 69 percent lower, robberies declined by 40 percent, and burglaries and grand larcenies were down 27 percent and 22 percent respectively. Examination of crime patterns in adjoining precincts revealed no increase as a result of displacement from the Pressure Point area. Perhaps the highest compliment the campaign received was the complaints of promoters of low-income housing who feared that the successful closing of the narcotics street market would encourage the gentrification of Alphabetville.

In Los Angeles, meanwhile, Darryl Gates, the chief who succeeded Ed Davis, would attempt community-rescue policing of a similar sort in the Wilshire area, which was overrun by prostitutes and drug dealers. A Community Mobilization Project revived the interest in maintaining order that had remained relatively moribund since the decline of the basic car plan and the reassignment of the senior lead officers (SLOs) to routine calls. Prodded by the "broken windows" article, L.A. commanders in 1985 ordered all eight of the SLOs in Wilshire to go back to finding out what the community saw as its crime problems and respond accordingly. "The SLO's went to block meetings, undertook special projects the meeting or their own sense of their area suggested, handled complaints that came through the local councilman's office, organized graffiti 'paintouts,' and the like." Where the department had focused on robberies, burglaries and auto thefts, one SLO told Kennedy, residents might be more concerned with a group of winos that had taken over a corner, prostitutes on the street, and the spread of graffiti. The responses would take the form of miniature Operation Pressure Points. "What we'll do is we'll send a 318, a vice investigation, to our vice unit, to start an investigation of the liquor store for selling to the drunks in the first place," an officer said. "We'll go down to the location three, four, five times a day. Every time we see someone we can take to jail for drinking in public, we'll take him to jail. We'll do a constant, constant patrol until the problem doesn't exist. It might take a week, it might take two months, but we just keep hitting." The Wilshire area police claim clear results. In January 1985, one officer said, "You'd drive down the street and they'd throw rocks and bottles at you." Now the area is cleaned up. "You can actually drive down the street and not have to unlock your shotgun and get the tear gas out."

Yet unlike police commanders in New York, where recent massive hirings meant the department could spare the officers necessary for a sustained commitment to cleaning up Alphabetville, Los Angeles commanders found that moving the SLOs so deeply into community policing meant a decline in response time to regular calls. As a result they cut back on the Community Mobilization Project, much to the dismay of the officers involved.

FIVE

However sporadic or halting the efforts have been, the continued interest in policing to uphold the quality of neighborhood life as well as the law inspires a bolder idea: Police have an important role to play as community social workers and ought not to hesitate to pursue it.

The early attempts at team policing were based on the idea of giving line officers responsibility for a geographic area, as opposed to fixed duties, and greater say in decisions about how that area should be patrolled. The purposes of this were to break down the alienation that had so eroded relations between the police and the citizenry and to improve the line officers' morale. A side effect might be that police would become more aware of crime or order-related problems that irritated people even more than crime. But the main focus remained on crime, as opposed to neighborhood conditions. If police teams organized neighbors, the purpose most likely would be to watch for burglars or auto thieves, or to receive instruction in resisting rape. They would be less likely to organize for the purpose of making a playground out of the empty lot that had become a haven for junkies, or doing something about all the hooky-playing kids who hung out at a pizza parlor.

Efforts like Operation Pressure Point would put the problem of correcting an intolerable condition before the need to convict drug dealers, but on a grand and obvious scale. How might that approach be reduced to a more routine level, in order to stop the potentially intolerable conditions before they had a chance to become intolerable in fact? The answer to that question would also be an answer to the "broken windows" question: How could police defend order on the street without resorting to vigilantism of their own?

In 1979, Herman Goldstein published an article that formulated a theoretical response. He called it "problem-oriented policing." However appropriate the years of effort to professionalize police may have been, given the chaos and corruption that went before, Goldstein points out that today police seem too comfortable with a "means over ends" syndrome—they prize administrative competence for its own sake without focusing too much on the results. "The situation is somewhat like that of a private industry that studies the speed of its assembly line, the productivity of its employees, and the nature of its public relations program, but does not examine the quality of its product."

What should be the product of the police? In Goldstein's view, it is solving a class of problems. "By problems I mean the incredibly broad range of troublesome situations that prompt citizens to turn to the police, such as street robberies, residential burglaries, battered wives, vandalism, speeding cars, runaway children, accidents, acts of terorism, even fear. These and similar problems are the essence of police work. They are the reason for having a police agency." One good defining principle, he adds, might be that the problems left to the police are those for which the community has no other answers. "They are the residual problems of society." Thus, for example, as housing and mental health policies have failed, police have in recent years had to spend more time dealing with the homeless and the mentally ill on the streets. In those terms, Goldstein argues, it ought not be the responsibility of the police to eliminate the problems that no one else seems able to eliminate. "It is more realistic to aim at reducing their volume, preventing repetition, alleviating suffering and minimizing the other adverse effects they produce."

To the extent that the police department is the social agency of last resort, then, what should be its operating strategy?

In the first place, Goldstein suggests, it should realize that police-related problems are problems whether or not they fall neatly into categories of criminal offenses. In that sense, for example, it misses the point to call for decriminalizing offenses like prostitution, vagrancy, and gambling in order to free the police for more serious law enforcement. "The public expects drunks to be picked up if only because they find their presence on the street annoying. . . . The public expects prostitutes who solicit openly on the streets to be stopped, because such conduct is offensive to innocent passersby, blocks pedestrian or motor traffic, and contributes to the deterioration of a neighborhood. The problem is a problem for the police whether or not it is defined as a criminal offense."

Recognizing a broader role isn't without precedent, Goldstein points out. Police once defined their responsibility in rape cases as responding quickly, securing evidence of the crime, and identifying and apprehending a suspect as quickly as possible. Today, in response to complaints of victims—and a belated common sense—police consider it part of their job to teach women methods of avoiding attack, to help deal with all sorts of sexual assaults beyond just those defined in the law, and to offer the victim psychological support.

Given such a mind-set for all police-related problems, how then to institutionalize procedures for researching and addressing them? Problems might be documented by police records, interviews with officers at work in communities, or outside sources, Goldstein suggests. In search of remedies, police ought to consider physical or technical changes, like better street lighting to reduce muggings or stronger locks to deter burglars, adjustments to other public services, such as garbage collection or housing code enforcement, even changes in zoning or other city laws. The police officer may wind up serving as ombudsman, promoting the cause of a community before other city agencies and rallying help from many sources.

The idea echoes the community development social work taught to Peace Corps volunteers serving in the Third World and once a familiar feature of life in some American city neighborhoods: researching a community's problems in its terms rather than those of any outsider, motivating the community to participate in finding a solution, coordinating the various available resources. The concept is certainly as valid for crime-ridden neighborhoods in the developed world. The spontaneous generation of block organizations reported by George Kelling makes a strong argument for that. Yet the role of community organizer and social worker requires much astuteness, tact, and skill. How would the police handle it?

The apparently positive, if preliminary, answer arises from the handful of experiments with this most advanced form of community policing. One was instituted in 1984 in New York City's 72nd Precinct, which encompasses the sprawling working-class neighborhood of Sunset Park, Brooklyn. It was subsequently expanded to forty-four other precincts around the city. A second was instituted to rescue a faltering special unit created to deal with fear in Baltimore County, Maryland. And a third guides the whole police department of Newport News, Virginia.

In New York, the 72nd Precinct was divided into nine "beat areas" and a volunteer "community patrol officer," or CPO, was assigned to each one. The CPOs were exempted from the regular work schedule and instructed to "deal proactively with crime and order-maintenance con-

ditions existing within the beat areas. The overriding goal
. . . is to effect permanent change, whether that change
can be measured by a reduction in crime, a reduction in
the community's perceptions of crime, or an increase in
the crime resistance of a community," according to a department report on the project, which was developed with
the assistance of the Vera Institute of Justice.

The officers were expected to communicate with residents and merchants in the beat area "to determine their
perceptions and priorities about crime and order-maintenance problems in the neighborhood." And they were not
to limit possible responses to their traditional training.
Instead, they were to call upon full resources of the whole
police department. And "where the identified problems deal
with matters that require the assistance of other public or
private agencies, the CPO is expected either to make an
appropriate referral, or when necessary, to initiate contact
with the appropriate agency himself and coordinate the
interagency response." In effect, they were to become community activists in uniform: "Increasing the consciousness
of the community about its problems, involving community people and organizations in developing strategies
to address the problems, motivating the people to help in
implementing the strategies, and coordinating their action
so that they may contribute maximally to the solution are
all aspects of the community organizing dimension of the
CPO role. The CPOs are encouraged to identify potential
resources and, where they are not adequate, to help in
organizing and motivating the citizenry."

What did that mean in practice? It was not long before

the project could claim to be vindicating the concept. Responding to perhaps the most glaring police problem in the precinct, the 72nd's CPOs decided to close down the notorious drug marketplace operating on a block of 61st Street. "The decent citizens who lived on the block existed in fear of the drug dealers and when the program began were afraid to be seen talking to the beat officer." The CPOs made a point of daily drug arrests on the block, however, and "after several weeks of this sustained attention, the decent citizens on the block began to have confidence in the CPOs and began to flood the unit with intelligence information on narcotics activities." That made it possible to make more arrests and bring in the borough narcotics unit. "As a result of this sustained attention, street sales on 61st Street have been substantially reduced, if not completely eliminated," reads a department report. "In some instances dealers have relocated, in others they have moved indoors. The change in the block is very evident to any informed observer, and street traffic is now limited to residents and their children."

Other CPO projects expanded the police role well beyond straight law enforcement. One oft-told tale of the 72nd Precinct concerns a weed-grown empty lot that had become a hangout for drug users and other disorderly folk. When nearby residents told community patrol officers that they felt menaced just walking past the place, the police persuaded them to revive a moribund block association. After the group discovered that the lot was owned by the city of New York, the CPOs were able to persuade the city to deed the property over to the block association.

The CPOs obtained the services of neighborhood young-sters paid by a youth employment project to clean up the property. The block association raised money to fence it off and install play equipment. A local artist even con-tributed his talents to produce a colorful mural on the side of an adjacent building. Thus was menace turned into amenity.

Aware that Halloween had become a night of vandalism and violence, the CPOs figured a party might serve to get some of the troublemakers off the street and at least provide a safe way for younger children to celebrate. Expecting a few dozen for the event, the police were amazed when several hundred appeared. In other ways, CPOs would vindicate the Goldstein social-agency-of-last-resort idea. In the 72nd and elsewhere, some would take a police van and drive around their beat after the first school bells had rung, rounding up all who appeared to be of school age but still on the street. Others would arrange with senior citizen centers to escort groups of old folks on evening walks about the neighborhood. "To many of the seniors, this simple program has afforded them the first opportunity they have had in years to see many of the changes which have occurred in the neighborhood," a department report notes.

The CPOs would even do rudimentary individual case-work: "Police Officer Maria Irizarry responding to the complaint of a resident, discovered that a 15-year-old boy had been sleeping on the roof of an apartment building for several nights. The boy, whose name is John, was not living at home because of difficulty he was having with his mother.

"Officer Irizarry interviewed John's mother and was told

that he had been a 'problem child' since he was very young and his mother was unable to deal with him. John did not want to return home that night and Officer Irizarry prevailed upon the priest at a local church to take the boy in for a few nights until his mother could present her case at Family Court and receive their assistance.

"As a result of the court hearing, John volunteered to be admitted into Jacobi Hospital for 30 days of psychiatric evaluation and treatment. After his release from the hospital, he returned home with his mother and Officer Irizarry continued to visit them and monitor the situation.

"Officer Irizarry has noticed that since John has stopped living on the roof of the building where she found him, there has been a significant reduction in burglaries there."

Baltimore County, Maryland, moved into community policing in 1982 with a "fear force" set up to reassure the public after two senseless murders generated widespread alarm and outrage. Forty-five "Citizen Oriented Police Enforcement" (COPE) officers were relieved of routine patrol duties but given only vague instructions on what to do to fight fear.

After several months, with the program foundering for lack of direction, the department decided to shape it around Goldstein's problem-oriented-policing idea. Though Goldstein had envisioned the theory as a tool with which upper levels of management could better deploy the line officers, the Baltimore police managers saw no reason not to bring problem-solving thinking right down to the street level. The results were much like those of the New York experiment.

"Fear problems were to be exhaustively researched,"

writes Philip B. Taft, "using surveys and other information-gathering techniques. Solutions to those problems would then be 'brainstormed' with other officers. Officers assigned to each project would then write a detailed 'action plan' that would diagnose the fear-causing problem and describe their proposed solutions. Public and private agencies were to be engaged to help. . . . 'We kept saying, "We don't care what you think the problem is, we care about what the community thinks the problem is" [said one superior officer]. 'We kept pounding that into them.' "

Before too long the Baltimore County police would have their own stories to tell about police as de facto Peace Corps volunteers or social workers of last resort. COPE's first real success came in a run-down blue-collar townhouse complex called Garden Village, where crowds of teenagers had the run of dimly lit streets after dark. Taft relates that everyone seemed to have given up on Garden Village. "It got so bad, no one bothered calling the police anymore," one resident said. And the police had little use for "Garbage Village."

Two COPE officers named Brandt Bradford and Guy Johnson took on Garden Village, helping residents to form an improvement association. They persuaded local officials to repair broken streetlights and fix potholes. They helped the association apply for federal neighborhood cleanup funds. They got the complex's management to trim hedges and provide deadbolt locks in order to deter burglaries. "After a few months, Garden Village looked and felt safer," Taft writes. Yet the community recognized a deeper need. Taft quotes Bradford as saying, "It wasn't too long into the fear surveys that Johnson and I realized that these parents were really concerned about their kids. They didn't focus on the crime so much as on the lack of recreational facilities for their kids." The two therefore spent eighteen months documenting the need, organizing the community, and lobbying the county's recreation agency, until it finally came through with $32,000 to fix up a long-neglected park. The effect was immediate on the complex's quality of life.

In another Baltimore County case, also involving a housing complex, COPE officers showed that focusing on a community's fears aroused by a series of robberies could have an even more direct effect on crime. This case, reported by John Eck and William Spelman of the Police Executive Research Forum, concerned elderly women living in Loch Raven Apartments. Because of the street attacks, "most were unwilling to leave their apartments after dark. Their feelings were exacerbated by the conditions of the complex: Many street and building lights were broken; unkempt trees and shrubs created many hiding places; rats, stray dogs, and unrepaired structural damage all contributed to the feeling—widespread among residents—that they were trapped. To break the apartments out of the trap, the COPE officers made them a local cause, to be pressed with everyone in sight.

"Representatives of two local neighborhood associations agreed to help Loch Raven Apartments residents form their own association. The police convinced a variety of organizations to assist the new neighborhood group: a local printer produced crime prevention information, free of charge; a local church donated its meeting facilities; a local baker contributed free donuts." The officers also got the power company to repair the streetlights and mobilized health, fire, animal-control, and housing inspectors to descend on the apartments en masse, forcing improvements by the managers.

The campaign to fix up the complex turned out to have an effect against crime. "Perhaps because of the deterrent effect of patrolling dog catchers, building inspectors, and the like, the string of robberies stopped completely. Burglaries in the complex, running at the rate of six per month prior to the COPE unit's intervention, dropped to one every two months. It has remained at that level ever since," Eck and Spelman write.

They offer another story that vindicates the approach with elegant, or perhaps brutal, simplicity. A park had fallen into disuse because residents of the area feared crowds of rowdy young people who had taken over a corner of it to drink and take drugs. One response might have been to make a lot of arrests for drinking and drug use. But COPE officers investigated and discovered that the young people were actually drawn to the corner by a shed they called the treehouse, which they had constructed on a wooded lot that adjoined the park. The quickest way to solve the problem, the officers decided, would be to demolish the shed. But no other agency took them seriously. The county roads, health, and fire departments said they found it hard to justify any action since no one actually lived in the treehouse. Then the police sought out the owner of the property. He said he would be glad to be rid of the treehouse but couldn't afford to tear it down and feared a confrontation with the youngsters who used it.

At that point, the COPE officers realized that the way was clear for the most direct and obvious course: "Armed with saws and sledgehammers, [they] quickly reduced the treehouse to rubble" and carted it off to a dump. Eck and Spelman note that the whole process, which caused the drinkers and drug users to disperse and allowed families to reclaim the park, had taken no more than two weeks.

Newport News also committed itself to problem-oriented policing, but with an important difference: Instead of assigning problem analysis and solving to a small group of street-patrol officers, Chief Darrel Stephens in 1984 decreed it to be the operating strategy for the whole department. A task force composed of patrol officers and detectives as well as higher-ranking officers worked out models for identifying, analyzing, and responding to problems, as well as for evaluating the effectiveness of the response. Though Newport News thus invested much more heavily in theorizing than Baltimore County had, it could still produce practical street results.

An officer told to do something about crowds of rowdy kids who disturbed a quiet residential neighborhood on Friday and Saturday nights discovered that they were coming from a roller rink that was trying to improve business with the offer of free transportation in from other areas. Since it offered no return transportation, large numbers of customers flooded into the streets at closing time. These were the cause of annoyance to the sleeping neighbors. The officer persuaded the rink owner to bus his customers out as well as in, thus restoring peace and quiet.

On a larger scale, an officer attempting to curb prostitution and related crime on Washington Avenue found that the courts had considerable powers that were going unused. Typically, prostitutes were given fifteen-day suspended sentences. The police officer got together with the commonwealth attorney and worked out a proposal that hookers be given twelve-month sentences and required to serve two months on conviction. The other ten months would be suspended on condition that the convicted prostitute refrain from all soliciting and stay away from the most notorious stretch of Washington Avenue. Violating those conditions could mean having to serve out the remaining ten months. The cop and the commonwealth attorney sold the plan to the other prosecutors and the district court judges, who agreed to hand out maps of the restricted area when sentencing the prostitutes. The police officer then mobilized state liquor agents to pressure the bars that were havens for prostitutes, and he informed the hotels they used that they would have to obey an ordinance that required a john to provide proof of his name and address when signing up for a room. The officer also met with the two thousand sailors stationed in Newport News, lecturing them on the risks of sex with prostitutes and spreading the salient information that some of the most beautiful hookers were transvestites.

The officer also spent plenty of time on Washington Avenue. "He learned the prostitutes' street and legal names; he made sure they learned his. He chatted with the streetwalkers whenever he could. Occasionally he joined conversations between streetwalkers and johns, often formally introducing the astonished johns to their male dates," Spelman and Eck report.

All this paid off handsomely. Within six months the number of identifiable prostitutes regularly working the area plunged from twenty-eight to six and remained at that level for another year. And robberies declined by 43 percent. "Since about half the robberies committed before this time were prostitution-related," Spelman and Eck note, "this is almost exactly the percentage decrease that would be expected, had all prostitution-related robberies been eliminated entirely."

SIX

Skepticism remains. Stories of neighborhoods rescued and playgrounds reclaimed may warm the heart. Yet the professionalism so easily denounced for removing the police from the people did not occur without good reason. In the early days the police manager's basic problem was simply to keep track of where his men were and what they were up to. The limits on his ability to do so meant that if line officers were not avoiding work, they were likely to be pursuing some ugly forms of "community policing": bribery and brutality. One need not look far for evidence that the potential for similar behavior remains strong among modern police. Even as New York accepted compliments for the achievements of its community patrol officers, regular police were being investigated for taking bribes and extorting money from drug dealers. In 1985, the department was shaken by the case of officers who thought a good way to clean up street-level narcotics dealing was to torture a suspect with an electronic stun gun. The incident added alarming weight to misgivings over the "we kick ass" approach reported by Wilson and Kelling.

A big achievement of professionalizing, furthermore, was to remove police from partisan politics. Wouldn't police working as community organizers and activists inevitably become deeply embroiled again? And anyone who has ever been involved in a block association knows how easily they may fall apart over neighborhood factionalism—leaving hard feelings that last for years. Is it really a good idea for cops to plunge into those potentially treacherous waters? And what if such an organization, having lobbied successfully for the new playground, then takes off in directions inappropriate for police—like seeking to block a shelter for the homeless, or to keep minority groups from moving in?

As germane, if not more so, are more practical questions. Pilot projects involving a small community patrol unit in a single precinct stand a good chance of succeeding simply because officers testing the new concept are likely to be highly motivated volunteers. They bask in favorable attention from the department, the news media, and academics interested in the experiment's progress. Yet so much depends on their special commitment and motivation that a demonstration's success hardly guarantees its replication.

In New York, some would criticize the commissioner's decision to expand the successful program in the 72nd Precinct to thirty others after only eighteen months. The move was prompted by a desire for some favorable publicity to offset negative headlines about other police scandals, the critics suggested. An early evaluation of the 72nd, while generally positive, also acknowledged that the CPOs felt most comfortable using their law enforcement powers to respond to problems, while they "engage in community outreach with some anxiety and hesitancy." Some also felt shaky about dealing with community groups or helping people to organize. "There is a clear need for more assistance with this dimension of the role."

The department proceeded to contract with a civic group to provide special training. But certainly it was appropriate to wonder whether officers could be found to carry out such responsibility in thirty more precincts if the hand-picked, well-motivated crew in the 72nd was already faltering. The demonstration-program CPOs themselves, meanwhile, "reacted with mixed emotions to the Department's decision to expand to other precincts. . . . it meant that the Department would be developing rules and procedures to regulate the behavior of CPOs. The officers were concerned that such regulations do not reduce their discretion and dull their initiative."

More anxiety arises over costs. Done right, community policing consumes significant manpower. Yet a department dare not let it drain resources from responding to emergency calls. Not all departments can afford simply to add officers in order to create a community patrol force.

While all such concerns are reasonable, they ought not

to be considered lethal to the idea. However it might disturb the tradition of professional law enforcement, there is nothing inappropriate about recasting the mission of a big-city police department to encompass a more intimate relationship with the community. Public hospitals and public schools routinely employ social workers to deal with troubled pupils or patients and carry on outreach activities. Once all that might have been considered beyond the legitimate scope of those institutions. Today it seems an obvious and comfortable way to enhance the delivery of education and health care. The capacity for community social work similarly enhances the police and ought be seen as an expansion of professionalism rather than a threat to it. More to the point, community patrol would bring new police resources to focus on the hosts of lesser offenders who remain untouched by any police effort at all so long as departments continue to give priority to the major felons. It therefore would respond directly to the problem of the funnel. In that sense, it finally would resolve the confusion over mission that has proved so demoralizing and alienating. No wonder community patrol inspires enthusiastic public support.

One can hardly blame a police chief for worrying about corruption, especially in the midst of a nationwide drug epidemic. But there is no real reason to believe that community patrol would make officers any more vulnerable than those on regular patrol so long as officers working in the community are kept fully accountable for their activities.

The need to avoid the snares of neighborhood politics

poses a more difficult challenge. Yet here again, the Peace Corps parallel is worth noting. It was of paramount importance to the agency's efforts and the standing of the whole U.S. diplomatic mission that the Peace Corps volunteers not run afoul of neighborhood factionalism or host-country partisan politics. Some did, and failed spectacularly, but most managed to maintain integrity and independence. They did this by making it absolutely clear from the day of their arrival that their interest was only in the welfare of the community as a whole, not the fortunes of any particular group. Much would then depend on the sensitivity and skill with which they pursued the basic course of community development.

Similarly, community patrol police officers ought to make clear from the outset that they are concerned only with community problems that relate to crime, order maintenance, and other police functions. Should the block association formed to improve street lighting bog down with internal conflict, the police would appropriately withdraw until the group was prepared to focus on the crime-related issue. Should the association that had fixed up the park move on to promoting a political candidate or fighting a halfway house for the retarded, the police would disavow any interest in those issues and leave the group to pursue them on its own. As long as the signals had been clear from the start, the police would need to suffer no hard feelings from such a turn of events. But as with the Peace Corps volunteers, much would depend on their astuteness and tact.

Wouldn't some community patrol officers find such detachment frustrating? Wouldn't they be tempted to assert more direct leadership, relish the idea of wading into a neighborhood dispute and resolving it for the better? Certainly many would, and such an impulse would be in the finest tradition of American politics. But to follow it, an officer's supervisors should make clear, he or she would have to resign from the force.

The practical questions of motivating officers to do community patrol and replicating demonstrations throughout a department are perhaps more troubling. The history of team policing suggests that the idea of getting officers more involved with citizens creates a need for profound organizational change likely to be resisted by the police bureaucracy's natural inertia. In some forms, the new community patrol might pose less of a threat, since regular patrols may remain in place as community patrol units, of a relatively modest and nonthreatening size, function separately. But that creates the opposite risk that community patrol, after the novelty wears off, might wind up trivialized, denied the attention and resources necessary to sustain a significant role. Succeeding with community patrol may require profound alteration of a police department's whole organizational structure—its leadership, its management, its reward system. Much would depend on the depth of a department's commitment to the concept. Ideally, it ought to consider recruiting new officers especially for community patrol and giving them special training.

As for cost, some promoters of community patrol now talk of its potential to reduce the volume of calls for service that tie up regular patrol officers for hours each day. Should it prove to do so substantially, then in theory at least, the manpower saved could mean the integration of community patrol at little extra cost. Such hopes remain speculative, however. Certainly the example of the Wilshire area in Los Angeles, where recommitment to maintaining order left the area short on emergency response, is not reassuring. Yet there is likely to be some saving as a result of community patrol, and that along with the obvious public benefit could make its net extra cost easy to justify to the taxpayers. The important point is that the police demonstrate that they know how to maintain order and reduce fear as well as crime. The question of how much that is worth in terms of tax dollars then becomes a choice for the voters.

The idea of recruiting and training officers especially for community patrol and the need to minimize costs raise another echo of the Peace Corps: a "police corps" of volunteers who would serve a few years at community patrol, perhaps in exchange for a benefit like a college scholarship. Such an idea has been developed by Adam Walinsky, a New York attorney, along with Jonathan Rubinstein, the scholar who patrolled with the Philadelphia police. They would have a state government set up the scholarship program for all who would agree to serve three years after graduation with a local police department. The volunteers would be tested and accepted before college, with training to begin during summer vacations. The scholarships might be expensive, but savings to the department would offset some of the cost. Since police corps officers would serve only three years, they would not require annual raises, nor would the department have to set up the elaborate pensions and other benefits that make up a big percentage of current payrolls. The three-year terms might also allay fears of the corruption hazard, since the cops most likely to succumb to temptation are those burned out after long years patrolling in the same area.

Though the police corps idea draws praise wherever it is introduced, no state has yet enacted it, mainly because police unions consider it a threat, police managers worry about how to integrate such a program given the skepticism and resistance of regular officers, and legislators remain wary of the cost of the scholarships. Still, it deserves a try. Assuming peer resistance could be overcome, the well-educated volunteers would make ideal candidates for community patrol. Many might decide on police careers, providing departments with rich reservoirs of future management talent sympathetic to community- and problem-oriented policing. And from those who did not, the police and the rest of society would gain a subtle benefit: the regular passage of civilians into police departments for long enough to appreciate what the police can and cannot do. Pursuing their subsequent civilian lives, they would disperse such understanding far and wide. Thus might the historical alienation of police finally be eroded.

Such speculations are of limited use without more practical experience. But the story of community patrol so far and the fact that it makes such new thinking possible suggest that the time is at hand for the third major era in the history of American police. After the confusion of beginnings and the insulation of professionalism, police are ready for a well-managed return to the community. The life of modern cities makes clearer than ever before the need for a social agency of last resort. If the police and politicians who worry about law enforcement would change its message, the way to do so is clear.

7

PUNISHMENT
without
PRISON

This time, a reprieve was unlikely. The courts were tired of [Robert] Sullivan's appeals of his 1973 conviction for the kidnap-murder of a restaurant manager. The media focused on rumors that a priest had heard a confession that might prove Sullivan's alibi, but no evidence of it came to light. The only real question was how Sullivan would conduct himself in those final thirty-eight hours.

Condemned men prepare in different ways. Some take "the Jesus route." Some go insane. Some go macho. Some give up. The hardest to take are those with the most human reaction of all: They must be pried out of their cells and dragged, shrieking and thrashing, down the Last Mile. . . .

In previous conversations, Sullivan had told me that he would fight the guards who came to get him. But [on the day before the execution] in a noon meeting with the warden, he announced that he would not struggle.

That evening, a countdown began that would turn out to be a dress rehearsal. His closest friends—Father Robert Boyle, a priest he had known since childhood; Susan Cary and Margaret Vandiver, supporters who had visited him every day—gathered for a Last Supper. Sullivan cried a few times, when he was reminiscing about his childhood and when he learned that the Pope had asked for mercy on his behalf, but he was more concerned about the reactions of his friends and supporters. He was trying to protect them more than himself. When the group ordered food, Sullivan decided they would all eat turkey sandwiches in honor of the governor.

In the last five minutes, during painful goodbyes, word came that a federal judge had granted a stay. Sullivan was whisked away to twist another night on the legal rotisserie. Even Christ skipped that Station of the Cross.

The stay was dissolved Tuesday afternoon, and the execution was reset for ten a.m. Wednesday. . . .

At seven, Sullivan was left alone to face the last three hours of preparations by the guard—hours that frightened him the most.

At 9:59 a.m., the door to the execution chamber swung open. Witnesses, separated by a window, saw Sullivan flanked by guards. His freshly shaven skull was shimmering with ointment to conduct electricity. He was plainly terrified—but he was walking under his own power.

Five minutes after ten: After Sullivan had been strapped in, an official put a microphone in front of him and held a clipboard with his statement. Sullivan's voice trembled at first, but he read the Sixty-second Psalm. It gathered together his theme: denunciation without bitterness, faith without submission. . . .

His voice was strong; he did not stammer.

At 10:11, after the hooded death cap was placed over Sullivan's head, the warden nodded, and Bob Sullivan discovered that which we do not yet know.

—Steve Gettinger, "Obit," Rolling Stone,
February 2, 1984

■ November 1986: Larry Davis, on probation after a felony conviction and numerous recent arrests for robbery, possession of stolen property, and attempted seconddegree murder, [allegedly] shot six police officers in the Bronx. At the time he had been cited for violation of probation, but his hearing on this charge had been postponed four times.

■ August 1986: Convicted felon Trevor Bailey [allegedly] shot two police officers on a Brooklyn street. He was on probation at the time and previously had assaulted two police officers.

■ August 1986: Mark Therezo, who had a history of burglary and drug conviction, [allegedly] murdered his invalid 85-year-old grandmother while robbing her Brooklyn home to get money to buy crack. He was on probation at the time.

■ August 1985: Convicted felon Alvin Rippy, while on probation, [was alleged to have] committed three rapes and was suspected by police of seven others.

■ November 1983: Convicted felon Anthony Germain, while on probation, [allegedly] broke into the Queens home of Charles and Helen Breslin, aged 81 and 79, and murdered them.

Despite these examples, city and state officials are examining the possibility of placing a greater number of felons on probation as a way of relieving prison overcrowding.

—New York State Senate Committee on Investigations, Taxation and Government Operations, The Collapse of the New York City Probation System, report, January 1987

ONE

*I*n the 1950s and 1960s, the public discussion of the courts focused on their capacity to abuse the innocent. Civil libertarians pressed for a "due process revolution" to protect the rights of defendants in ways that would fundamentally alter the life of American courts. The revolution would help to shape the legal handling of urban disorders and the principled disobediences of civil rights and anti–Vietnam War protesters.

But as the era of riots and protests gave way to the era of hard-core street crime, the debate changed. The new issue was not the innocent defendant railroaded to conviction for reasons of politics or racism—although surely there were some—but the guilty defendants who routinely got away with auto thefts, burglaries, armed robberies, even murder and rape. The courts, much like the police, appeared confounded by street crime and incapable of more than the passive reactions that had seemed sufficient for years.

It would become fashionable on the political right to link the earlier due process debate with this apparent new paralysis. How better to justify campaigns against the exclusionary rule, which forbade the use in court of evidence obtained through an illegal search or seizure? How better to demand that the courts reexamine landmark decisions guaranteeing defendants the right to lawyers and guarding against forced confessions?

Yet that was a simplistic reaction. The due process revolution had been based on real abuses. Obviously a totalitarian abandonment of civil liberties would make the control of street crime somewhat easier (though given the degree to which street crime eludes even the attention of the police, the extent of any such benefit remains unclear). But to argue that due process was responsible for crime was to argue that democracy was responsible for it.

The debate over such questions, however, tended to obscure issues far more central to the functioning of the courts, for better and worse: plea bargaining and the "triaging" of cases in the lower courts, and indeterminate sentencing in the higher courts. Misunderstanding of these activities hardly perturbed judges and prosecutors, many of whom no doubt welcomed efforts to blame the civil liberties movement. The new concern about street crime, however, would finally shed some light on these dimmer corners of criminal justice. The stresses on courts as a result of fiscal problems and increasing caseloads made plea bargaining and triaging even more germane.

Plea bargains settle criminal charges in advance of trial as the defendant's attorney and the prosecutor negotiate terms of conviction in exchange for the defendant's willingness to plead guilty:

Damian tears Sue's purse from her grasp and pushes her to the sidewalk. She's humiliated and bruised. He removes some cash from the purse and ditches it as he runs off.

He is arrested a couple of blocks away after police responding to a neighbor's 911 call note that his jacket matches the caller's description.

The prosecutor charges Damian with felonious assault and robbery. But the case looks weak. Summoned to a lineup that includes Damian, Sue has trouble picking him out. Damian produces some friends who are willing to say he was playing video games with them at the time of the mugging. The neighbor who called 911 isn't sure he can identify Damian either, and resists getting any more involved. Yet the prosecutor hesitates simply to drop all charges. Damian is no stranger. He's been arrested a few times for burglary and muggings—once even did a few months in jail. He's also known to have a drug habit. His alibi is based on the word of friends whose good faith is as dubious as his own. So the prosecutor would like to shake Damian up a bit and try to keep him off the street for a while.

As he sits in jail, a negotiation begins. The prosecutor offers to drop assault charges if Damian will plead guilty to robbery and serve a minimum of two years. Damian's lawyer, worried about the ability of Damian and his friends to impress a jury with their sincerity, likes the offer, but Damian, confident that he can beat the rap, refuses to take it. His lawyer goes back to the prosecutor suggesting his client might be willing to do a few months on a misdemeanor assault or larceny charge. The prosecutor holds out for felony time—at least a year behind bars. Weeks pass. The prosecutor moves along to other cases. Damian grows restive in jail. Finally he pleads guilty to minor charges in exchange for a sentence of the three months he has already served waiting for a deal. The prosecutor, no longer interested, accepts.

Such a case, however typical, raises disturbing questions. By what right does the prosecutor assert his judgment of the case in a way that preempts a jury's? And in what possible sense does such a negotiated settlement, resulting in a "sentence" that simply ratifies the situation in place, constitute justice? In the end, the prosecutor and judge may find some satisfaction in having kept Damian off the street for three months. Sue, however, is likely to feel slighted by the system—and doubly fearful of running into Damian again. Damian, meanwhile, tells himself that he pretty much beat the rap and will elaborate mightily on his experiences in jail for his friends at the video-game parlor.

The roots of this process stretch back at least to the nineteenth century. Albert W. Alschuler points out that through the early 1800s, guilty pleas were rare in English and American courts. Because trial processes were less formal, cases were handled rapidly and there was little administrative pressure to plea-bargain cases in order to avoid costly or time-consuming trials. So long as many defendants were not represented by counsel, judges felt obliged to insist that they protect their own interests by standing trial. The most salient deterrent to a guilty plea was that most felonies were punishable by death.

The development of the penitentiary, invented by American Quakers as a humane alternative to death, corporal punishment, or public humiliation, provided more room for negotiation, and by the end of the Civil War, plea bargaining had emerged as a common feature of American justice. A study of convictions in Manhattan and Brooklyn published by Raymond Moley in 1928 found that in 1839 only 15 percent of felony convictions were the result of guilty pleas. By 1879, the figure had risen to 80 percent. By 1926 it was 90 percent. Fifty years later, a study conducted by the Vera Institute of Justice found that in New York City the rate of felony convictions by guilty plea had risen to 97 percent. Alschuler quotes other studies confirming the trend nationwide. "In urban jurisdictions in Virginia, half of all convictions were by guilty plea in 1917, but three-quarters were by guilty plea in 1927. . . . In New Haven in 1888, fully 75 percent of all felony convictions were by plea of guilty; a steady increase brought the figure to over 90 percent by 1921."

In the early decades of this century, plea bargaining all too often reflected old-fashioned corruption. One's lawyer arranged directly with a magistrate, or perhaps with an influential police officer or other "fixer," to purchase a lenient sentence with a bribe. Alschuler quotes one 1914 account of a New York defense attorney who would "stand out on the street in front of the Night Court and dicker away sentences in this form: $300 for ten days, $200 for twenty days, $150 for thirty days." By the postwar era, plea bargaining accounted for so many convictions that it became hard to see how the courts could function without it. As important, the criminal courts embraced a set of mores every bit as alienated from the concerns and expectations of the public as the mores of the police, and plea bargaining was woven deeply into their fabric. "I don't see any value in another study about plea bargaining," a New York judge told a researcher for the Vera Institute of Justice. "In criminal court there is a subculture unrelated to the rest of the world. The rest of society has no idea what goes on in court. . . . You can't really understand."

Critics of plea bargaining would continue to argue that it appeared to cheapen justice, that it granted far too much discretion to prosecutors, and that it unfairly suggested to the defendant, unconsciously if not overtly, that his insistence on a trial could cost him the sentencing judge's sympathy should he wind up convicted. Still, in 1967, both the American Bar Association Project on Standards for Criminal Justice and President Johnson's Commission on Law Enforcement and Administration of Justice recognized the pervasiveness of plea bargaining and asserted that it could make a valuable contribution. "The quality of justice in all cases would suffer if overloaded courts were faced with a great increase in the number of trials," the Johnson commission's report stated. "Tremendous investments of time, talent, and money, all of which are in short supply and can be better used elsewhere, would be necessary if all cases were tried." Plea bargaining, the commission observed, "relieves both the defendant and the prosecution of the inevitable risks and uncertainties of trial. It imparts a degree of certainty and flexibility into a rigid, yet frequently erratic system." Negotiated pleas, the report said, make possible more individualized justice and are "frequently called upon to serve important law enforcement needs by agreements through which leniency is exchanged for information, assistance, and testimony about other serious offenders." The ABA and Johnson commission reports, however, called for tighter administration of a practice that afforded prosecutors such broad discretion and took place out of public view.

Supreme Court decisions in 1970 upheld the constitutionality of plea bargaining. In 1973, the National Advisory Commission on Criminal Justice Standards and Goals called for its abolition within five years, an appeal that generally fell on deaf ears. A notable exception was the state of Alaska, where a reform-minded attorney general, Avrum Gross, in 1975 ordered an end to all plea bargaining in state courts. An evaluation of the policy published in 1980 by the Alaska Judicial Council found that it succeeded to the extent that plea bargaining did end, that defendants continued to plead guilty at about the same rates as before, and that while the number of trials increased, it did not reach burdensome levels. The study also found that conviction rates did not change much because of the policy, but that it appeared to have increased sentences for lesser offenders. Students of plea bargaining cautioned against making too much of these generally positive findings, however: Alaska remains a sparsely populated state with a low volume of crime, and its attorney general, unlike those in the rest of the states, has the power to order and enforce such a policy statewide.

Should the Alaska approach be expanded? That depends on the extent to which plea bargaining and other unchecked exercises of the prosecutors' and judges' discretion actually result in their indulging laziness or carelessness and otherwise weakening justice. The answer isn't obvious.

In 1977, the idea that prosecutors were making sound use of their discretion gained some support when the Vera Institute of Justice published a remarkable study that sought to learn more precisely why so many felony arrests did not result in felony convictions. They analyzed court records for 1,888 felony arrest cases, a sample of the 100,739 total felony arrests in 1971 in New York City. And for another 369 cases that reached dispositions in 1973, they conducted interviews with the police, prosecutors, defense attorneys, and lawyers involved in an effort to find out why they handled the cases as they did.

Examination of the 1,888 cases confirmed the funnel and the appearance of turnstile justice. Only 56 percent of the felony cases resulted in conviction of anything. The rest were dismissed or acquitted. And only 15 percent of the total ended in conviction on a felony charge. Twenty-seven percent of the defendants received some jail or prison time, but only 5 percent got felony time of more than a year in prison.

Yet interviewing all the players in the 369 cases made clear the glibness of denouncing the system as ineffective on the basis of the statistics alone. The most striking finding of the interviews was that in nearly half of all the felony arrest cases that involved victims, the victims knew the criminals.

"Prior relationships included husbands and wives, lovers, prostitutes and their pimps or customers, neighbors, in-laws, junkies and dealers, even landlords and tenants," the Vera study noted. For violent crimes the rate of prior relationships was 56 percent; for property crimes like burglary and grand larceny, it was a somewhat surprising 35 percent. "Prior relationships were often mentioned by prosecutors as their reasons for offering reduced charges and light sentences in return for a plea of guilty." What purpose would be served, the prosecutors could ask, by investing the state's resources in trying and imprisoning people whose backyard dispute or lovers' quarrel had come to blows?

When charges were dropped altogether, the most common explanation (69 percent of the dismissals) was that the complainants had refused to cooperate in the prosecution. "Often the complainant simply never appeared and his reasons were not accurately known," the study states. Such behavior is not hard to figure. Victims of an angry exchange between friends, relatives, or neighbors either thought better of pursuing the case after their anger subsided or preferred to do so outside the law. In some cases, the victims may also have felt intimidated by the criminals.

The Vera study concludes with "an obvious but overlooked reality: Criminal conduct is often the explosive spillover from ruptured personal relations among neighbors, friends and former spouses. . . . Of course, this kind of 'familial' crime is still crime, and its victims often as strongly aggrieved as the victims of stranger crime. But there can be no doubt that the relatively close defendant-victim relationship is responsible for much of the case deterioration in court."

A second big factor that resulted in reduced charges or dismissals was the defendant's prior criminal record. The interviews with prosecutors, lawyers, and judges showed strong agreement that defendants who were before the court for the first time deserved a break. Fully 77 percent of convicts with no prior record were not sent to jail or prison. Only 16 percent of those with prison records were able to get off on the subsequent conviction.

In conclusion, the researchers asserted that the courts don't deserve all the criticism they are subjected to for treating felony cases too lightly. If prior relationships and lack of criminal record could result in light treatment, the researchers found, other circumstances led to real punishment. "Where crimes are serious, evidence is strong, and victims are willing to prosecute, felons with previous criminal histories ended up with relatively heavy sentences."

Others would make much of the Vera study's apparent conclusion that the court system actually works much better than is suggested by the statistics and the conventional wisdom about plea bargaining. They gained more ammunition from a study conducted by the Institute for Law and Social Research (known as INSLAW), published about the same time, that came to similar conclusions about the fate of felony cases in Washington, D.C. The INSLAW researchers found that in 35 percent of Washington robbery arrests, victim and offender knew each other. And they found that unwillingness of complainants to cooperate led to dismissals in more than half of the Washington felony cases where there were victims.

"By and large, prosecutors distinguish between 'real crimes'—crimes committed by strangers—and 'junk (or garbage) cases,' i.e., those which grow out of a dispute between people who know one another," Charles Silberman concluded from the two studies in *Criminal Violence, Criminal Justice*. "As the Vera Institute study makes clear, this dichotomy is central to any understanding of what happens in criminal court. . . . It would be hard to exaggerate the significance of this finding."

He goes so far as to call the statistics that outline the funnel "grossly misleading." He observes that some narrowing of the funnel after arrest must be discounted because perhaps a third of those arrested on felony charges turn out to be juveniles whose cases must be turned over to family courts. For the adults who remain, he asserts, it is wrong to say that only those sentenced to felony time in prison are punished. Many more experience some incarceration in local jails as the result of conviction for misdemeanors after felony charges are reduced. When they are added in, the total incarcerated approaches 40 percent. Jail time, he declares, may be even worse punishment than prison time, though shorter, because jails are notoriously more squalid and violent than prisons.

These arguments strain. In many jurisdictions, the ineffectiveness of juvenile courts amounts to an open scandal. And it is simply naive to say that a jail term of a few weeks or months, during which the inmate remains close to home and in touch with family and friends, is somehow worse than years of isolation in a forbidding state penitentiary. The best conclusion to be drawn from the Vera Institute and INSLAW studies was not that the courts are doing a wonderful job but that the police ought to arrest more stranger-felons. The Vera researchers had found that though prior-relationship robberies accounted for 36 percent of robbery arrests, they constituted only 2 to 6 percent of all robberies. The INSLAW group found that in Washington, prior relationships were involved in only 7 percent of robberies but 35 percent of robbery arrests. There is little reason for reassurance in the news that the police arrest a disproportionate number of "familial" suspects because they are easy to identify and locate, and that prosecutors then treat such arrests as garbage. The Vera study, furthermore, made clear its awareness of problems in the courts: "Because our society has not found adequate alternatives to arrest and adjudication for coping with interpersonal anger publicly expressed, we pay a price. The price includes large court caseloads, long delays in processing and, ultimately, high dismissal rates. . . . The congestion and drain on resources . . . weakens the ability of the criminal justice system to deal quickly and decisively with the 'real' felons who may be getting lost in the shuffle."

To the extent that the Vera and INSLAW studies demonstrated that prosecutors and judges are capable of rational selection of cases for serious treatment, they demonstrated an ability to triage. In times when court resources were a match for court business, selection could be based on reasonable criteria having to do only with justice. But stretch the resources, and suddenly issues of economy come into play as well. In the seventies, as arrests held up while fiscal crises strained court budgets, that appears to have happened. As a result, the courts would share in the process the police had begun of decriminalizing certain categories of crimes and criminals.

Unable to afford more judgeships and court space, court administrators made conscious decisions to concentrate scarce resources on the higher courts, which dealt with serious felony cases. The strategy worked to the extent that states retained the capacity to try the felony cases that survived the earlier stages of arraignment and preliminary pleadings. Despite fiscal shortages, higher courts in those years continued to send an increasing flood of felons to state prisons, producing a national crisis in prison crowding.

But husbanding resources for higher courts meant neglecting lower ones. Such neglect might sound reasonable—with no more money to hire more judges, let those available sit in the higher court to send the armed robbers and rapists to prison, rather than wasting time in the lower court handing out fines or brief jail terms to prostitutes and small-time drug pushers. Yet the consequences of such a policy could be devastating. In New York City, ample anecdotal evidence documented the near collapse of the lower court, called the criminal court.

In 1983, *The New York Times* published a series of articles on the court that began by declaring, "Rarely has any public institution been held in such open contempt by those who work for it and those who pass through it. Judges call it a sham and a fraud. Lawyers say that justice is unpredictable at best and that the tawdry surroundings and atmosphere of deal making deprive the court of even a feeling of justice."

In 1982, a writer named Howard Senzel, who had held a minor administrative job in the criminal court, published a book describing it in vivid terms. The courtroom where he worked, he wrote, "is famous for being a dump and a disgrace. . . . from the ceiling, just shy of cathedral height, little clumps of plaster fall occasionally into the lights and the proceedings. At the end of each row of the audience, sleeping policemen rest the pomade on their weary heads on dark spots in the oak paneling that mark the ghosts of millions of dollars in police overtime. The velvet rope guarding access to the court leaks crumbled sponge rubber where it has split from being overhandled. Thick ridges of greasy dirt balance on the folds of the limp flag hanging behind the judge. Above the flag, there is a bullet hole in the wall, right under the 'r' in "In God We Trust." . . . The clock on the wall . . . reads twenty minutes past eight; it stopped in May 1978."

Such reports echoed a study that had been published recently by the city's bar association. It said, "The failure of the Criminal Court . . . has been obvious and extreme. Because of the staggering volume of its caseload and its inability to provide trials, the Criminal Court has been virtually incapacitated in the last few years. Everyone exposed to the court knows this. . . ." With some judges' daily caseloads approaching two hundred, the court had spun "out of control—a crowded, heavily time-pressured continually depressing marketplace in which the need simply to dispose of cases has overshadowed everything else," including "separating out the innocent and imposing sensible penalties on the guilty."

Even such scathing and authoritative criticism, however, failed to produce any immediate remedy. In 1986, the state's chief judge conducted another study and found that little had changed. A judge's average daily load still commonly exceeded one hundred cases, and the average time spent on each appearance was 3.4 minutes. Since a case was disposed of, on average, in 3.7 appearances, the average amount of courtroom time devoted to each case was 12.6 minutes, spread over several months. Cases that could not be quickly disposed of, the study added, "tended to chronically 'churn' in the system, meaning that they moved from one adjournment to the next without resolution because there are not enough judges to try them."

Central to the court's weakness was the historical reliance on plea bargaining. In plea negotiations, the prosecutor's strongest card is the threat of taking a case to trial. "A judicial system is legally dead," the New York bar report stated, "if the defendant who insists on his innocence cannot get a trial and if the prosecution, itself having no credible threat of trial with which to obtain guilty pleas at serious levels, must settle for meaningless disposition, often after endless adjournments." Experts say credible trial capacity means being able to bring to trial at least 10 percent of the defendants coming before the court. In New York's lower court the figure had sunk to no more than 0.5 percent.

However much the prosecutors' and judges' desire to separate the garbage from the serious cases once might have served efficiency with no loss of justice, there was good reason to believe that the spreading rot at the basis of the court system had forced real sacrifice. The Vera study had found that judges and prosecutors treated the nighttime burglaries of commercial premises as garbage, along with family and neighborhood disputes. "Judges and prosecutors consider these crimes 'nuisances' rather than felonies, and it was the policy in several prosecutors' offices routinely to reduce them to misdemeanors." Though the crimes usually were committed against strangers by offenders with prior records, "commercial burglaries rarely result in prison sentences, because they are acknowledged to present little risk of violence. Congestion is almost certainly an important reason" for the policy, which "is not condoned by statute but is the product of priorities which place greater weight on crimes of violence or potential violence." The Vera study found a similar informal policy toward grand larcenies, especially auto thefts. The unstated guidelines appeared to be that "virtually no one will be prosecuted for the felony if the car is not worth more than $500; unless the defendant is believed to be a professional car thief or part of a ring, he will be allowed to plead guilty to a misdemeanor no matter what the value of the car; the compulsive joyrider is usually given a taste of jail in the hope that he will soon grow up." A subsequent survey of felony-arrest dispositions in 1981 confirmed that such policies remained well entrenched. More than 72 percent of burglaries were disposed of in the criminal court, while the figure for grand larcenies was more than 93 percent.

More disturbing was evidence that the rot affected drug enforcement. A 1984 examination of drug cases generated by the police department's Operation Pressure Point campaign on the Lower East Side showed that nearly 40 percent of felony charges were reduced to misdemeanors in criminal court. Two years later, a state study of felony drug cases concluded that though the vast majority of felony drug cases were made in the city rather than the suburbs or upstate towns, "New York City prosecutes fewer drug sale felonies through the upper courts, convicts a lower proportion overall and a lower proportion of felonies." Specifically, the study found that the city disposed of 44 percent of felony sale arrests in the upper courts compared with more than 70 percent upstate, and that in the city only 39 percent of dispositions were felony convictions, compared with 72 percent upstate.

With such statistics, the media would make much of cases like that of one Jerome Harrison, whose recidivism seemed to earn him easier, rather than harsher, treatment. On July 23, 1985, he was arrested on the felony charge of possessing narcotic drugs with intent to sell. It was reduced to criminal possession of a controlled substance, a misdemeanor, for which he was sentenced to a maximum of ninety days in jail. He was back on the street to be arrested again on September 23 for criminal sale of a narcotic drug. He was allowed to plead guilty to loitering and given thirty days. Then on February 24, 1986, he was arrested yet again for criminal sale of a narcotic drug. He pled guilty to the lesser charge of criminal sale of a controlled substance and walked out of court with a sentence of five years probation.

That the plea-bargaining system could break down to the point that burglaries, auto thefts, and drug peddling are routinely assigned to the prosecutor's garbage heap raises deeper questions about the triage mind-set. Why does only the threat of personal violence validate crimes for serious attention? Don't burglaries, auto thefts, and drug sales assault a person's sense of security, a neighborhood's atmosphere? On what authority do judges and prosecutors dismiss that kind of violence as garbage?

TWO

The higher courts, the arenas for the cases that survive triage, provoke questions of their own. They do not revolve around issues of overwork and inattention so much as the formal rules by which the courts work, specifically those having to do with sentencing.

Modern sentencing procedures evolved in intimate association with beliefs about punishment and rehabilitation. In colonial times, sentences were inflexible, since punishments—fines, whipping, branding, the stocks, death—were strictly fixed by law and in any case permitted little variation. Death awaited those found guilty of witchcraft and adultery as well as more violent crimes, and even those caught repeating petty offenses. Though defendants were locked up to await trial, incarceration as a punishment was rare. Where prescribed punishments appeared too harsh for the circumstances of a case, it is likely that juries simply declined to convict.

A reform movement gained force after the publication in 1764 of *On Crimes and Punishments* by Cesare Beccaria, the Italian criminologist and economist. He called for a more systematic approach to sentencing, safeguards for rights of defendants, and the abolition of torture and capital punishment. Anticipating the findings of criminal justice research two centuries hence, he argued that the clarity of the law and the certainty of punishment were far more likely to deter crime than "the fear of another which is more terrible but combined with the hope of impunity."

In 1787, in a meeting at the Philadelphia home of Benjamin Franklin, an influential Quaker named Benjamin Rush proposed that prisons, where inmates would follow strict regimens of work and solitary reflection, should replace capital and corporal punishments. The meeting led to such an experiment at Philadelphia's Walnut Street Jail in 1790. In 1796, Virginia adopted a bill proposed by Thomas Jefferson, who was impressed by Beccaria. It restricted the death penalty and established prisons where inmates did hard labor. Other states soon joined the move to penitentiaries.

In the first decades of the nineteenth century, however, as the nation's crime problems expanded with its population, criminal justice would begin its struggle with prison crowding. Prison managers learned quickly that courts following inflexible sentencing laws could rapidly fill up a prison, but provided no way to accommodate the overflow. Legislatures therefore began to allow time off for good behavior, to be awarded as prisons found necessary, and governors made liberal use of their powers to grant pardons.

At the same time, prison wardens developed new theories about the importance of reclaiming lost souls as well as punishing misbehavior. Flexible prison terms, linked to the process of recovery, were central to the strategy. "You ask me for how long a time he should be sentenced to such confinement?" wrote S. J. May, a New York prison reformer, in 1847. "Obviously, it seems to me, until the evil disposition is removed from his heart; until his disqualification to go at large no longer exists; that is, until he is a reformed man. How long this may be, no human sagacity certainly can predetermine." Zebulon Brockway, superintendent of the reformatory at Elmira, New York, believed in rigorous schedules of education, religious observance, and work. He pushed for indeterminate sentences to accommodate the process in the 1860s and 1870s. The movement gained much force with the first Congress of the National Prison Association, which took place in Cincinnati in 1870. The group declared that "preemptory sentences ought to be replaced by those of indeterminate length. Sentences limited only by satisfactory proof of reformation should be substituted for those measured by the mere lapse of time."

What eventually evolved were codes that required judges to sentence according to broad ranges—two years to ten years for armed robbery, for example—leaving it up to a parole board to decide when the convict would actually be released. By 1911, nine states had adopted the system. It gained widespread support after that, as it was continually promoted by the nation's leading prison wardens, who promoted the "treatment model" of corrections. As the twentieth century progressed, they would add drug and alcohol treatment and psychotherapy to the rehabilitation menu. Indeterminate sentencing was the rule in every state by the 1960s.

Then, in the 1970s, the indeterminate approach suddenly came under attack. To an extent this reflected the growing sense that the treatment model no longer worked, if ever it had. In the best of times for American prisons, no one had been able to come up with objective proof that any kind of therapy or education consistently rehabilitated criminals. Now crowding and neglect of prisons in many, if not most, states rendered the idea absurd. What kind of rehabilitative treatment could go on in a place where guards had acquiesced in the sharing of power with fearsome inmate gangs and many prisoners felt pressure to prey violently upon their fellows lest they be taken for weak and vulnerable themselves?

Stripped of its rehabilitation rationale, the indeterminate sentence suddenly faced pointed questions. In 1971, the American Friends Service Committee, descendants of the eighteenth-century Quaker reformers who had invented the penitentiary, published a report called *Struggle for Justice*. It challenged indeterminacy on practical and political grounds. The uncertainty of rehabilitation was one reason to doubt the system, the Friends group asserted. Another was that permitting judges and parole boards such broad discretion invited discrimination against minorities, the poor, and the powerless. The following year, Marvin Frankel, a federal judge, published an acerbic attack on indeterminacy, suggesting that his colleagues on the bench were not prepared to handle it responsibly. "An assault upon a federal officer may be punishable by a fine and imprisonment for 'not more than' ten years. The federal kidnapping law authorized 'imprisonment for any term of years or for life.' Rape . . . leads to 'death, or imprisonment for any term of years or for life.' " Judges, he observed, exercise this broad authority in the absence of any legislated guidelines about the relative values of different crimes or the purpose of imprisonment. "Left at large, wandering in deserts of uncharted discretion, the judges suit their own value systems insofar as they think about the problem at all," Frankel wrote.

In 1976, Andrew von Hirsch, in a report for the privately funded Committee for the Study of Incarceration, advanced the idea that "desert"—a more neutral term than "retribution"—ought to supplant rehabilitation as the purpose of sentencing. "Those who violate others' rights deserve punishment. That, of itself, constitutes a prima facie justification for maintaining a system of criminal sanctions." That same year, Alan Dershowitz of the Harvard Law School wrote a background paper for the Twentieth Century Fund's Task Force on Criminal Sentencing. It, too, criticized indeterminacy and argued that the power to deny a person's liberty ought not to be so diffused among judges, prison administrators, and parole boards. "Democratic theory would seem to indicate that such important decisions concerning human liberty should be made by the most representative elected body. . . . It is clear that no democratic society would ever leave it to judges, administrators, or experts to decide which acts should constitute crimes. That decision is quintessentially legislative, involving, as it does, fundamental questions of policy. Likewise, it should not be left to judges, administrators, or experts to determine the bases on which criminal offenders in a democratic society should be deprived lawfully of their freedom." The move against indeterminacy gained somewhat less high-minded support from prison inmates, who were perhaps the best witnesses against the treatment model. From their point of view, indeterminate sentences offered an annoying opportunity to sadistic prison guards, who could torment inmates simply by threatening to submit unfavorable comments for their files as parole hearings approached. ("Don't eyeball me that way, boy, or I'll write you up.")

Meanwhile, the mounting public frustration with street crime was beginning to focus on indeterminate sentencing and the parole system. The question guiding public opinion was James Q. Wilson's: "What do we do tomorrow that will reduce the chance of my wife having her purse snatched by some punk on the way to the supermarket?" And an answer that seemed obvious was: "When we catch such a punk, lock him up for a long time so that he doesn't do it again." Beyond the practical doubts, political poison tainted the idea of rehabilitation. Worse still, confusion over the workings of indeterminate sentencing and parole often left the public feeling defrauded. The vicious armed robber or rapist is convicted and led off to prison. The media, having devoted yards of space and miles of videotape to the investigation and trial, approvingly report the judge's stern tongue-lashing of the offender and his sentence of "twenty-five years." No one would focus much on a fact that defendant, judge, and prosecutor all understood full well: a twenty-five-year term usually results in parole release after eight years. Why couldn't a criminal's victim and the public—not to mention the criminal himself—know at the time of conviction what his punishment would actually be?

The question would turn venomous at times when paroled convicts committed new crimes. There was little
evidence that "failures" of parole were a pervasive problem.
For the most part, parole boards were doing a good job of
determining prisoners' abilities to cope with freedom. But
their mistakes could be spectacular. In 1984, a parole board
released George Acosta, who was serving time for manslaughter in a New York state prison. He came to New
York City and wound up in a gas-station shootout that left
a city police officer dead. The public outrage intensified
as it was revealed that not only had Acosta been released;
prior to the murder he had been found to have twice violated
terms of his parole and might have been returned to prison
had parole officers pursued that option.

What fed the public reaction in such cases was not so
much the idea that parole boards could err as that they
were permitted to do so in private. Not only were the terms
of punishment unknowable at the time of conviction; the
process of release occurred in remote, secret hearings from
which no explanations were offered. In the growing belief
that criminal justice was too important to be left to the
experts, the public began to demand greater truth in sentencing and the accountability it would seem to afford,
along with harsher sentences however administered. The
result was a rapid retreat from the thinking that had shaped
sentencing policies for more than a century.

THREE

Of all the forms the search for sterner, more certain sentences would take, the most dramatic was the return of the death penalty—with a vengeance many would find gratifying.

Execution was a fact of American criminal justice until 1967. States executed 199 convicts in 1935, the highest number on record. After that, the number began to decline until only two were killed in 1967. The last to die in that era was Luis Jose Monge, a Denver furniture salesman who had murdered his wife and three of their eleven children in 1963.

The decline in executions and the de facto moratorium that began after Monge went to the gas chamber in 1967 were due to the aggressive efforts of civil rights attorneys who mounted an all-out legal assault on capital punishment. Previously, opposition to the death penalty had arisen mainly from religious groups, whose campaigns failed to inspire broad public support. The civil rights lawyers, led by the Legal Defense Fund of the National Association for the Advancement of Colored People, saw capital punishment as the ultimate manifestation of systemic racism, since a disproportionate number of death-row inmates were black.

Civil rights lawyers began handling the appeals of condemned convicts and sought a Supreme Court ruling that execution was an unconstitutionally "cruel and unusual" form of punishment. Though no executions occurred for ten years as the litigation proceeded, the civil rights campaign ultimately failed. In the 1972 *Furman* v. *Georgia* case, the court found unconstitutional the arbitrary and capricious application of the death penalty, but not the penalty itself. That led to a flurry of activity in state legislatures to make death-penalty laws less arbitrary and capricious. Some states made death mandatory for certain offenses. North Carolina, for example, prescribed automatic death for first-degree murder, armed robbery, rape, and nighttime burglary. Other states established a two-step process for condemning a convict to death. The first trial would determine guilt or innocence. If the verdict was guilty, a second would decide whether the sentence should be death or life imprisonment, depending on how specific aggravating and mitigating circumstances applied to the case.

The NAACP Legal Defense Fund challenged both systems but fell short of victory in 1976 when the court in two decisions struck down mandatory death sentences (*Woodson* v. *North Carolina*) but allowed the two-trial procedure (*Gregg* v. *Georgia*). The following year a firing squad in the state of Utah brought the moratorium to an end by executing Gary Gilmore, who had murdered two men during armed robberies. The moral and legal issues were complicated by the fact that Gilmore had ordered an end to further appeals and claimed to welcome execution.

His last words were "Let's do it." Two years later, John Spenkelink, convicted of murdering a companion in a Florida motel room, died in the electric chair at the hands of the state of Florida. He was the first to be executed against his will under the new laws.

A second convict, Jesse Bishop, called off appeals and asked for death that year, and the state of Nevada obliged. Another "voluntary" execution, of Steven Judy, took place in Indiana in 1981, and two more executions, of Frank Coppola, voluntary in Virginia, and Charlie Brooks, not voluntary in Texas, occurred in 1982. Then the pace quickened. Five executions took place in 1983, eighteen in 1984, twenty-one in 1985, and eighteen in 1986. By 1987, thirty-seven states had enacted new death-penalty statutes to meet the Supreme Court's conditions, though the death penalty appeared to have a strong regional flavor: Nearly all of the new-law executions were in the South.

By 1986 most executions no longer rated more than a few paragraphs of newspaper coverage and got virtually no attention at all on the evening news. Yet public support for state-sanctioned death remained strong. From a low of 42 percent in 1966, the percentage of Americans favoring capital punishment for murder climbed to 70 percent by 1985. As the idea of Bernhard Goetz gunning down potential muggers restored a sense of power to citizens grown used to fear, so did the idea of murderers writhing in the electric chair, gagging in the gas chamber, or succumbing to the smothering sleep of the newest execution technique, lethal injection.

For criminals convicted of less than murder, meanwhile,

pressure grew on all sides for tougher sentences short of death. One response was simply that judges and parole boards sensed the shifting wind: The judges tended to scale up the brackets around sentence ranges, while parole boards grew more reluctant to release.

The informal stiffening of sentences was reinforced by a remarkable spate of legislative activity. A 1985 Justice Department survey of sentencing state by state found that "during the past 10 years, all 50 states and the District of Columbia have at some time considered or drafted legislation to alter extant indeterminate sentencing structures to some other sentencing plan. This apparently trivial piece of information represents a wholesale shift in thinking about criminal sanctions. . . ." Nearly everywhere, the revisions were in the direction of limited discretion and increased penalties.

By 1985, every state but Wisconsin had enacted mandatory prison terms for certain offenses. Twenty-seven states had tightened eligibility for parole, while eight had abolished it altogether, though such drastic blows for more certain sentences were sometimes hedged by the creation of a de facto parole board under a new name. In Illinois, for example, it was called the Prisoner Review Board.

Another popular idea was to identify the most active criminals (dubbed "career criminals," "dangerous offenders," or "habitual offenders") and make sure they were imprisoned for long terms. The idea gained force with research published in the early 1970s by Marvin Wolfgang and his colleagues at the University of Pennsylvania, who studied juvenile delinquency in Philadelphia. They found that of about ten thousand boys born in 1945, 6 percent accounted for more than half of the crimes committed by the whole group, including 60 percent of the aggravated assaults and 75 percent of the rapes. A second study of boys born in 1958 found that 7.5 percent committed 69 percent of the group's serious crimes.

Such statistics kindled ideas of "selective incapacitation"—making a cost-effective dent in the crime rate by getting the superactive 6 or 7 percent off the streets for long terms. In 1982, a Rand Corporation researcher named Peter Greenwood, assisted by Allan Abrahamse, pursued the concept to provocative lengths with his analysis of data collected from prison inmates in California, Texas, and Michigan. The data revealed a clear pattern of career criminality. Of all who reported committing robberies, for example, 10 percent said they committed eighty-seven or more per year, and while 50 percent of burglars committed fewer than six burglaries per year, more than 230 per year were committed by 10 percent.

Greenwood decided to dirty his hands with a question others might consider off-limits: What could distinguish the high-rate offenders besides high rates of offending? Working with the data, he came up with factors associated with career criminality that included a record of conviction and recent incarceration, a history of juvenile criminality, a history of drug use, and recent unemployment. The more these factors appeared in a person's record, the more likely he was to be a dangerous offender.

Using the factors to screen offenders, Greenwood figured, could reduce both crime and the prison population. If one took the California robbers, for example, and reduced prison sentences for those who committed the crime infrequently while increasing them for the careerists, one might reduce the prison population by 5 percent while reducing robbery by 15 percent. Such fine tuning of relatively soft data, not to mention the ethical questions raised by the idea of increasing a person's punishment because of his unemployment, provoked sharp controversy, and no jurisdiction ever tried sentencing according to Greenwood's dangerousness factors.

But one did not have to accept the precision of Greenwood's approach to find appealing the idea of focusing resources on the worst offenders at a time of general state and local austerity. Prosecutors in many cities set up special units to ensure the vigorous prosecution of career criminals. The federal sentencing study found that thirty-three states had enacted or increased special penalties for repeat offenders.

Some legislatures would go so far as to junk the indeterminate system and set up whole new sentencing procedures. The federal survey found that in 1985, fifteen states could qualify as "determinate." Maine and California led the way in the late seventies with sentencing-code revisions that got rid of parole and left fixed prison terms. Convicts were to serve them in full, minus allowances for good time. Such ambitious undertakings would reflect ideas about fairness and desert as developed by Marvin Frankel, Alan Dershowitz, Andrew von Hirsch, and David Fogel, who had served as a correctional administrator in Minnesota and as head of the Illinois Law Enforcement Commission.

The most elaborate model called for the legislature to

authorize a politically balanced panel representing all branches of criminal justice as well as the public. It would prepare sentencing guidelines to be administered according to a grid. One axis would rank categories of offenses in order of severity; the other would gauge an offender's criminal record. To find the appropriate sentence the judge would match up the offense and the record the way one might find the distance between two towns on a roadmap mileage chart. In addition, the commission would prepare a schedule of aggravating factors ("the crime involved excessive cruelty") or mitigating ones ("the victim was a participant in the crime") that could justify deviation from the chart. Deviations would have to be justified by one of the aggravating or mitigating factors, stated on the record. The grid sentence might still be stated as a range, but one narrowed to a matter of months rather than years. The convict would serve out the full term, with only modest time off for good behavior. Parole would be eliminated.

Though the commission-guidelines model would arouse much interest, only Minnesota and Washington managed to implement it in full. Other states pursued the same basic idea but authorized committees of judges, the state bar association, or other groups to prepare guidelines. Some retained parole but subjected it to a system of guidelines as well.

FOUR

The efforts to reverse a century of indeterminate sentencing raised new questions that had nothing to do with nostalgia for the discredited idea of rehabilitation.

The return of the death penalty, for example, did little to settle the long-running debate over its purpose, a debate that could starkly expose the gap between common assumptions and criminal justice scholarship.

The most obvious purpose of capital punishment would appear to be incapacitation—it could be stated with grim certainty that the executed murderer would never kill again. The possibility of pardons or paroles from life sentences appears to argue strongly for the need to incapacitate absolutely. In 1957, Edgar Smith, despite his claims of innocence, was convicted in New Jersey of killing a cheerleader. He became a model prisoner, winning reprieves from his death sentence. After the columnist William F. Buckley, Jr., took up his cause, Smith won a new trial and freedom in 1971. But in 1976, he was arrested again for kidnapping and attempted murder and confessed to the crime along with the 1957 murder.

Yet studies show that such cases are rare. First-degree murderers for the most part are not inclined to repeat the crime. On parole they behave themselves better than those convicted of other crimes. Stephen Gettinger, in his thoughtful study of the death penalty, *Sentenced to Die*, reports that "a nine-state study of 1,293 first-degree murderers who were paroled showed that only nine subsequently committed new felonies. One of these was murder. The execution of 1,293 people to prevent one death seems hard to justify."

A second argument for the death penalty, heard more frequently in times of exorbitant prison costs, is that it is cheaper than life imprisonment. Researchers, however, find plenty of reason to doubt this apparently obvious idea, too. Cells on death row, where a single convict may remain for decades, are the most secure and heavily staffed and therefore the costliest to maintain in a prison. The heaviest expenses associated with capital punishment, however, arise from all the litigation that occurs before an execution can take place. The New York State Defenders Association calculated in 1982 that if the New York legislature enacted a death-penalty law, each prosecution would cost $1.8 million, or double the cost of imprisoning a criminal for life.

The greatest controversy surrounds the third claimed purpose of capital punishment, the deterrence of criminal behavior in others. Even given that some murders are committed by people either permanently deranged or made momentarily irrational by jealousy, rage, or fear, shouldn't the prospect of execution stay the hands of at least some potential killers? Proof that it does so has remained surprisingly elusive.

Or, on reflection, maybe not so surprisingly. If one

grants that people bent on murder are inclined to think about the consequences, they would first calculate their chances of arrest and successful prosecution. How many more would be deterred by the added possibility of death? And how would they make such calculations, given that the percentage of murderers executed always will be tiny? There were 20,613 homicides in the United States in 1986. Yet even in the high-volume death-penalty years of the 1930s, the number executed in any one year never topped two hundred. Today they are still running way below one hundred a year. Even accounting for the fact that not all homicides wind up with convictions for first-degree murder, potential killers can count on immensely favorable odds for avoiding capital punishment.

Social scientists like Thorstin Sellin have sought to discern a deterrent effect by comparing murder rates in states with the death penalty and neighboring states without it, and in time periods before and after death-penalty laws were passed. But none of the studies produced conclusive results. The researcher who came closest was the economist Isaac Ehrlich, who applied the statistical process of regression analysis to data from the years between 1933 and 1969 to isolate from other social factors (race, age, employment) the effects of capital punishment on murders. He concluded that "an additional execution per year over the period in question may have resulted, on average, in seven or eight fewer murders."

The study caused a sensation in criminal justice circles until other scholars examined it and found that, excluding data from 1960 to 1969, when few executions took place, eliminated any suggestion of a deterrent effect. James Q. Wilson, hardly soft on murder and murderers, concluded that "the available scholarly work ought to make one an agnostic on the deterrence issue."

The commonsense assumptions about so seemingly logical an idea as longer terms for career criminals would also wear thin as researchers continued their work. The whole idea of selective incapacitation was anathema to scholars like Andrew von Hirsch, who believe passionately that however wicked a person might be, he ought to be punished only for crimes he has already committed, not for ones he might commit in the future.

But one did not need to wrestle with the ethical issue to doubt the wisdom of such a policy. Elliott Currie pointed out that Marvin Wolfgang's 7.5 percent of superdelinquent Philadelphia boys born in 1958 numbered about 1,000. Extrapolating their number nationally would mean about 160,000 new career criminals added to the population in a single year. Furthermore, the 7.5 percent were those who had accumulated five arrests by the time they were eighteen. Adding in those who had two to four arrests increased the figure to 19 percent, implying a national one-year total of 400,000 recidivists. Yet the number of prisoners incarcerated for felonies in all states and the federal prison system now totals 547,000. A serious program of selective incapacitation would apparently require levels of incarceration much beyond our current capacity to afford, or even imagine.

Others find reason to question the practical soundness of the whole idea. Wolfgang and Greenwood made much of incidence, the rate at which each individual commits crimes. Yet the level of crime in a community also depends on its prevalence, the number of people who commit some crime in a given time period. Alfred Blumstein and Elizabeth Graddy found that prevalence as well as incidence are high in American cities of more than 250,000. In such cities, they found, about a quarter of all men, and half of all black men, were likely to be arrested at least once before the age of fifty-five for one of the FBI's "index" crimes.

Researchers studying violent crime in Columbus, Ohio, discovered that high-incidence criminals actually committed a small proportion of all the crimes committed. More than two-thirds of the violent criminals were first-time felons. And because so few violent criminals are arrested by police, the Columbus researchers found, requiring mandatory sentences of five years for all felony convictions—a step that would massively strain prison resources—would reduce violent crime by no more than 4 percent.

Promoters of incapacitation could object that many of the crimes for which no arrests were made might well have been committed by the incidence offenders, and adjusting the calculations for that supposition would increase the crime-control benefit from the mandatory five-year terms. But even a substantial reduction would have to be squared with the cost of new prison space, which would have to accommodate five times the number of prisoners that Ohio was already struggling to keep locked up.

Nor were the benefits of efforts to restructure the sentencing process always so clear. Those who pushed to abolish parole, for example, tended to assume that parole boards were too lenient. Yet ending parole discretion also made it impossible for anyone to be reasonably strict—that is, to keep a prisoner locked up when it was obvious that it would be irresponsible to allow him back on the street.

Thus California, having abolished parole for new convictions, learned a painful lesson. One day in 1978, Dan White, a former county supervisor, walked into San Francisco's city hall, pulled out a gun, and shot to death the mayor, George Moscone, and a supervisor named Harvey Milk, who had won election after a campaign in which he acknowledged proudly that he was gay. Had White been convicted of first-degree murder, he would have had to serve at least sixteen years and might have been held for life. But his lawyer managed to persuade the jury to convict him only of manslaughter on the ground that an overindulgence in sugary junk food (the "Twinkie defense") had impaired his judgment. For manslaughter, however, the fixed sentencing system permitted only seven years and eight months. When he had served the time, the prison had to release him, in the face of a huge public outcry. Helpless, prison officials arranged for his secret release. Had he been convicted of manslaughter under the indeterminate system, a California judge might have authorized a maximum term of fifteen years, and a parole board could have made sure that he stayed put. (So far as anyone knows, he stayed out of trouble for the short time after his release until he committed suicide.)

Even more troubling, however, was the fact that the

return to determinacy again engaged the issue that had attracted prison administrators to indeterminate sentences in the first place: prison crowding. The formal and informal efforts of the 1970s to make prison sentences more certain and increase their lengths had produced the greatest run-up of prison population in history. In the fifty years from 1927 to 1977, the nation's state and federal prison population had grown from 109,983 to 285,456, an increase of 175,473. But in the next ten years, more than a quarter million more flooded into the correctional system, bringing the 1987 total to 570,000.

Thus as state legislators discovered the heady politics of sentencing reform, state budget directors looked on with alarm. In California, the prison population surged from 21,525 in 1977 to 62,822 in 1987. In New York, mandatory minimums enacted for drug and habitual offenders and tightening of parole eligibility combined with the greater willingness of judges to send more convicts to prison. As a result, the prison population would more than triple from 12,444 in 1973 to 39,489 in 1986. The federal survey of sentencing changes pointed out with a touch of dismay that "amid a decade of focus on sentencing and sentencing reform, only 11 states have provided for research on their reforms or conducted statewide studies to ascertain the impact of the reforms." The state of Michigan enacted an emergency prison-release law to go along with tougher sentencing. It provided for the automatic *rollback* of parole dates once the prison population reached 95 percent of capacity. The new sternness at the front door, in other words, would be matched by new lenience at the back.

The more formal and inflexible the determinate sentencing apparatus, the greater the danger that it would become a device for ratcheting up prison sentences and populations as each new sensational crime stirred public outrage. It was partly in response to that concern that promoters of sentence guidelines suggested turning over the task of writing the grids to independent commisions. But even such politically insulated bodies found it hard to overcome the effects of the fraud that years of indeterminate sentencing had perpetuated upon the citizenry. The public had little sense that average time served fell far below the maximums a judge might have authorized at the time of conviction. The armed robber with a prior conviction would be sentenced to five to fifteen years but would serve closer to five than to fifteen. To avoid an overload of armed robbers in prison, the sentence chart would therefore have to fix the sentence for a similar armed robber at, say, six years. Yet to prescribe so seemingly lenient a term would ignite a firestorm of criticism from politicians and the press. The appeal of the commission guidelines system would fade somewhat as legislators understood the politically unpalatable fine print: fixed sentences would have to be short sentences.

Guidelines could also disappoint those who hoped to make punishments more certain, because the existence of a chart would make only a slight dent in plea bargaining, which settled the vast majority of criminal cases. Prosecutors and defense lawyers who want to negotiate pleas simply settle on the amount of time the defendant should serve and then select the charges for which the chart prescribes the right number of months or years. When pressed on this point, promoters of the chart system respond that its real purpose is to move the decision of how much time a convict will actually serve from the obscurity of the parole hearing, at the end of the criminal justice process, into the healthy sunshine of open court, near the beginning. That is certainly desirable, but it is not the point on which the guidelines idea tends to be sold.

FIVE

The neglect of lower courts and the efforts to toughen up sentencing in the higher courts send messages of frustration. The triage policy of neglecting the lesser offenses and offenders for the sake of more violent ones only dubiously addressed public safety and did violence of its own to public values. Victims of burglars, muggers, and auto thieves, aware the courts would do little in the absence of an airtight case and a multiple recidivist for an offender, were not particularly comforted to know that the courts might do better if the crime was murder or rape. Nor were the residents of neighborhoods taken over by drug dealing. The return of the death penalty and increases in incarcerations, while obviously meaningful to the individual convicts involved, still had no demonstrable effect on public safety. While they addressed, and in a symbolic sense no doubt gratified, public lusts for the kind of vengeance that would discharge outrage and fear, the basic arithmetic—and message—of the funnel remained in place.

Were no more constructive responses possible? The answer could be yes for those willing to entertain an idea that had not seen much attention in the decade or so of focus on prison sentences: Find ways to punish apart from prison.

Having invented the penitentiary as the uniquely American way of punishment, Americans would grow used to it to the point they would believe that a criminal who had not been sentenced to prison had not been punished. By the 1980s, that attitude would inhibit efforts to improve the message of the courts.

In concept, at least, the courts do have a sanction to impose short of prison. It is called probation. Typically, a judge imposes a prison sentence on a convict but suspends it and allows release under supervision of a probation officer. In addition to seeing that convicts stay out of trouble, the probation officer is expected to function as a social caseworker, or "resource broker," helping convicts to find schooling, employment, and counseling. The judge can impose specific conditions on the probationer depending on the circumstances of his case ("Stay away from that video-game parlor where your unsavory friends hang out"). A probationer who fails to meet such conditions could find himself in prison, serving out the balance of the suspended term.

The idea of allowing some criminals to escape the court's discipline stretches back for centuries in Western history. In medieval times, the right to sanctuary established certain places to which offenders might flee to avoid punishment. In feudal England, ordained clerics might escape the king's court by claiming "benefit of clergy," which permitted their cases to be resolved in more lenient ecclesiastical courts. The benefit was extended in the fifteenth century to lay persons who could prove literacy by reading the "neck verse"—so called because it so commonly was used to avoid hanging: "Have mercy upon me, O God, according to thy loving kindness, according to the multitude of thy tender mercies blot out my transgressions." The benefit would continue in England until the nineteenth century.

The modern practice of probation was originated in 1841 in Boston by John Augustus, a shoemaker who believed that "the object of the law is to reform criminals and to prevent crime and not to punish maliciously or from a spirit of revenge." One day he went to police court, bailed out a drunk, and helped him find a job. When the offender returned to court three weeks later, he appeared rehabilitated, and the judge imposed no more than a fine of one cent and costs. In the eighteen years that followed, Augustus would perform the same service for 1,152 men and 794 women. He evidently had a sharp eye for a good risk: Of his first 1,100 clients, only one jumped bail. Before long, other volunteers had joined Augustus in attempting to salvage prisoners, and in 1878, Massachusetts passed a law making probation a more formal option. The idea of supervised release began to spread, especially as a sanction for juvenile offenders, and by 1900 six states had authorized it. By 1940 all states granted probation to juveniles. Twenty years later, most states had established it for at least some categories of adults.

Probation would eventually become the sentence most commonly imposed by the courts on cases that were not dismissed outright. Though the public remains only faintly aware of it, more than 2 million Americans are serving terms of probation today, more than triple the number in prison and nearly double the 1979 figure. The growth apparently reflects the courts' increasing reliance on probation as they are overwhelmed with cases and prisons fill up. Probation, in other words, is what happens to cases that fall outside the funnel.

But virtually no one takes probation seriously as a sanction. It was originally conceived of as a way to give offenders for whom there might be some hope—especially youngsters—a second chance. The years of LEAA experiments spawned scores of programs to which probationers might be assigned: drug and alcohol treatments, group and individual psychotherapies, job training and other schooling. Such "community corrections" activities, conducted in a variety of thoughtfully devised settings and facilities, would to some extent pick up on the rehabilitation that prisons were fumbling. But as LEAA funding lapsed and localities suffered fiscal crises, such programs, and then probation departments themselves, would be sacrificed along with lower courts. By the end of the 1970s, in many cities, prosecutors, judges, defense attorneys, and criminals and their victims would no longer think of probation as a second chance so much as a free ride—you're guilty, the court would say to the young burglar or mugger, but we don't think you've done enough yet to deserve prison, and since we can't figure out anything else to do with you, we're going to let you go.

Experienced probation workers consider caseloads of thirty-five to fifty manageable. Yet in some urban jurisdictions, especially since the fiscal crises of the seventies, caseloads run into the hundreds. A 1980 *Corrections Magazine* article found that "caseloads of individual officers sometimes run as high as 500, with most falling between 75 and 150. . . . Large caseloads sometimes frustrate officers from seeing their clients at all." The magazine referred to the increasingly common practice of " 'postcard probation,' in which the client sends a preaddressed postcard once or twice a month reporting on his activities. In some jurisdictions, postcard probation ends when the client misplaces his postcards."

Philadelphia criminal court judge Lois Forer asserts that "probation is not a penalty. The offender continues with his life-style. . . . If he is a wealthy doctor, he continues with his practice; if he is an unemployed youth, he continues to be unemployed. Probation is a meaningless rite; it is a sop to the conscience of the court."

The neglect continues. A 1985 Rand Corporation study of probation in California documented the starvation of probation services in that state and called the system "a serious threat to public safety." The study examined 1,672 felons granted probation in Los Angeles and Alameda counties. In a forty-month period, the researchers found, "65 percent of the probationers in our subsample were rearrested, 51 percent were reconvicted, 18 percent were reconvicted of serious violent crimes, and 34 percent were reincarcerated."

"Since the mid-1970s," the study states, "probation has fallen on hard times. The mood of the country has grown more punitive, and the public has increasingly demanded consistent, harsher sentencing, not 'lenient' probation." The study found that while total criminal justice spending in California increased 30 percent between 1975 and 1983, from $4.15 billion to $5.35 billion (in constant dollars), spending on probation actually decreased 10 percent from $435 million to $390 million. Yet the number of probationers expanded by 32,000. In 1975, California spent $2,060 on each probationer each year. By 1983, the figure had declined by nearly 25 percent to $1,600.

A committee of New York's state senate examined the New York City probation system in 1986 and found it in an advanced state of collapse. Caseloads exceeded two hundred per probation worker and turnover of the workers was 25 percent annually. Yet, the report stated, "there is essentially no relevant training of incoming probation officers and little supervision of officers at any stage in their careers." The need for training may have been academic, however, since "New York City probation officers usually spend only one day a week actually counseling probationers. Most of the time, the other four days on the job are spent doing paperwork. For nonviolent and less serious offenders, the agency was not even so rigorous as to require postcards. "These individuals are only required to phone into the office at given intervals, and leave word with either a clerk or an answering machine."

Even where better funded and staffed, probation suffers from a problem of identity. Some observers are deeply perturbed by the fundamental conflict between the probation officer's roles of surveillance and social work. Truly helping an offender to pursue a job or schooling, support his family, and stay out of trouble, they point out, requires a relationship of trust and mutual respect. But the probation officer must remain cop as well as therapist, standing ready to haul his client forcibly before a judge to answer for violations of probation rules. David Rothman, the historian, would call the probation officer a "gun-carrying psychiatrist. . . . The probation officer is the ultimate reflection of the failure of the idea in American corrections that you can guard and treat at the same time. . . . It's a patently absurd notion."

Overwork compounded by the difficulty of resolving such a conflict makes burnout a common malady of probation officers. Walter Lide, who spent seven years as a probation officer in New York and Arizona, writes that "although the manipulators, the self-indulgent and the chronic offenders made up only a small part of my caseload, they stood out and overshadowed the rest. They required the most time and work. . . . Repeaters were usually a mental, emotional and spiritual drain, unable or unwilling to give anything positive in return." Though as many as 75 percent of those on probation stay out of trouble on their own, "the insincere and trouble-prone require intense contact for the entire period of their probation. Economics of time and human energy limit contact with the positive aspects of the job in favor of the most hopeless."

"I was asked to believe some of the most phenomenal

tall tales imaginable," Lide writes. "It was a depressing thing to live with and soon found its way into my personal life. My liquor intake increased . . . and I was suspicious and mistrustful of everybody. . . . Family, friends and even my wife were targets for unrelenting accusations. Paranoia strikes deep. I had changed and everyone noticed but me and the people I worked with. No more mister nice guy. Life was serious and I had to cover my ass at all times. I soon became a statistic in the profession's abnormally high divorce rate."

Role conflict and burnout are further aggravated by the increasing pressure on probation to sponge up the cases that spill out of crowded courts and prisons. In the Rand study of California probation, the researchers identified "basic factors"—criminal record, use of a weapon, drug addiction, injury to the victim—that would normally cause a judge to sentence a felon to prison. Between 20 and 25 percent of the felony probationers, they found, should have qualified for incarceration instead of probation. "These data suggest that many offenders who are granted felony probation are indistinguishable in terms of their crimes or criminal record from those who are imprisoned."

That might not be reason for concern if it resulted from judges' ability to identify felons who do well on probation despite a background that would qualify them for prison. Yet the prison-qualifying felons actually did poorly on probation: 78 percent were eventually rearrested, while recidivism among those whose backgrounds would suggest a good probation risk was 55 percent.

The senate committee's study of New York City probation found that the 58,000 offenders on probation included 38,000 who had been convicted of felonies, compared with only 20,000 five years before. Since 1980, the study found, the average caseload per probation officer had risen from 157 to 204. The 38,000 felony probationers included 12,000 "who were sentenced to probation despite recommendations by the Probation Department that they receive prison sentences." "Rather than serving as a counseling and rehabilitation service for low-risk, first offenders, who might well benefit from this type of supervision," the study concludes, "it is being used as an alternative to overcrowded prisons for thousands of violent criminals, for whom it serves little useful purpose, and who often prove to be a real risk to society."

How best to beef up probation? In a number of places, necessity has already fostered some attempts. Despite the common wisdom about the conflict between punitive surveillance and treatment, such experiments are best measured by the extent to which they accommodate the conflict, combining punishment with social work, or, better, making clear the importance of punishment and tailoring the social work to it.

This may not be necessary for that many probationers. James Byrne of the University of Lowell in Massachusetts cites studies showing that about 15 percent of all probationers are responsible for the bulk of "failures"—new crimes or other violations of terms set by the court. These presumably are the "manipulators, the self-indulgent and the chronic offenders" that drove Walter Lide to paranoia and divorce. "It is this group," Byrne writes, "that poses a threat to community safety, not the majority of offenders under supervision." Changing the message of probation might require tougher sanctions for all, but they ought to be designed with the problem 15 percent first and foremost in mind.

Perhaps the simplest approach is to combine traditional probation with a sobering dose of prison. Some judges make a common practice of "split" sentences—a few weeks or months of jail followed by a longer term on probation. Others may prefer sentencing the offender to weekends in jail and weekdays on probation, an arrangement that permits the convict to hold a job and remain with his family. But such sentences require some use of scarce jail space.

A few states therefore are experimenting with "work camps" inexpensively constructed on the grounds of a state penitentiary. The judge sentences the convict to a standard felony term—three years, say, for burglary—but suspends all but six months on condition that he function successfully at the work camp. The regimen might include mornings of hard outdoor labor in woods or fields under the supervision of "drill instructors," followed by afternoons of education, counseling, and job training.

The camps are typically reserved for nonviolent offenders who submit to the camp discipline on pain of transfer to the nearby penitentiary. At one such program in Georgia, the campers are reminded of that pain every day. As they march to work past the penitentiary yard, the hardened cons peer out at them through the fence, taunting them with offers of homosexual sex that, but for the fence, the vulnerable youngsters would no doubt find impossible to refuse.

A New York State proposal for such camps to accommodate nine hundred prisoners per year estimated the cost at $3 million for construction and $9.5 million annually for operating costs, compared with $50 million for construction and $23 million annually to add another nine hundred conventional cells. Can such a dose of old-time chain gangs, basic training, and modern treatment actually straighten out young burglars and car thieves? Whether it does or not, the idea certainly sends a stronger message to the public than simple release on probation.

A second area of experimentation involves trying to enforce some control on an offender's movements even though he has been released to the community. Given the caseload problem, it once seemed ludicrously impractical to impose curfews on offenders or restrict them to their homes except for excursions to buy food or visit a doctor. Now technology makes it seem less so. A number of enterprising companies, eyeing a potentially vast market, produce devices designed to let probation officers monitor convicts in their homes. The device might be a transmitter, worn by the convict, that continuously emits a signal. A receiver in the convict's home telephone relays the signal to a computer at the probation office, indicating times when the signal is received and when it disappears. Probation officers monitor printouts and check up on the offender when the computer suggests he's gone out when he should have stayed in.

Another version of the system is based on an automatic telephone dialer in the probation office. It rings the convict's home phone at random times during periods he is supposed to be there. When he answers, he verifies his identity with a device strapped to his wrist that plugs into another device on his phone.

Since 1984, a number of states have experimented with such systems. Florida counts more than 4,750 convicts on this form of house arrest. Oklahoma, Alabama, Connecticut, Delaware, Indiana, Georgia, Texas, and South Carolina also report state-run house-arrest programs. Those at the county level bring to thirty the total number of states trying out the idea. Though such programs are too new for definitive conclusions, some tentative ones are possible. Electronics appears to work fairly well in controlling convicts. Florida reports that only 1 percent of its home detainees have escaped, and a modest 14 percent had their probation revoked for violations. Those who argue for house arrest as an alternative to jail or prison express concern that convicts selected for it are the better risks who would not have been sent to prison anyway, that such programs only "widen the net" of social control. They may well do so, but there is a good case to be made that the net ought to be widened. No one gains from an ineffective probation system that the public views with contempt.

The devices involved remain fairly expensive—house arrest with the more sophisticated electronic monitors may cost as much as $8,500 a year, a figure that approaches the cost of incarceration in a county jail. Whether that cost will come down as use of the devices spreads remains to be seen. In the meantime, some jurisdictions offset the cost by charging the convicts a "supervision fee" that may run to $200 per month. That raises a serious issue of fairness, since it effectively bars the option of house arrest to poorer convicts.

Yet another set of objections involves the totalitarian overtones of such electronic surveillance. As long as it only approximates the use of beepers by doctors and other busy professionals, the intrusiveness issue seems slight. But Joan Petersilia of the Rand Corporation reports that producers of the house-arrest transmitters, seeking to develop their market, are "already considering the potential of including home video and audio surveillance and remote-control testing of blood alcohol content." That would exceed even George Orwell's direst fantasies.

For now, however, the more important problem with house arrest is that it offers only surveillance, no social work. Yet a role for social work remains, even in a probation service that would put surveillance and punishment before rehabilitation. The models for it are the "intensive" approaches that are the subject of experiment in a number of jurisdictions. Their strategy is to reduce the caseload per probation officer. The most acclaimed, and imitated, program began in Georgia in response to severe prison crowding in 1982. Thirteen two-person teams work caseloads of no more than twenty-five. They may visit clients as often as five days per week, sometimes even twice a day, and they become heavily involved in helping them manage their lives. Probationers in the intensive program are required to get and keep jobs, pay restitution and a fine, do 132 hours of community service, and be home each evening by 7:00.

Stephen Gettinger, writing in *Corrections Magazine* in 1983, told the story of Harry Brock, "a 41-year-old white male who by his own admission has been charged with or has served time for almost every crime known to man except child molestation and murder." For two decades of his adult life "his major occupations had been drinking . . . committing petty crimes, and playing softball. . . ." He landed in the intensive probation program after a skeptical judge decided to test the program with the most difficult case he could find. The program rose to the challenge.

"The first two weeks Brock was on probation," Gettinger writes, his probation officers "visited him 12 times. Since then they have seen him five times a week, at all hours of the day and night. They turned his softball playing into an asset; his community-service work at a recreation center became a paying job. They recruited his girlfriend (a no-nonsense nurse who had been his high school sweetheart) and other acquaintances to help keep him in line. Except for one minor curfew violation, at this writing Brock had walked the straight and narrow for six months, and appeared to be making a strong effort to pull his life together." According to Georgia corrections officials, Brock successfully completed his probation in 1986 and at this writing, so far as the authorities know, he has remained out of trouble.

Billie S. Erwin, writing in the journal *Federal Probation*, reported that by 1985, the Georgia program had expanded to thirty-three jurisdictions and had supervised 2,322 convicts. Sixteen percent were dropped from the program because they committed new crimes or otherwise violated its terms. Yet, Ms. Erwin reported, the program did not draw much blame for threatening public safety. The most serious crime committed by a probationer in the intensive program was an armed robbery that did not result in injury. The rest of the crimes consisted mostly of a handful of assaults and burglaries, one being "the burglary of a gum ball machine in a hallway outside the probation office." To be sure, such figures did not include any crimes that did not come to official attention. Yet Ms. Erwin appears on solid ground when she asserts, "The citizens of Georgia have had little reason to fear. . . . The pervasive methods of surveillance of all aspects of the probationer's life may be considered not only as community control over the offender but also as control of the risk for the community."

The benefits, meanwhile, were substantial. Analysis of the offenders sentenced to intensive probation suggested that after three years, the program had succeeded in reducing the number sent to prison by 10 percent. Prison costs per inmate per year were $12,537, while the intensive probation cost was $1,622. For every offender the program kept out of prison, the state of Georgia netted a saving of $10,915 per year. More important benefits had nothing to do with money. Georgia judges professed to be pleased with so genuinely viable a sentencing option. And instead of complaining about burnout, probation workers praised the program as finally approximating ideal concepts of probation practice.

"All the resources of the community are tapped through probation staff in behalf of the probationer who is willing to obey the rules and try to straighten out his life," Ms. Erwin wrote. "IPS staff members have taken on cases that everyone else in the system had given up on. Staff members live inside probationers' shoes for a while, and some of the greatest job satisfaction comes from seeing their charges self-supporting and assuming the responsibilities of law-abiding citizens." The Georgia probation officers apparently have no trouble combining heavy surveillance with helping. "Georgia's experience," Ms. Erwin writes, "has, in fact, led notable criminal justice authors to rethink the assumptions of inherent role conflict."

The probationers themselves, meanwhile, "express positive reactions to the feeling that somebody in the criminal justice system really cares enough to get involved." Gettinger recounts the case of Angela Cantrell, a nineteen-year-old ex-convict who was on probation for forgery when she was arrested for shoplifting. She was also about to give birth to her son. On intensive probation because probation officers persuaded the judge to give the new mother another chance, she held a restaurant job and felt grateful for the probation support. "This is the first time I ever had any probation officers I liked," she says.

SIX

The most intriguing attempts to make more of probation involve restitution—the convicts' payment of money to a victim to compensate for material loss, pain, and trouble. Roots of the idea reach back at least to the Dark Ages. In Anglo-Saxon England, a criminal might "buy back the peace" disrupted by his crime with a payment of restitution to the victim and a fine to the lord who administered the settlement. Laws of Kings Aethelberht and Alfred the Great spelled out fines to be paid to victims of injuries. Alfred's were precise: "If a wound an inch long is made under the hair, one shilling shall be paid. . . . If an ear is cut off, 30 shillings shall be paid. . . . If one knocks out another's eye, he shall pay 66 shillings, 6⅓ pence. . . . If the eye is still in the head but the injured man can see nothing with it, one-third of the payment shall be withheld. . . ." In the ninth and tenth centuries the Frankish Penitentials sentenced criminals to prayers and pilgrimages but also to do their victim's work, pay medical costs, and give them money directly.

As the Middle Ages progressed, however, the state grew more and more involved in codifying and administering an increasingly complex legal system. Concern for the crime victim gave way to the interest of the state in collecting fines and administering other punishments. Restitution moved over to the civil law of torts and faded from criminal justice, to be acknowledged only occasionally in the theories of thinkers like Sir Thomas More and, in the nineteenth century, Jeremy Bentham.

The first modern promoter of restitution apparently was an English magistrate named Margery Fry, who in 1951 published a book, *Arms and the Law*, that proposed payments to crime victims. "Compensation cannot undo the wrong," she wrote, but "it will often assuage the injury, and it has a real educative value for the offender, whether adult or child." Though her ideas stirred interest in Great Britain, they were not implemented.

In her 1980 book *Criminals and Victims*, Lois Forer, the Philadelphia judge, noted the long history of restitution, pointing out that it has a much longer tradition than the relatively modern sanction of imprisonment. She called for including restitution payments in criminal sentences but proposed that they be paid into a state fund from which victims could be compensated according to their needs, an idea also endorsed by Ms. Fry. Judge Forer took a more guarded view of direct payments from criminal to victim. "From my limited experience, I find that sentences requiring the offender to make payments to the victim can work. But a concerted unremitting effort by the judge and the probation department to compel enforcement of such orders is required."

As she was writing her book, a number of jurisdictions around the country had begun to experiment with just such direct-payment restitution efforts, particularly for juvenile offenders. Several states passed laws encouraging restitution in criminal sentencing, and in 1978, the state of Washington made money available for restitution programs in eighty-five juvenile courts. A 1981 survey by the American Correctional Association counted forty-four formal restitution programs for adults and/or juveniles in twenty-seven states. Of these, twelve operated out of halfway houses where residents were supervised as they worked off their restitution obligations.

Not all such programs would survive, however, especially with the subsequent collapse of federal funding for local criminal justice. And where they did exist in name, the extent to which they actually functioned to make sure victims got paid remained unclear. In a few places, however, promoters of restitution demonstrated beyond any doubt that it could be made to work.

The Victim Offender Reconciliation Program that began in Elkhart, Indiana, for example, pioneered a constructive if radical idea: Arrange for the victim and the offender to meet. Each year about 135 offenders, mostly juveniles, are referred to the program, which is run by the Mennonite-funded PACT Institute of Justice. Mennonite volunteers work as mediators. In about 70 percent of cases referred to the program, they manage to arrange conferences between criminals and victims, who negotiate a contract for the payment of restitution. In the last five years, the program has spread to about forty other communities in the Midwest and Northwest.

The program's promoters consider it part of a religious mission. "Christ's emphasis is clearly upon unconditional love—on forgiveness and reconciliation as a way to change persons, rather than coercion," writes Howard Zehr, director of PACT. The prescription of "an eye for an eye and a tooth for a tooth," he writes, was never meant to authorize revenge. "In fact this statement could be seen as a limitation on violence and not a command. In a society unused to the rule of law, an act of retaliation often led to another in a rising crescendo of violence. In that situation, the Israelites were told to limit their response—to do this much and only this much."

The meetings, PACT mediators say, tend to humanize

offender and victim to each other. In the victim's mind, the mugger had become the fearsome focus for impotent rage. In person he looks more like a pathetic, troubled kid. To the mugger the victim had been no more than the vulnerable middle-aged man in the three-piece suit: fair game. Now he looks more complicated—injured, angry, yet inclined to forgive as the meeting goes on. In addition to a schedule of restitution payments, the eventual contract may include the mugger's formal apology to the victim. And the victim may come away from the encounter with answers to questions that could have nagged forever: What made him single me out for crime? Why did he have to knock me down in addition to taking my wallet? What did he do with the money? In some cases victim and criminal wind up friends after restitution is paid. So far, the program has been most successful in smaller, homogeneous middle-class communities, but its promoters are hopeful for attempts to get it going in such large urban centers as Minneapolis, Detroit, and St. Louis.

In Genesee County, New York, a sheriff sought to develop another restitution model based on the powers of his own office. He would arrange for victim-offender conferences in hopes of negotiating settlements requiring the criminal to confess to civil liability for damages caused in the course of the crime. When the court accepts that confession as part of the plea bargain, it falls to the sheriff, charged with enforcing civil judgments, to make sure the restitution gets paid. His powers to do so are considerable, extending to the garnishment of wages and seizure of assets.

By far the most interesting restitution program, however, developed in Quincy, Massachusetts, a blue-collar Boston suburb, from the activism of Judge Albert Kramer. His contribution was to combine restitution sentencing with a court-run employment service, so that no offender could avoid repaying a victim for lack of a way to earn the money. As the judge tells the story, the program he would call "Earn It" began one day in 1976 when he faced a lawyer arguing for lenience on the grounds that the damage his young client had caused would be repaid by his parents.

"The parents didn't do it," the judge said. "What will *he* do?" When the lawyer explained that the youngster couldn't pay because he had no job, the judge said, "I'll get him work long enough to pay back the victim. No restitution, no second chance." That night, the judge called a friend who owned a business and persuaded him to provide a job.

To the considerable surprise of everyone involved, the boy reported faithfully for work and paid off the victim. That emboldened the judge to pursue the idea further. He convened meetings of local businessmen in his courtroom and persuaded them to contribute minimum-wage-level jobs for offenders sentenced to repay their victims. Mostly he simply appealed to their community spirit, but he also suggested that if businesses cooperated, the court might expedite bad-check cases and other cases of concern to the business community. Eventually more than sixty businesses signed up, including caterers and restaurants, supermarkets, a nursery, a warehouse, a construction company, an auto body shop, a lumber yard, and various retail stores.

The judge hired a man to work as an employment agent, screening the offenders and matching them with appropriate jobs. The businesses were told to pay the court-assigned employees whatever they would pay regular workers for similar work, and to fire them should they not show up or cause trouble on the job. In such cases, the court pledged to provide quick replacements. About 20 percent failed for one reason or another. The rest continued to work until they paid off their obligation.

The restitution amount would either be set by the court or, if the victim was willing, negotiated in a conference similar to those conducted by the PACT program in Indiana. The offenders had to pay a hefty portion of their weekly earnings to their victims, but could keep the rest. Thus a young man named Joe, convicted of burglarizing a gas station and making off with $75, faced a restitution bill of $784, which included costs of repairing the break-in damage and compensating the owner for lost time. The court found him a job preparing graves at a cemetery, and he paid $40 a week to the gas station until he was laid off. Then the court sent him to a restaurant to wash dishes, and he paid $50 a week to complete the sentence. "I'm glad they didn't put me in jail," he said. "They could have given me six months to a year. I sort of, like, learned my lesson."

Such cases would boost the annual total of restitution earned and paid back to victims through the Quincy court to about $200,000, compared with $37,000 before the program began. Businesses in the community, meanwhile, found that the court program actually filled a need. It could reliably provide low-wage help on short notice. "If I need someone this afternoon at five o'clock, I can't put an ad in the paper," explained the restaurant owner who hired Joe to wash dishes. "But I can call the court, and they'll have somebody. It's convenient."

As important, the program filled a need of the Quincy probation department. No probation worker could ever supervise clients for all the hours employers would supervise them on the job. As long as they were at work and the employers had no complaints, the probation officers could rest assured that the clients were staying out of trouble. (Of course, the program was hardly trouble-free. An example of the failed 20 percent was the offender who went to work in a factory, didn't get along with his boss, and got fired. In response, he returned to the factory, stole a van, and set it on fire.) The need to keep the restitution-paying offenders' accounts also forced probation officers to pay regular attention to them. And in at least some cases it was apparent that the discipline of work and the lure of legitimate money turned some youngsters back from a fascination with crime. Some could argue that restitution was rehabilitative in and of itself. Joe Hudson and Burt Galaway, two students of restitution, point to "a fairly substantial body of research on equity theory propositions" that "indicates that if harmdoers are given opportunities, they will make efforts to complete restitution and as a result, not use rationalizations in attempts to excuse their behavior." They quote Gilbert Geis: "Fiscal atonement could produce in the offender a feeling of having been cleansed, a kind of redemptive purging process, which might inhibit subsequent wrongdoing."

The Kramer program enjoyed a wonderful press, winning praise from the liberal Boston papers but also from the ultraconservative *Manchester* (New Hampshire) *Union Leader*: "Judge Kramer is a delightfully forthright man, exceptionally sober and not at all a namby-pamby fellow." The response underscores the special appeal of restitution, satisfying as it does the liberal's desire for a constructive approach to punishment and the conservative's desire for strict accountability.

Taken altogether, the efforts to elaborate on probation so far present a rich opportunity to the judge who would punish without prison. A probation department given substantial resources might, for example, negotiate a restitution contract between a convict and his victim, find the offender a job to pay off the agreed amount, subject him to electronically monitored house arrest for the times he was not supposed to be at work, and assign intensive supervision officers to keep track of him and provide moral support. Such a system might safely include even offenders who had committed violent crimes. Run properly, it would enjoy popular support. It still might be cheaper than a prison term, and the victim would get his money back.

Why then does probation in most places continue to languish? Why aren't the state legislatures that are so aware of their constituents' frustration with crime also rushing to rescue probation from years of neglect? Why don't they grasp the wisdom of realizing its promise?

Perhaps no other issue so dismayingly reveals the failure of politics to serve justice. Probation suffers because it is so broadly misunderstood. Few political leaders develop much interest in probation because the voting public remains so focused on prison as the only real punishment. It's safe to say that a poll of the general population would reveal relative ignorance even of the existence of the most widely used criminal sanction. In recent years, the only people interested in developing probation have been reformers fundamentally opposed to prisons. To make so unpopular an approach palatable, they relied on the fearsome economics of incarceration. For the slightest crime-control benefit, they would point out, correctly, legislatures were prepared to spend as much as $100,000 to construct a single maximum-security cell and more than $20,000 per year ("more than the tuition at Harvard!") to keep a convict locked up.

The trouble with promoting probation in those terms, however, was that it had to be measured by its ability to "divert" prison-bound convicts into programs in the community. Judges refused to go along. Study after study of such diversion programs found that most of those diverted were not likely candidates for prison sentences under the prevailing practices and would have been released under minimal probation supervision if they had not been placed in the community program. As a result the reformers quickly lost interest. Enhanced probation, they would say, was no good if it merely "widened the net" of social control.

Such thinking betrayed drastic misunderstanding of the need. The most glaring problem the courts present isn't that they send too many to prison; it's that they don't know what to do with the hundreds of thousands more found guilty but, for reasons of justice or available space, not ready for prison. In that sense, the "net" of punishment is too narrow, and no one need apologize for seeking ways to widen its reach.

Such widening could turn out to be a logical adjunct to the emergent community policing. Another benefit of Judge Kramer's restitution employment program, after all, is the extent to which it directly involves the community's businesses in the normally remote and alienated process of corrections—and does so in a way business finds useful. A court system that so successfully integrates the community in the process of responding to the crime it spawns makes the audience itself a part of the message. And well it should.

8

The
CRISIS
of
CONTROL

It is not too much to say that the change is from a prison in which force and intimidation by force were monopolized by custody to one in which the most intimidating force is now in the hands of prisoners. It is a community of fear. In many prisons, the surest hope of survival for the unaffiliated prisoner is voluntary segregation in protective units. Increasing numbers of prisoners are choosing to survive by this means, even at the cost of serving their sentences in solitary confinement.

—*John P. Conrad and Simon Dinitz*, In Fear of Each Other, *1977*

After I was attacked, I asked my friends what to do. They all said, "Man, you work over there in the stamp plant [licence-plate shop]. Make yourself a knife, and if a guy bothers you, just cut his heart out." I said, "No. I know that's wrong. I don't want to do that." But now, I don't know. . . . If I'd stabbed somebody and got caught, they'd put me in segregation anyway. It's all the same. They put you in if you hurt somebody, and they put you in if you're afraid of being hurt.

—"The Price of Safety: 'I Can't Go Back Out There,' " Corrections Magazine, *August 1980*

After only a couple of days, it was clear to me that the prison was barely under control. The guards, massed in a cavernous, spooky central hall for the daily roll call, seemed an unkempt, shiftless lot who had long since made their accommodation with a formidable inmate power structure. Inmates, in conversation about mundane matters, casually referred to horrible events: suicide leaps from high cellblock galleries; pipings and stabbings for cigarettes, or just for fun; homosexual rapes committed by predatory gangs that apparently roamed the vast penitentiary at will.

Arriving at the office of the deputy warden at 7:30 each morning, I would find him already at his desk, phoning in to the state police his reports of the night's violent happenings, or calling the local hospital to check on the condition of inmates admitted since he had left the previous day. An official who supervised the wing of the prison that housed the protective custody unit explained to me that the system had degenerated into a grim game of musical chairs.

The policy of the prison was to give protective custody to any inmate who asked for it by saying that his life was in danger, since the legal risk of ignoring such a request is substantial. Protective custody inmates were housed right next to the disciplinary segregation inmates, those locked up as punishment for violent acts. When the protective custody cells were full, the official explained, the only way to make room for another inmate who requested protection was to release one of the disciplinary cases back to the general population. But once he returned to the yard, he was likely to cause several more inmates to request protection.

"This thing has grown," the official complained. "It's gotten out of hand."

On the last day of my visit, I sought a final interview with the warden. But in his outer office, a new sense of anxiety was palpably in the air, and his secretary insisted that he would be tied up in emergency meetings all day. It didn't take long to find out what had happened: The state's governor, faced with reduced tax revenues and inflationary costs, had decided to bite the bullet. He had requested all state agencies to reduce their operating budgets by 2 percent for the coming fiscal year.

By the end of the day, when the warden finally admitted me to his office, another round of conversations with inmates and corrections officers had left me in a perverse mood.

"Well, warden," I began, "what are you going to do? Release 2 percent of the inmates?"

He smiled bitterly. "No," he said. "I've decided to lay off 20 percent of the guards."

—*"A Letter from America's Prisons,"* **Across the Board, September 1981**

ONE

*T*he penitentiary is a relatively recent, largely American invention—some of the original structures built in the early decades of the nineteenth century remain in use today. Their inventors did not envision them as forbidding Bastilles of stone and iron, enclosing bizarre or barbaric subcultures. America's prisons were born of the new republic's surging idealism, practical optimism, and high-minded confidence.

Public tortures, humiliations, and executions were Old World traditions that demonstrated the power of society to exact revenge for the violation of its rules. Until the revolution, the tradition prevailed in the American colonies. The historian David Rothman points out that colonial Americans entertained no thoughts of wiping out wickedness. "They would combat the evil, warn, chastise, correct, banish, flog or execute the offender. But they saw no prospect of eliminating deviancy from their midst. Crime, like poverty, was endemic to society." Social control, the colonials believed, depended on the influence of the church, the strength of the family, and the tightness of the community. The stocks, the whipping post, and the gallows gave painful and lethal authority to these basic institutions.

The founding fathers believed they could do better. The new Constitution's Eighth Amendment banned "cruel and unusual punishments." But that wasn't all: Promoters of the new penitentiaries asserted that they could actually reclaim lost souls. Beyond punishment, they would turn bad men into good. Thus was born the "rehabilitative ideal." Its history, quintessentially American, would demonstrate how thoroughly some men could disappoint the faith of others in their better nature.

At first, the idea was simply to substitute more objective, rational laws and a belief in the malleability of man for the severely localized controls and Calvinist determinism of colonial communities. Beccaria had written that certainty of punishment is more important than severity, and that overly brutal sanctions were counterproductive, since they left a legacy of rage that led to further crime. Thus new states of the union rushed to enact enlightened criminal codes. "In this first burst of enthusiasm," Rothman writes, "Americans expected that a rational system of correction, which made punishment certain but humane, would dissuade all but a few offenders from a life of crime." So rational a system would depend on prison as the basic sanction.

By the 1830s, however, it was clear that more would be required. The first decades of the nineteenth century saw the rise of large urban centers, while manufacturing in factories began to supplement farming as the nation's basic ·economic activity. America's population, furthermore, was surging, along with its idealism. Crime increased despite the rationalized criminal law. The early penologists therefore began to focus on what happened inside prisons. Now the abandonment of Calvinism seemed complete, for the reformers denied that evil lurked within any individual heart. Men were born innocent and were turned bad by the external influences of society. In the best American spirit of practical optimism, managers of the early prisons declared that the proper programs could reverse the forces of corruption and turn the bad back to good. Prisons would demonstrate the best America had to offer, Rothman writes. They would attempt to "join practicality to humanitarianism, reform the criminal, stabilize American society, and demonstrate how to improve the condition of mankind. . . ."

The basic strategy would be to isolate the offender from all outside influences. New York developed one model at the Auburn penitentiary between 1819 and 1823, then transplanted it to the penitentiary at Ossining known as Sing Sing. Pennsylvania officials tried another version in the penitentiary at Pittsburgh in 1826, moving it into the prison at Philadelphia three years later. Both schemes emphasized total silence. Prisoners in New York stayed alone in individual cells but worked and ate together in shops and dining halls. Whether alone in their cells or in the company of others, however, they were forbidden to talk, or even to look at their fellow inmates. The Pennsylvania plan took the isolation a step further. The inmates worked, ate, and slept alone in their cells; one might pass a whole prison term without ever seeing another inmate.

Separating the deviant from the evils of free society and forcing him into a regime of order and work would cure him of crime, the early penologists believed, and their new penitentiaries were a source of national pride and the focus of world attention. Tourists visited them, as did distinguished guests from overseas, who wanted to see for themselves what the new democracy could teach the world about the ancient problem of crime. One was the Frenchman Alexis de Tocqueville, who would write a broad report on democracy in America.

All found Americans furiously debating the merits of the Auburn and Philadelphia approaches. Both called for separation, obedience, and productive work, while emphasizing silence and the rigors of orderly institutional life. The Pennsylvanians, however, argued that theirs was the purer penology, since an inmate might pass a whole term associating only with his work, his Bible, and occasional visitors selected for their wholesomeness. The Pennsylvanians even went so far as to march a new inmate to his cell with a bag over his head to prevent his seeing any of the other convicts. The New Yorkers responded that the extreme isolation of the Pennsylvania model was so unnatural as to breed insanity. They spread the word that the Pennsylvania penitentiaries' walls were thin enough and plumbing exposed enough to permit the inmates some communication despite the efforts of wardens to stamp it out. In any case, they added, the additional costs of full isolation were substantial and hardly justified by the marginal rehabilitation advantage.

The substance of the debate is far less remarkable than its intensity. "The fervor brought many of the leading reformers of the period to frequently bitter recriminations, and often set one benevolent society against another," Rothman reports. The emotion invested in the controversy at once bore witness to the expectations America had loaded onto the new penology of the 1830s and betrayed an insecurity about its possibilities.

The insecurity would soon be vindicated. Louis Dwight, founder of the Boston Prison Discipline Society and the leading promoter of the New York system, would succeed in selling it to a few other places in the Northeast, notably in Connecticut, Massachusetts, and New Jersey. The Pennsylvania system, meanwhile, did not spread much beyond Pennsylvania. Western and Southern states simply began building prisons without worrying too much about the philosophy of running them. In effect, the early American penologists succeeded in establishing incarceration as the nation's basic criminal sanction—no small achievement—while leaving open the question of rehabilitation.

As time went on, it became obvious that the new penitentiaries had done little either to control crime or to

reform American society. The theology of silence, obedience, and work stood revealed as empty. Prison wardens
enforced it to maintain order and produce income from the
sale of inmate labor or manufactured goods rather than to
reclaim lost souls. Education programs, a useful and sensible reform, were totally incompatible with the classic
regimen that forbade speech or even eye contact. Gradually
the Auburn system began to wither away. Blake Mc-
Kelvey, another historian of American prisons, reports that
in the 1840s, "the prison in Maine and that at Clinton,
New York, went so far as to permit talking at labor 'when
necessary.' " By 1852, a New York investigatory commission found that the state's prisons did a good job of
keeping dangerous criminals locked up. "But if the object
is to make him a better member of society, so that he may
safely again mingle with it . . . that purpose cannot be
answered by matters as they now stand."

The years following the Civil War saw a surge of crime
and criminal convictions. The resulting crowding of penitentiaries in most places overwhelmed any remnants of
the rehabilitative ideal. McKelvey notes that the crowding
that forced wardens to put two men in a single cell or bed
down others in corridors made the old rule of silence impossible to enforce. Yet it remained nominally in effect,
meaning that guards could choose to invoke it when they
felt like harassing inmates.

By 1870, such leaders of American corrections as Enoch
Wines, Daniel Gilman, F. B. Sanborn, Theodore Dwight,
Amos Pilsbury, and Zebulon Brockway were concerned
enough about the deterioration to call a national convention

in Cincinnati. The result was a kind of revival meeting of penologists who declared themselves reborn in the rehabilitative ideal. "Overwhelmed with inspired addresses, with prayer and song and much exhortation, even the hardheaded wardens were carried up for a mountaintop experience," McKelvey writes. "In their enthusiasm for the ideal they rose above the monotony of four gray walls, men in stripes shuffling in lockstep, sullen faces staring through the bars, coarse mush and coffee made of bread crusts, armed sentries stalking the walls." The wardens issued a statement of principles that acknowledged their responsibility to reform criminals by means of education, religion, and job training. It called for discipline that built up self-esteem rather than destroying it and endorsed the idea of indeterminate sentences with release based on progress toward rehabilitation.

Despite the level of emotion at Cincinnati, only one warden apparently followed through with a sustained effort. He was Brockway, who established the reformatory at Elmira, New York, in 1876. He secured legislation that provided indeterminate sentences for Elmira convicts, who would be released when a board of prison administrators found they had made enough progress according to a rehabilitation grading system. In addition to putting inmates to work manufacturing products that brought in revenues to support the prison, Elmira offered an extensive education progam that earned it a reputation as a "free college" for New York's criminals. Brockway brought in public-school teachers to conduct elementary classes for the inmates. For those who showed greater aptitude, he hired college professors to teach geometry, bookkeeping, human physiology, Bible study, ethics, and psychology. He invited prominent speakers in to address the inmates, and even experimented with "the recently imported Swedish technique" to bring around the more intractable convicts. "The training included carefully planned and measured diets, steam or hot-water baths with rubbing and kneading of muscles by an expert trainer, and extended drills in calisthenics," McKelvey writes.

McKelvey credits Brockway with establishing "that the criminal was an erring brother deserving of society's special care until he should be refitted for a normal life in its midst." Rothman takes a dimmer view. However much the fact of convicts studying ethics or bookkeeping might stir the enthusiasm of reformers, Brockway would produce only spongy statistics to document that such studies had a positive effect on the convicts' subsequent behavior. Furthermore, Elmira had a darker side, eventually exposed to the harsh light of a state investigation. Though Brockway would be exonerated of more dramatic abuses, the 1894 hearings revealed that whippings had become a common event at Elmira, as was prolonged solitary confinement with the subject shackled to the cell door. Brockway was reduced to explaining that the leather whip, twenty-two inches long, was first soaked in water in order to soften its bite, and that "in no case . . . has a convict been shackled both by his hands and his feet at the same time."

Perhaps most germane, however, was the point that no other wardens had been sufficiently moved by the Elmira example to emulate it. For the majority of prisoners up to

1900, and beyond in many places, prison meant day after day of idleness, meals of mush and questionable meat, monthly congregate baths in giant tanks, cellblocks that trapped smoke from kerosene lamps and coal stoves along with odors arising from the massed humanity, and sanitation based on a "night bucket" made of wood.

Where crowding and poor staffing threatened control, Rothman writes, "wardens had regular recourse to amazingly bizarre punishments." These included devices for the binding of an inmate's wrists so that he might be hauled off his feet and suspended in air, and iron cages, weighing as much as eight pounds, that rested on a man's shoulders, enclosing his head. Inmates might be flogged with heavy leather paddles while bent over a wooden "horse." Their feet were laced into shoes nailed to the floor on one side, while their wrists were secured on the other. Bread-and-water rations and straitjackets were common "and so was the brick bag—the convict who would not work was forced to wear it until he changed his mind." Kansas inmates learned to fear the "water crib," a coffinlike box. The recalcitrant lay face down with his hands cuffed. Then a guard would begin to fill the crib with water. "The effect was of slow drowning, with the inmate struggling to keep his head up above the rising water line." Guards spoke of the device with satisfaction: "You take a man and put him in there and turn the water on him and that wilts him at once. He wilts and says he will be good. It might take days in a blind cell. . . ."

None doubted that such conditions and punishments might discipline lost souls. The hope of reclaiming them had long since faded.

TWO

Penologists of the 1820s and 1830s had isolated the criminal from society and sought the redemption of flawed spirits by hammering them into institutional molds. A century later, they would focus on the criminal's individual needs. The new specialty of psychiatry encouraged a "medical model" of corrections: Criminality was a disease caused by poverty, the failures of family and community, and other stresses of modern life. Instead of punishing guilt, the psychiatrists wanted to search out the roots of a person's misbehavior in the particular circumstances of his upbringing and his relationships. Prison was the place to diagnose the criminal "patient" and administer the appropriate treatment. Indeterminate sentences were fundamental to the trend. They left prison and parole officials with broad discretion to link an inmate's release to the extent of his "cure."

The medical model, however, proved no more effective than the old Auburn and Pennsylvania routines of silence. The erudition of psychiatrists and psychologists might brilliantly describe the sources of inmate deviance and permit its classification into neat types. They might, for example, distinguish between inmates who showed some promise for improvement, those who made a profession of crime, the retarded, and the psychotic. "But such divisions were of little use," Rothman writes. "There was nothing that any warden could do with them, really nothing that the professionals themselves could do with them. They fit offenders into boxes but did not explain how they came to enter such a box, nor how they could be moved out of it."

If the psychologists failed to cure, however, they at least succeeded in effecting some big changes in prison life. Where the early-nineteenth-century reformers had sought to remove inmates from the community, the twentieth-century penologists now would try to "normalize" the prison—make it as much like the community as possible. They got rid of silence rules and the lockstep and permitted inmates hours of free socializing on the yard. Striped uniforms were replaced by more conventional clothes. Wardens allowed baseball leagues, weekly movies, and individual radios. They also liberalized rules for correspondence and visiting. But such changes only acknowledged basic humanity.

Nowhere would the gap between the reformer's claims and the harsher realities of prison management be better revealed than at the Norfolk, Massachusetts, "Prison Colony" in 1932 under the leadership of Howard Gill. A Harvard efficiency expert who had served in the Hoover administration, Gill was appointed to superintend the building of a new Massachusetts penitentiary. To save money he put the inmates to work on the construction and soon became intrigued with the possibilities for rehabilitating men who seemed so capable of hard work and some measure of individual responsibility.

"Norfolk seeks not only to guard securely the men committed to its safekeeping, but as a fundamental policy to assume its responsibility for returning them to society . . . as better men capable of leading useful, law-abiding lives," said Gill's manual for the new institution. The prison, the manual said, "accepts its charges as delinquent, socially maladjusted human beings . . . who need help, understanding and guidance in rebuilding their lives and characters. Each man is looked upon as an individual with individual needs and problems."

Though enclosed by massive walls, the colony consisted of small buildings where inmates might live dormitory-style or in single rooms. The staff consisted of guards responsible solely for security and "house officers" who were supposed to act as caseworkers for the inmates. The prisoners were classified according to five categories: those whose life situation forced them to crime, the mentally defective, the professional criminals, the physically disabled, and those with personality problems.

By all accounts, including Gill's own diary, the result was a disaster. The men Gill recruited as house officers lacked social work skills. Even had they possessed them, it remained unclear how casework might effectively reform criminals, even granting the potential Gill had seen during the construction project. The guards, furthermore, often clashed with the caseworkers, insisting that security had to come before individual inmate's needs. "Ultimately," Rothman writes, "Norfolk was the scene of a fierce war between custodians and therapists, and Gill proved to be an inept peacekeeper. The staff could not balance custody and rehabilitation." In the end, security would win out.

Before escapes and other lapses resulted in his dismissal, Gill would go so far as to set up a "hole"—solitary confinement cells where recalcitrant inmates were subjected to bread-and-water diets. The Norfolk story, Rothman wrote, amounted to a "powerful parable" about the difficulties of humane imprisonment and the innate hyprocrisy of attempting to rehabilitate men behind walls and bars.

He concludes that the hypocrisy serves the public's desire for denial. "In effect, the state and the prison had struck a mutually agreeable bargain: As long as the warden ran a secure institution which did not attract adverse publicity (through a high number of deaths or riots or inhumane practices becoming publicly known), he would have a free hand to administer his prison as he liked. And most of the time, the wardens fulfilled their side of the arrangement." Indeed, Gill's problem could be seen as taking the rehabilitative ideal too seriously.

A more classically successful warden would emerge between the wars at the Stateville penitentiary in Illinois. His name was Joseph Ragen, and he would reign for a few decades after 1936 as one of the most prominent wardens in America. He was the apotheosis of security based on authoritarian administration, the diametric opposite of men like Howard Gill, who denounced Ragen's prison as a "monolithic monstrosity."

Stateville in those years consisted of three giant cell houses constructed according to the "panopticon" design of the nineteenth-century English philosopher Jeremy Bentham. The panopticon buildings were circular, theoretically maximizing light and air while allowing a handful of guards in a guard post at the center to supervise efficiently the hundreds of prisoners in cells around the circumference. At Stateville, however, the effect was spooky. For a fourth cell house, Illinois officials had abandoned Bentham for a conventional rectangular block, in 1932 the largest in existence, with six hundred cells.

Ragen ruled over this small empire of convicts, whose numbers approached four thousand in the thirties, with the guile and ruthlessness of Stalin. If Gill had hired house officers to counsel inmates and advocate for their individual needs, Ragen forbade officers to pursue any constructive relationships with inmates that went beyond the bare minimum necessary to keep them moving to their assignments. At the same time, he encouraged guard captains and lieutenants to compete for his favor by producing intelligence from networks of informers. "The goal was always to be one step ahead of the inmates, thereby perpetuating the myth of the administration's omniscience," writes James Jacobs in his study of Stateville. "Informers were the backbone of the system." Ragen would brag, "Whenever you see three inmates standing together, two of them are mine."

To run the place, Ragen developed a code of rules so elaborate that no inmate could hope to observe all of them at all times. "Failure to button a shirt or to salute a white cap [captain] was reason enough to be brought before the disciplinary captain," Jacobs writes. " 'Silent insolence' was an actionable offense." Once brought in for discipline, "the inmate might admit to the rule infraction and 'take his weight' [take the blame] or try to dispute the 'ticket' and thereby be found guilty of calling a guard a liar, itself a violation of the rules." Discipline resulted in either case. The basic sanction was an isolation cell, where an inmate might be forced to stand at attention for eight hours a day.

In Ragen's terms, the system worked beautifully. Guards wrote only twenty-five to thirty disciplinary tickets each day, and a relatively small isolation unit was sufficient to keep order. Ragen did not have to contend with a single riot or escape in twenty-five years as warden. For all that Howard Gill might denounce the "monstrosity," who could say that he had done better?

THREE

Ragen would reign over Stateville as warden until 1961, when he was appointed Illinois's director of public safety, a post in which he continued until 1965. By that time the era of prisons dominated by authoritarian administrators, virtually omnipotent within their domains of stone and iron, had begun to wane. The walls that could hold back the rest of the world, permitting the social fungus of the prison subculture to flourish in dank alienation, were simply no match for the forces that shook American society in the sixties and seventies.

When rising concern about crime forced the public to scrutinize the institutions that men like Joseph Ragen kept so discreetly under control, it did not like what it saw. President Johnson's 1967 crime commission found that "life in many institutions is at best barren and futile, at worst unspeakably brutal and degrading. . . . These conditions are to a great extent the result of a drastic shortage of resources together with widespread ignorance as to how to use the resources available."

The commission's report spoke disapprovingly of "a special inmate culture . . . that is deleterious to everyone. . . . Certain inmates—often the most aggressive—assume control over the others with tacit staff consent. . . . Rackets, violence, corruption, coerced homosexuality, and other abuses may exist without staff intervention."

The following year, a riot at the prison in Salem, Oregon, began a string of prison disorders that would culminate at the forbidding penitentiary in Attica, New York, in September 1971. In order to recapture the prison from rebellious inmates, heavily armed state police invaded, killing thirty-nine prisoners in fifteen minutes of gunfire. The final death toll was forty-three. The bloodshed riveted national attention on prisons, stirring sympathy for inmates in a broader climate of challenge to the "establishment."

As blacks and Hispanics increased as a proportion of the inmate population, sympathizers of the civil rights movement looked to prisons as the ultimate instruments of white oppression. Eldridge Cleaver, the California inmate, published his popular *Soul on Ice* in 1968. George Jackson produced a similar work.

Revelations of prison abuses attracted civil liberties lawyers interested in establishing a new body of legal rights for inmates. Litigation often led to even more gruesome revelations—Arkansas guards, for example, were found to have tortured convicts with a device called the "Tucker Telephone," which cranked jolts of electricity to the subject's genitals. In the developing climate, judges would abandon the hands-off attitude that had long allowed authoritarian wardens unfettered discretion over convict discipline. Courts intervened to require due process before an inmate could be ordered into segregation or otherwise disciplined. Judges, legislatures, and prison administrators also relaxed the rules governing prisoners' communication with each other and the outside world. No longer would mail be routinely opened and censored, and inmates gained greater access to telephones. Guards and wardens once secure in the knowledge that they might abuse inmates at will now were forced to hesitate: Should the abuse come to light, as it easily might, the administrators, not the inmates, would be subject to discipline. Inmates were quick to sense the erosion of authority.

As official control ebbed, powerful inmate organizations emerged to give more rigid structure to the subculture. To the consternation of prison administrators used to cracking down on troublesome groups with doses of solitary or transfer to other prisons, Black Muslims won court sympathy for their recognition as a legitimate religion. Wardens and guards had to accommodate inmates who claimed adherence to the faith. They were entitled to visits from Muslim ministers, access to the Quran, and time and space for religious services.

Secular gangs gathered followers as they offered inmates a sense of identity and self-assertion, along with protection in penitentiaries that were growing increasingly dangerous. Most such groups formed along racial lines: blacks and Hispanics set up prison subsidiaries of the street gangs that had long dominated ghetto neighborhoods on the outside. Whites, whose share of the prison population had begun to shrink in big urban states, sought refuge in white-supremacist fraternities. On the West Coast, "bikers"—motorcycle gangs—readily transplanted their distinctive culture to the prison yard, where they stuck up for each other and pined for their beloved machines.

James Jacobs traces the growth of Chicago's street gangs during the late 1960s as they gained legitimacy and even federal and foundation money for their participation in job training and other social-action programs. By 1969, however, the gangs had fallen out of favor with local politicians and Mayor Daley ordered the police to curb gang violence. As a result of the crackdown, scores of gang members moved into Illinois prisons, where they would permanently alter a relatively traditional convict society based on prestige attached to convicts' offenses and their ability to manipulate the system to win choice job assignments. Jacobs reports that by 1972 it was estimated that at least half the inmates in Stateville were affiliated with one of four "super-gangs"—the Black P Stone Nation, the Disciples, the Vice Lords, and the Latin Kings.

Gang leaders published rules for their members to follow: "There will not at any time, be any unnecessary commotion while entering the cellhouse. . . . Homosexual confrontation toward another Disciple, will definitely not be tolerated. . . . Fighting another Disciple, without consulting a Governing chief will result in strict disciplining." Wardens might have to worry about the new due process requirements imposed by the courts, but the gang administrators did not. After traditional intake processing by prison guards, the gang-member inmate would report for what was probably the more germane briefing by the inmate chief of his cell house.

Gangs developed unabated in the West and Midwest, less so in the East and South. By 1982 the federal Bureau of Prisons had formed a prison-gang task force and Western state corrections departments were trading intelligence on gang activities. By 1983, the Illinois gangs were reported to have enrolled fully 75 percent of the state's 14,000 prisoners, and chapters of the Vice Lords were causing new headaches for prisons in the neighboring state of Iowa.

In California, meanwhile, four supergangs—the Mexican Mafia, Nuestra Familia, the Black Guerrilla Family, and the Aryan Brotherhood—were said to have murdered 111 in California prisons over the previous eight years. The two Mexican-American gangs were a source of constant worry because their members hated each other. The Mexican Mafia had sprung up in the barrios of East Los Angeles, while Nuestra Familia was composed of rural Mexican Americans from northern California, "country bumpkins" who had organized to defend themselves against the predations of the streetwise urbanites from the south. In Arizona, members of the white-supremacist Aryan Brotherhood were convicted of smuggling guns and ammunition into the penitentiary at Florence. In Walla Walla,

Washington, two inmate gangs called the Wells Spring Commune and the George Jackson Brigade were discovered to have smuggled a quantity of cyanide into the prison, apparently in hopes of lacing the food with it. "They wanted to create chaos and anarchy," a prison official said.

As gangs altered the character of prison life in many states, so did drugs. Crime grew more drug-related in the sixties and seventies, and so did the proportion of drug-involved prisoners. Drug dealing made an obvious focus for gang activity and a way to bankroll gang operations. Though prisons banned cash, inmates in many places were encouraged to maintain outside bank accounts as a way to learn financial responsibility and provide for the difficult days following release. With a mail drop at the address of a relative or friend, the inmate dealer could receive drug payments and order them deposited in his bank. Then they might be transferred to the account of a wholesaler for the purchase of new inventory.

Addicted inmates would go to imaginative extremes to outwit guards seeking to control the smuggling of drugs. Were strip searches routine after any contact with a visitor from the outside? Not to worry, experienced inmates advised. Simply instruct a female visitor to insert the contraband in a balloon, or perhaps a condom. Then tell her to put it in her mouth. It could be transferred to the inmate's mouth during a parting kiss. He would swallow hard, then wait for the package to turn up in his toilet bowl the following day.

Did the warden institute a policy of mass urinalysis,

with the promise of dire punishments for anyone whose urine tested positively for drugs? No problem, savvy inmates counseled. Simply find a friend with "clean" urine and persuade him to lend a specimen shortly before the test. It could be deposited in a jar that might be concealed underneath one's shirt. A slender, flexible plastic tube running from the jar's stopper to the groin would, with a bit of practice, permit one to "urinate" the safe sample persuasively, even as a guard watched.

Inmate wholesalers found that guards might easily be bribed to bring in the goods. The economics were powerful. Theodore Davison, who studied Chicano inmates at the San Quentin penitentiary in California, estimated that a guard willing to smuggle heroin might supplement his $18,000 salary by more than $60,000 a year. John McCoy, a writer who spent several weeks in 1978 wandering freely through the penitentiary at Walla Walla, Washington, quoted a guard declaring that "the surest, easiest and quickest way [for an inmate] to make a grubstake is drugs." The leader of a gang called the Lifers "collected eight hundred to twelve hundred dollars to buy a pound of marijuana on the street," McCoy wrote. "After they smuggled it inside, they each took an ounce for personal use and then broke the rest into nickel bags. They passed the nickel bags on to dealers who kept one bag for each three that they sold. 'The lifers triple their money on the dope deal,' [one inmate] figured."

The drug trade inspired new gang violence as rival organizations vied for their shares of the lucrative business. It encouraged individual bloodshed as addicted inmates, desperate for drugs, would finagle money, merchandise, or drugs from their companions, then welsh on their debts.

Drugs were by no means the only sources of money, however. The law permitted convicts to continue receiving Social Security and veterans' or pension benefit payments. Some might also bank the small amounts they earned from prison jobs, received as gifts from family or other outside sources, and acquired from dealing in the inmate consumer economy. Relaxed rules about what an inmate might keep in his cell combined with the growing affluence to energize traffic in all sorts of merchandise besides drugs. Once rules requiring uniforms were eased, few self-respecting inmates would let themselves be seen in rumpled prison-issue outfits. Jeans, flashy shirts, and top-of-the-line basketball sneakers were always in demand. So were television sets, radios, tape decks, automatic coffee makers, hot plates, clocks, typewriters, and most other small appliances. The centerfolds from pornographic magazines were the standard decor for cell walls. Most inmates might also feel the need for a knife or other personal-defense weapon.

David B. Kalinich studied the inmate economy at the big State Prison of Southern Michigan at Jackson, where, he found in 1976, 5,071 inmates earned $839,835 from prison jobs and received another $2,589,945 from the outside. The total of $3,429,780 meant that per capita income in the prison population exceeded $600 annually. Inmates without access to cash dealt in the time-honored prison currency, cigarettes. Kalinich's survey of prisoners and parolees yielded a price schedule: A blackjack cost $2 or one carton of cigarettes, while a joint of marijuana sold for $4 or five packs (he does not explain the discrepancies between cash prices and cigarette prices). A pint of liquor was priced at $15 or six cartons, a hot plate at $6.50 or fifteen packs, and a stolen television set at $50 or twenty cartons. One might purchase a tattoo for $5 or two cartons, while an ounce of heroin cost $8,000 and could not be had for any quantity of cigarettes.

The survey revealed that inmates were not the only ones participating in the economy. Ten dollars or four cartons of cigarettes would purchase a cell transfer, while $25 or eight cartons might persuade a counselor to write a favorable report, $150 would purchase a furlough, and $125 could improve the attitude of the parole board.

Kalinich argued that despite the potential and actual corruption, a free market for goods and services in a prison provided them to inmates far more efficiently than any officially sanctioned bureaucracy might. And he asserted that the prison economy served to stabilize the institution. As long as they were making money on the orderly distribution of contraband, he pointed out, inmate leaders had a powerful interest in keeping the prison quiet. To the extent that prison administrators tolerated, encouraged, and shared in the economy, however, they legitimized the inmate power structure and acknowledged some loss of authority to it.

In fact, the gangs, the drugs, and the money had forced a general crisis of authority and control for prison wardens and guards in the seventies and eighties. It was exacerbated severely by a historical expansion of the prison population. The number of convicts in the nation's prisons declined through the 1960s until it reached a low of 188,000 in 1968. Then it began climbing steadily, to the point that it exceeded 570,000 by the middle of 1987. States spent hundreds of millions on new prisons to accommodate the flow but kept pace only barely. Crowding became the basic preoccupation for wardens in nearly every state. The result was a climate of fear unlike anything the prisons had seen in modern times.

"Whereas at one time prisoners had to fear possible brutality by prison guards, today the chief perpetrators of violence against prisoners are other prisoners," wrote Stanley Rothman, a professor of government, and Kathleen Engel, a social work researcher, in a 1983 study of prison violence. Today's prisoner, they observed, "can attempt to avoid violent encounters, and thus be labeled weak and live in fear; he can join a gang and receive protection, and in so doing risk his life in intergang disputes; or he can 'marry' an inmate leader and thereby be protected in exchange for submitting to periodic rapes. Or he can try to fend for himself. Whatever course an inmate chooses, he quickly learns that most guards will not protect him from the aggressive inmates who run the prison. It used to be the case that rebellious inmates suffered more than passive inmates; now, in most prisons, the less rebellious, nonaggressive inmates face the greatest abuses."

As conditions deteriorated, the guards, never particularly well paid or trained, grew demoralized and burnt-out. As they began to desert prisons for better-paying jobs, administrators were forced to replace them with young, inexperienced recruits who might be no match for the powerful convict leaders with their tight gang organizations. The result would be to accelerate an institution's spiral out of control. For a time that happened at Stateville in the 1970s. "Stateville had acquired a reputation for being such a snake pit that no one wanted to work there, especially for the wretched pay scales that were offered," wrote Kevin Krajick in *Corrections Magazine*. "Periodic wildcat strikes erupted, and guards stayed away from work. Old-timers quit in fear and disgust, and newly hired guards often quit after two or three weeks. In order to keep enough warm bodies in uniform to run the prison, assistant wardens toured unemployment offices in smaller cities and slum streets in Chicago, using bullhorns to offer jobs to nearly anyone who would take them. Job applicants received little screening. The recruiting took place in the same neighborhoods where the gangs flourished. As a result, some gang members and sympathizers were hired. They then supplied weapons, drugs, and other contraband to prisoners."

FOUR

To a great extent, prison administration in the seventies and eighties became a matter of holding the line against collapse. The line did not always hold. By the end of 1986, a total of thirty-six states were operating their prison systems under the supervision of federal judges persuaded that state officials could not be trusted to maintain minimally decent conditions on their own. In some places, wardens would welcome such orders because they finally forced legislatures to focus on prison problems and provide the resources they demanded.

But officials in some states also showed they were capable of alarming compromises. At the Walla Walla, Washington, penitentiary in 1974, Superintendent James Rhay preferred to acknowledge the power of inmate organizations rather than trying to break them. He called upon the resident bikers gang to help subdue a riot and followed up by assigning them other police duties. In the vast Texas prison system, administrators formalized inmate power even more with a system of "building tenders"—inmates whose official duty was to sweep halls, but who also were relied upon to help keep order. "It was control from within, with reinforcements," explained one Texas prison employee who went on to become a criminal justice student. "To put it in sociological terms, we co-opted a group of the subculture and, through that, we controlled behavior. We reinforced it with a kick in the ass or a slap upside the head. That was pretty much the philosophy."

Like drill sergeants, the building tenders shaped up the inmates for work details, kept discipline, and reported any troublemakers to higher authorities. In return, a *Newsweek* article on a Texas prison reported, the building tenders were granted special privileges and had more authority than many guards. " 'Anytime we were beating someone on the run [cellblock] and a guard would tell us to stop, we'd say, "Shove it," and "If you don't like it, call the major," ' says onetime tender Tommy B. 'And we'd tell the major, "You've got an idiot working here who doesn't like us whupping these inmates," and the next thing, the officer would be put on one of the outside towers.' "

A challenge to the building-tender system brought by an inmate named Danny Ruiz would lead to a massive lawsuit that consolidated numerous complaints about conditions in Texas prisons. In 1980, Federal Judge William Wayne Justice handed down a withering opinion: "When the legislature says that you're to be imprisoned, they don't also say that you are to be anally raped or subject to inferior medical care or have someone assaulting you on a day-to-day basis. The incarceration is punishment. The rest is punishment above what is authorized by law."

Prison officials who formalized inmate-to-inmate brutality at least were willing to face reality. In other places, it appeared, corrections administrators preferred denial. In 1982, Loretta Tofani, a reporter for *The Washington Post*, published a series of articles that would win a Pulitzer Prize but were extraordinary by any measure. The subject was sexual abuse in the Prince George's County, Maryland, jail. The articles provided a rare glimpse of prisoners beyond control, and though it concerned a local jail rather than a state penitentiary, what it depicted might be found in crowded, severely demoralized state institutions as well.

An inmate in the jail, Ms. Tofani reported, could expect to be beaten, forced to perform oral sex, or anally raped by other inmates unless he took to such predatory behavior himself. "If I can completely destroy this person here, it tells everyone I'm OK," an inmate explained.

The series made it clear that jail officials no longer were able to prevent inmates from raping each other and instead seemed to accept the situation. "In interviews, 10 current or former guards and a jail medical worker said they have come to accept that rape is a normal part of life in the detention center," Ms. Tofani wrote. " 'At first it shocks you, but then after a while it's just another rape,' said one current guard. . . . 'Even though you don't like it to happen, you get used to it because it happens all the time.' "

The inmate rapists considered the practice to be so acceptable that they freely admitted to raping other inmates and allowed Ms. Tofani to identify them by name in her articles. One such inmate, Tim Lipscomb, told the reporter that he considered rape a way to relieve the boredom of jail life. "There's nothing to do but play cards there. There's no recreation on the outside so you get recreation on the inside. Rape for rec."

Another inmate seemed to consider rape a matter of right: "I get tired of masturbating. Why should I masturbate when I got freaks who will do it for me?" The acceptance even extended to the judges whose business it was to send people to the jail. Circuit Court Judge David Ross told Ms. Tofani, "One of the reasons you shouldn't break the law is that you get raped in that jail."

The director of the jail denied that the sexual violence occurred on a scale that Ms. Tofani seemed able to confirm with little difficulty. It was apparently the kind of situation that encouraged denial. That was the most disturbing aspect of a highly disturbing report. Circuit Court Judge Vincent Femia told Ms. Tofani that "this is the kind of thing that's so bad you shut your mind to it. It's easier to blot it out than to come to grips with the fact that it's happening in our own society."

At the state level, such denial, compounded by incompetence, burnout, and bureaucratic instability, would at times come close to posing a threat to the public as well as prisoners. James Jacobs concluded his 1977 study of Illinois's Stateville penitentiary on a guardedly hopeful note, suggesting that the efforts of Warden David Brierton to develop professional managers might permit control of the gangs, drugs, and crowding. But two years later, Warden Brierton was gone and the prison appeared on the brink of catastrophe. The massive defection of guards had contributed to a general collapse of morale. "There was not a sufficient core of experienced people who knew how to deal with hostile and aggressive inmates in a positive way," Lou Brewer, who served a short stint as warden from September 1978 to May 1979, told *Corrections Magazine*. "On many days, not enough people showed up to even do the basic necessities, like feeding and showering the inmates." The staffing crisis also produced severe neglect of the most fundamental maintenance: When locks on cell doors broke, nobody fixed them. Inmates were free to come and go as they pleased.

"In most prisons, inmates run small daily affairs to a certain degree. But, at this point, Stateville inmates, especially the gangs, took over the whole prison. They stole and distributed food from the dining hall and moved freely throughout the prison. Officers, thinly spread, inexperienced and frightened, were afraid to stop them. In fact, the guards were afraid to enter many parts of the prison; inmates had declared certain areas off-limits to them, and threatened to kill those who trespassed." Perhaps the ultimate humiliation for the administration came at Christmas in 1978, when about three hundred inmates gathered for an unauthorized holiday party. They got drunk on homemade "hooch" ladled from a trash barrel while others smoked marijuana openly and feasted on steaks stolen from the dining hall.

News of the Christmas festivities led Governor James Thompson to install a new director of corrections, Gayle Franzen, who immediately called in a fact-finding panel from the American Correctional Association to assess the situation at Stateville. "They spent only a few hours at Stateville; that was all they needed," *Corrections Magazine* reports. "According to Franzen, Anthony Travisono, executive director of the ACA, emerged from Stateville ashen. Travisono immediately dragged him into a private room in the administration building and told him that extreme violence could erupt at any time." Later, Travisono told the magazine, "The situation at Stateville was extremely volatile and critical. I think they had given up trying to run the institution."

Franzen regained some purchase on the prison several weeks later with an elaborately staged "retaking" and shakedown. A force of sixty state troopers and two hundred guards, some imported from other prisons, donned bright-orange jumpsuits and riot gear and marched the corridors of Stateville, chanting in unison. They removed gang leaders to prisons in other states and harvested an astonishing inventory of weapons. According to *Corrections Magazine*, it included "542 knives, two guns, 14 saw blades, 82 clubs, three hatchets, one grappling hook, an improvised flame thrower, two gas masks, gasoline, kerosene, liquid mercury (used for detonating bombs), electric bomb detonators and a copy of *The Anarchist Cookbook*, a guide to homemade explosives."

A year later, in February 1980, the Penitentiary of New Mexico at Santa Fe was convulsed in rioting that realized the worst nightmares of failed prison management. The riot began in the wee hours of a Saturday morning, when a group of inmates jumped a few guards who were checking out a dormitory. The convicts managed to break into the prison's main control center and take over the whole institution. They held it for a day and a half, during which thirty-three inmates were reported to have died and scores more beaten and raped. By that measure, it was not the worst prison riot in American history—forty-three had eventually died as a result of the 1971 riot at New York's Attica penitentiary. But at Santa Fe, unlike Attica, most of the brutality suffered by inmates occurred at the hands of other inmates, in ways that plumbed the depths of human cruelty.

Beyond the predictable orgies of beating and sexual assault, marauding Santa Fe convicts revealed a rage untamed by any civilizing force. They broke into one man's cell, beat him, dragged him out, tied one end of a rope to the bars and another to his neck, then tossed his body over the catwalk. Fortunately, he died the moment the noose snapped his neck, for then his assailants hauled his body back up and slashed it to ribbons with knives. When the death squads could not get into cells, they threw gasoline on the occupants, followed by lighted matches. A reporter examining the aftermath of one such assault found only the victim's shinbone uncharred. Perhaps the most hideous murder was carried out with the more focused fire of blowtorches the inmates found in an area of the prison that was being renovated. They dragged the victim from his cell, used the torches to burn off his genitals, then methodically worked their way up his body, silencing his screams only as the flames obliterated his face.

To this day, no one has come up with a satisfactory explanation for this outburst of inhumanity. Early reports that the death squads had been high on drugs were later discounted. Some would also make much of the fact that some of the victims were informers or subjects of special hatred for other reasons. The blowtorch victim, for example, had been convicted of raping a mother and her two little girls before murdering all three of them. Yet many of the victims seemed chosen at random.

If the riot raised unanswerable questions about the nature of man, however, the answer to the question of how it came to pass seemed all too plain. As in Illinois, the breakdown of order in New Mexico was the wholly predictable result of the prison's chronic maladministration. The penitentiary's problems were hardly a secret. Two weeks before the riot, the state's attorney general released a report on an escape in December. It noted the prison's "history of instability and poor planning," "factionalism, poor communication and apathy" among its middle managers, and the general frustration of administrators with their responsibility for "holding the institution together despite inadequate staffing and training."

A *Corrections Magazine* report on the riot pointed out that "as individuals, the correction officers had long complained that there were not enough of them, that they were underpaid, and that they didn't get adequate training. Many of them were so young and inexperienced—more than half had been on the job for less than a year—that they didn't even realize the danger they were putting themselves in day after day." Guarding at the prison was considered "seasonal" work, like picking vegetables. Annual turnover was 80 percent.

Roger Morris, a White House and National Security Council aide in the Johnson and Nixon administrations, happened to be living in New Mexico, working as a writer, at the time of the riot. He produced a devastating account. Santa Fe, he concluded, "was a prison ruled by a craven, unstable coalition between a few of the dominant felons of maximum security and an administration that could govern no other way. . . . It was an alliance of keepers and kept that filled the vacuum of management and political oversight." He quotes a former counselor at the prison: "Inadequate people were surrounded by inadequate people. The officials became indistinguishable from the inmates, and the riot, in a way, was simply a continuation of administration."

FIVE

The Attica riot of 1971 and the Santa Fe riot of 1982 framed the modern debate over prisons. Attica had focused the crisis of oppression: Rioting inmates protested the violation of their humanity by guards and the institutional regime. To put down the revolt, New York officials resorted to a brutality that seemed to confirm the inmates' moral case. Santa Fe focused the crisis of control: Prolonged mismanagement had produced an environment of neglect and decay that nourished exploitive violence among the inmates. Instead of asserting humanity, they vented naked rage.

Some would point out the link between the two modes of bloodletting. Hadn't the perceived crisis of oppression led to new sympathy for inmates in ways that interfered with prison administrators' ability to run their institutions? They had been used to controlling inmates with swift, rough justice: solitary confinement and corporal punishments administered at the virtually total discretion of the warden and his lieutenants. Now they had to worry about due process. What restrictions might further lawsuits bring?

Hadn't that erosion of power allowed the gangs to grow up inside the walls? And didn't the loss of authority make the job of running the place that much harder, contributing to the collapse of guard morale?

By such arguments, the episodes of lost control would appear to vindicate resistance to reform. To the extent one might sympathize with inmates at Attica, Santa Fe became inevitable. In any case, the crisis of control would eclipse more talk of rehabilitation. How could a prison reclaim lost souls and turn bad men into good if the bad men, organized into gangs, found it possible to negotiate the sharing of power with terrified guards? What were the chances for counseling and therapy when an inmate believed, with reason, that the only way to avoid beating and rape was to learn how to beat and rape for himself?

Not all American prisons would experience the agonies of the Statevilles and the Santa Fes. But in most, the stress of overcrowding would lay bare a profound confusion of purpose. Did prisons help to control crime by incapacitating actual criminals and deterring potential ones? The research proved as inconclusive for incarceration as for death. Michael Sherman and Gordon Hawkins, in their study "Imprisonment in America," report the nearly comical "conclusion" of the National Academy of Sciences that "we cannot assert that the evidence warrants an affirmative conclusion regarding deterrence," but that this does not "imply . . . that deterrence does not exist, since the evidence certainly favors a proposition supporting deterrence more than it favors one asserting that deterrence is absent." Sherman and Hawkins add that "it is likely that the question will remain open, or more accurately, open and shut and open again."

The uncertainty hardly defies common sense. The problem is implicit in the numbers. So long as only a small percentage of felons wind up in prison, others are not likely to take the threat seriously, nor will their removal from society have much impact on the overall level of crime. Sherman and Hawkins summarize a study of defendants convicted of serious charges over a two-year period in Denver, Colorado. The researchers, Joan Petersilia and Peter Greenwood, sought to determine how crime rates would have been affected if those arrested had been subjected to harsher prison terms for previous crimes. Their calculations suggest that given the returns in terms of crime control, prison is a poor investment:

"Only a severely stringent policy, under which every offender convicted of any adult felony, violent or not, regardless of prior record, were sentenced to a mandatory prison term of five years, might lessen violent crime by one-third. This policy incidentally would increase prison population by close to 450 perecent. A sentencing policy which would impose a five-year sentence for any person previously convicted of at least one adult felony would have prevented 16 percent of violent crimes and increased prison population by 190 percent. A sentencing policy requiring offenders to have prior convictions for violent offenses would have reduced violent crime by less than 7 percent, even with mandatory five-year terms."

If the prison's contribution to crime control remained in doubt, so did the "rehabilitative ideal," the philosophical cornerstone of the modern penitentiary. The optimism of the early penologists had become a remote memory by the

1960s. But more important, as Michigan law professor Frances Allen pointed out, rehabilitating a wrongdoer required consensus on his wrongdoing, a basic agreement on social values, and that had broken down. What should prison do to change the character of a ghetto dweller whose criminality, social science confirms, arises from the effects of poverty and racism many Americans believe are an embarrassment to a modern society? To the alienated, rehabilitation would appear to be the tool of a corrupt establishment. They might point out how the Soviet Union sends dissidents to psychiatric hospitals for "rehabilitation," while in the People's Republic of China, it may involve heavy doses of public humiliation and political reindoctrination.

In *The Decline of the Rehabilitative Ideal*, Allen laments that the confusion over rehabilitation too often resulted in its "debasement." He was especially fascinated by the euphemisms common to modern penitentiaries. "In one place or another solitary confinement has been called 'constructive meditation,' and a cell for such confinement 'the quiet room.' Incarceration without treatment of any kind is seen as 'milieu therapy,' and a detention facility is labeled 'Cloud Nine.' Disciplinary measures such as the use of cattle prods on inmates become 'aversion therapy' and the playing of a powerful firehose on the backs of recalcitrant adolescents 'hydrotherapy.' Cell blocks are hospitals, dormitories or wards, latrine cleaning 'work therapy.' The catalog is almost endless. Some of the euphemisms are conscious distortions of reality and are employed sardonically or with deliberate purpose to deceive. The more serious distortions, however, are those that reflect the self-deception of correctional functionaries."

Lois Forer, in *Criminals and Victims*, took a long step back from the whole debate to point out that assuming criminal behavior always reflects sinful character vastly oversimplifies the problem. "I have . . . seen good, decent people who acted impulsively or on misperceived facts or who were convicted on very shaky evidence," she writes. As an example, she describes Rochelle, a barmaid, who began to be romanced by Seymour, "a fast-talking man with a shiny new car and elegant clothes. He courted her assiduously and in very gentlemanly fashion. . . . He spoke of marriage." Having won her trust, Seymour began asking Rochelle to deliver packages for him. Eventually, she was arrested for delivering heroin. Seymour disappeared, and Rochelle was convicted. "Does Rochelle need rehabilitation?" Judge Forer asks.

Yet it isn't even necessary to wrestle with such issues to question the rehabilitative ideal, for the simple reason that no one has ever succeeded in showing that it works. For all their efforts over the years, and for all the heartwarming anecdotes that might document individual criminals' return to self-respecting lives, the penologists and psychotherapists could not devise any treatment that would reliably prevent large numbers of inmates from going out and committing more crimes. The scholar Robert Martinson shook the world of criminal justice in 1974 when he published a survey of correctional programs that had been sponsored by New York State officials promoting prison reform. Its stark conclusion was that "with few isolated exceptions, the rehabilitative effects that have been reported so far have had no appreciable effect on recidivism." The sponsors were so dismayed that they refused to publish the study. They "ended by viewing the study as a document whose disturbing conclusions posed a serious threat to the programs which, in the meantime, they had determined to carry forward," Martinson wrote later. They even refused Martinson permission to publish the study himself. It only saw print after an attorney subpoenaed it to use as evidence in a criminal case.

The Martinson research became known as the "nothing works" study. It extinguished any residual optimism about prisons. In the 1980s, sensible students of penology like Norval Morris of the University of Chicago Law School would conclude that only those inmates who had reached a decision to reform on their own might become rehabilitated by programs in prisons. Instead of hoping to impose personal reformation on the unwilling, institutions could only make available a variety of therapies and vocational and education programs. They might facilitate the transformations of those who had decided for themselves that the time had come to change.

The uncertainties of incarceration as a way to promote either crime control or rehabilitation would lead some critics of the 1970s and 1980s to argue that prisons are absurd, especially as the cost of constructing maximum security space for a single inmate approached $100,000 and the cost of keeping him in it for a year surpassed the cost of an Ivy League tuition. Such critics would propose that reliance on prisons be drastically reduced. This argument, advanced by groups like the National Council on Crime and Delinquency, recognized that some criminals were so bad that they needed to be locked up. But these were the baddest of the bad, the "dangerous offenders" and "violent recidivists" and "career criminals" for whom there could be no realistic hope of rehabilitation. The penitentiaries should be reserved for them, for long terms whose acknowledged purpose would be to keep these incorrigibles off the streets so that they could no longer threaten the innocent. But after locking up the hard core, what to do with the rest?

The adherents of the strategy talked vaguely about dispersing them to "community corrections"—small locally based programs of therapy and training. Such a strategy would echo the policy of deinstitutionalization underway in mental health, where the gothic old state hospitals were being systematically emptied, often under pressure from the courts, on the promise that the patients could be better cared for in the community.

Given the outcome of that policy—the failure of community treatment to follow up on the released mental patients, with the result that tens of thousands walk the streets of American cities, homeless and desperate, to this day—it is perhaps fortunate that the community corrections strategy never moved much beyond the enlightened policy paper or newspaper editorial. The problem for the reformers was not just that the public was in no mood to talk about reducing the number of people being sent to prison. The community corrections strategy assumed that thousands of nonviolent first or second offenders were crowding the prisons. That wasn't always true. When reformers sought to make that argument in New York State, for example, corrections officials responded with figures showing that in fact, vast majorities of state penitentiary inmates had been convicted of violent felonies and had substantial criminal records. They also pointed out that many wound up in prison after bargaining and pleading guilty to reduced charges. As a result, their recorded crimes of conviction were less serious than what they had actually done. The reformers were reduced to arguing that many of those classified as violent were in for burglary, which some might consider a nonviolent crime if it occurred when no one was home or the victims had not been confronted. But there was simply no chance that the legislature would consider writing off prison as a punishment for burglary.

Others, like Charles Silberman, would try to make the case for a return to optimism about the penitentiary. He concludes a discussion of corrections with a description of the relatively new Illinois correctional center at Vienna, designed to provide a positive experience for inmates. The facility "looks more like a suburb, or college campus, than a prison. Instead of a prison yard, there is a 'town square,' surrounded by two chapels, a large school building, kitchen and dining room, library, gym, and small, detached buildings containing a commissary, barbershop, and other services." This community is presided over by a warden committed to the idea that "only a minority of prisoners are unwilling to abide by prison rules; instead of gearing everything to that minority, it makes more sense to erect a prison government around the majority of conforming inmates, and then to zero in on those who refuse to conform."

All well and good: Silberman reports that the prison functions peacefully; there have been no riots, strikes or other disturbances; the atmosphere is relaxed and there is little violence among inmates. Morale of guards is high.

But there is a catch. Vienna rejects inmates its staff considers "troublemakers." It will take in only those who have been locked up at other Illinois prisons and demonstrated their willingness to behave. Transfer to Vienna becomes a reward; once there, inmates tasting the pleasanter atmosphere know that should they slide back they will be returned to Stateville or one of the other more violent places. Illinois prison officials are to be complimented, perhaps, for turning their problems of control elsewhere to this positive use at Vienna. But there should be no illusions: In addition to suburban layout and a staff willing to give prisoners some respect, the success of the institution also rests on old-fashioned fear. The crisis of control remains the central problem.

How to gain some purchase on it? As the 1980s continued, some sort of disaster began to look inevitable. States continued to spend hundreds of millions expanding prisons, only barely containing an inexorably rising tide of new convicts. New York spent $657 million to increase its capacity to 38,000 by 1987. The estimates for 1988 exceeded 40,000. In Texas, the prison population approaches 40,000, after the expenditure of several hundred million; building plans call for spending another $134 million in 1988. California officials estimate that their nation of convicts could total an incomprehensible 97,000 by 1991. Current plans call for spending more than $2 billion by that time, an undertaking likely to keep the prisons barely under control.

Such projections would encourage reformers to hope that the public would finally tire of paying for more cells and give up on the penitentiary as America's basic sanction for wrongdoing. Such hopes were neither politically realistic nor even practically sound. While the voting public might be disappointed to learn that a prison term could not reliably deter crime or rehabilitate criminals, it could not be easily persuaded to share the reformer's conclusion that therefore prison was an absurd waste of money.

In fact, prison continues to do just what the public wants it to do: punish. To the extent conditions inside prisons have deteriorated, their punishment value might even be said to increase. If tales of gang warfare and homosexual rape appall the reform-minded, they could also secretly gratify the crime-weary. Indeed, even the Supreme Court, deciding the case of *Bell* v. *Wolfish* in 1977, seemed to countenance a certain degree of crowding by refusing to find unconstitutionally cruel the practice of confining two inmates in a single small cell.

And while reformers might continue to gag on the word, there is in fact nothing wrong with the idea of punishment or with the penitentiary as a way to deliver it for serious and repeated criminality, especially when such punishments are required in substantial volume. Programs of drug and alcohol treatment, psychotherapy, community service, and restitution—especially restitution—deserve a huge and expanding place in modern corrections. But they are best imposed at the early stages of a criminal's career, when they might plausibly do the most good. It's not unreasonable to hope they might thereby inhibit greater incorrigibility. But it's unrealistic to consider them more than a partial response. For the foreseeable future, America is going to need to do something else with hundreds of thousands of criminals who simply won't be reached by the helping programs. And there need be no apologies for the idea of punishing them. Whether or not punishment helps criminals—as it might—it helps to reinforce values for the rest of us.

To accept that idea, however, does not mean one may ignore the crisis of control. Instead it makes it more imperative than ever to restore proper and humane management to prisons. While punishment clearly has a place in an enlightened society, barbaric punishment does not. The question remains, therefore, how society can afford to expand the infrastructure of punishment to humanely accommodate the tide of criminals that is likely to keep rising at least for another decade. While there is no certain answer to this question, there is one that deserves more urgent exploration, for its promise is substantial, and as yet barely realized.

S I X

In 1977, a riot of capitalism erupted inside the maximum-security state penitentiary at Thomaston, Maine. The engine of economic activity was the prison's handicraft program. The fuel was money.

For years, inmates had been allowed to earn spending money by using prison woodworking machinery to make "novelties"—handcrafted lamps, stools, jewelry boxes, model ships, and other knickknacks—for sale in a gift shop located on a busy highway near the prison. But the amount an individual inmate could earn had been restricted, and no single inmate could own more than four of the patterns for the novelty items. Then in 1977, a warden intrigued with the program's potential to keep the inmates constructively occupied and relatively contented raised the limit on patterns to ten per prisoner and the individual income ceiling to $10,000. With that, the invisible hand of profit motivation reached into the prison and transformed it.

The more entrepreneurial inmates realized that simply turning out individual items one by one was no way to maximize productivity. They set up assembly lines and hired other prisoners to work on them for pay. Output increased so much that an inmate committee set up to supervise the novelty program persuaded the warden to lift the ceiling on individual income to $15,000. A pleasant wave of affluence swept through the cellblocks. Inmate managers took loans at local banks to purchase more materials and expand their operations. They invested their money in certificates of deposit. Allowed access to some of the earnings in accounts with the prison business office, inmates developed a secondary service economy. They did each other's laundry, rented television sets, gave haircuts. Some were able to carpet and pine-panel their cells. One claimed to have declared income of $38,000 on his 1979 tax return.

The expanding novelty industry converted an idle, somnolent institution into a hive of activity. "Inmates were whittling, carving, sanding and gluing wherever there was enough space for a single worker," wrote Edgar May in *Corrections Magazine*. He quotes a prison official: "Hey, they were making things all over the damn place. In the cells, in the basement of the kitchen, in the gymnasium. . . . They had little shops all over the place. They were working like beavers. We seldom had any problems from the standpoint of fights or other disturbances."

But the experiment also reflected the darker side of free enterprise. The more dynamic entrepreneurs sought to expand their power and wealth by evading the limit on pattern ownership. They secretly purchased patterns from others. "The system created successful businessmen who started buying other businesses," the warden said. "They bought out other guys who still owned patterns but didn't have the talent or the drive to mass-produce them. It led to subsidiary industries, dummy companies."

The rise of these "novelty kings" spelled the end of the experiment. Corrections officials realized that power in the prison was slowly shifting to the inmate entrepreneurs. In some cases, they were believed to have intimidated weaker inmates into handing over patterns and exploited the labor of others. Though charges of collusion with the prison staff were never proved, the potential remained obvious. A consulting group called in to assess the program charged that "the staff do not control the prison. . . . The inmate economy generated by the novelty program dominates the entire social structure and operation of the prison."

In 1980, the warden resigned as state corrections officials ordered a lockdown to cut back the novelty industry, now a thriving weed. After being confined to their cells for ten weeks, inmates were allowed to resume novelty production, but only in a single room of the prison, for no more than fifteen hours a week. And no inmate could earn more than $5,000 a year.

The experiment deserved to be denounced as a gross failure of prison administration. The group called in to evaluate it found that "current operations at the Maine State Prison violate nearly every accepted principle of prudent correctional management as practiced in this country today. . . ." At the same time, however, the experiment served to confirm an obvious if too often overlooked point: Offering inmates real pay for real work could motivate them to constructive activity, sustain morale, and drastically reduce traditional problems of discipline. Why not try to offer such pay for such work in circumstances that would permit greater control and allow the public to share in some of the financial benefit?

The idea is hardly new. The early American penologists associated idleness with evil and sought to include work in their prison routines. In Pennsylvania, convicts worked alone in their cells, while in New York they worked in congregate shops. As the decades passed and idealism faded, prison managers resorted to selling inmate labor in order to offset the costs of running prisons. They leased out inmates to work on farms, in mines, and in factories. Or they invited businessmen to set up factories within the prison walls. Convict workers manufactured wagons, shoes, furniture, and stoves. But they got no money themselves. The prisons took all the money either according to terms of the leased labor agreement or a "piece-price" system.

Predictably enough, however, the practice eventually came under attack by labor unions and businessmen who weren't in a position to take advantage of the cheap convicts for hire. Their campaign gained support with charges, often well founded, that convict workers were exploited and abused. The practice appeared as offensive as slavery. By the turn of the century, the movement against free-market convict labor had won state and federal restrictions that forced prison managers to think in other terms. Inmates would no longer be put to work in order to bring in money to run the prison. Instead, work programs would be designed to teach job skills; their products would be sold only to state governments.

Under those conditions, however, prison wardens could not find enough work to keep inmates busy. An Attorney General's survey of prisons found that in 1935–36, only 51,000 of the nation's 106,800 prisoners were working at jobs or prison maintenance. The other 55,800—60 percent—had nothing to do. Chronic idleness had become an entrenched problem of American prisons, one that plagues them to this day.

It was in those Depression years that Congress nailed down the legal lid on the commercial use of prison labor. The Hawes-Cooper Act, which took effect in 1934, said that prison-made goods from one state couldn't be sold in another that barred the sale of goods manufactured in its own prisons. The next year, the Ashurst-Sumners Act barred interstate carriers from hauling goods that might violate Hawes-Cooper. In 1940, the Sumners-Ashurst Act imposed a total ban on interstate transportation of prison-made products intended for the private market. That left open the possibility of prison labor for products purchased by state and federal governments. But the Walsh-Healy Act put a $10,000 ceiling on such contracts.

There the issue stood until the 1970s, when the run-up in prison populations and costs forced new attention to prisoners' work as a source of revenue. In 1973, when state and federal prisons held 200,000 inmates, an economist, Neil Singer, estimated the cost of their wasted manpower at more than $700 million. The manpower available in jails would double the figure. By 1979, the prison population had climbed by 100,000, and Senator Charles Percy of Illinois introduced a bill that would outline the modern approach to a role for prisons in private enterprise.

It authorized exemptions to the Sumners-Ashurst restrictions for seven pilot projects that met conditions designed to meet objections of organized labor and make the exemptions otherwise politically palatable. Prisoners would have to be paid prevailing local wages for comparable work and could not be denied benefits available to similar workers in the free world; their participation could not be coerced; their work could not displace free-world thinkers or existing contracts; local unions would have to be consulted. Perhaps most intriguing, prison officials could deduct up to 80 percent of an inmate's wages for taxes, room and board, support payments to his family, and restitution payments to the victim of his crime.

Meanwhile, a few voices had begun to promote the concept that the relaxed laws would permit. In 1975, the LEAA had funded a Philadelphia organization—it would come to be known as Criminal Justice Associates—to improve on prison industries. It began by offering financial help and advice for the upgrading of traditional state-use prison enterprises. But it would become a leading developer of industries aimed at the general market. In the 1980s the movement gained a prestigious and enthusiastic adherent in the person of Warren Burger, then Chief Justice of the United States. Converted to a belief in the virtues of massive prison work programs that provided real-world wages, he devoted speaking engagements all over the country to his call for "factories with fences."

In 1984, Congress expanded the number of projects under the Percy law guidelines. By 1986, a Criminal Justice Associates survey counted thirty-five projects operating in prisons of fourteen states and two county jails. They employed more than a thousand inmates in activities ranging from data processing to the manufacture of mattresses for water beds. An earlier survey, at the end of

1984, found that twenty-six private-market prison businesses had paid $4.4 million in wages to convicts, who paid $750,000 in taxes and reimbursed prisons $470,000 for room and board.

The earliest real-pay prison industries developed in the 1970s in Minnesota, a progressive state that had never imposed restrictions on the sale of prison-made goods to the general public. Corrections officials managed to interest the state's leading businesses in the problems of prison industries. Today, more than forty Minnesota inmates are employed in businesses that assemble toner boxes for photocopy machines, set up customized data processing for businesses in the Twin Cities area, and enter purchase-order data for B. Dalton, the book retailer. Meanwhile, more than two hundred prisoners at two prisons are employed for wages approaching real-world rates in print shops and the manufacture of furniture and farm machinery.

The most interesting real-pay prison industry projects developed in Kansas. In 1979, an entrepreneur named Fred Braun assembled $1.1 million in capital, including a $500,000 industrial revenue bond, $70,000 of his own money, and additional borrowings, to purchase Zephyr Products, Inc., a sheet-metal processor. His purpose was to create a business with a convict work force as an antidote to idleness in prisons. On a small scale, he proved his point. Zephyr employs about a dozen Kansas inmates, busing them each day to and from the Kansas Correctional Institute at Lansing. The inmates earn $3.35 to $3.60 per hour, and the project has cost the state of Kansas nothing either for capital or operations. Instead, the prisoners who work at Zephyr pay taxes and reimburse the prison for room and board. They are able to send money home to their families and save the rest for their release. The company has been profitable since 1985 and in 1986 had sales of $1.39 million. In 1985, Braun purchased a second company, Heatron, Inc., which employs another dozen inmates to make heating elements.

A somewhat simpler success story occurred in Arizona, where Best Western International, the big motel chain headquartered in Phoenix, hired thirty inmates at the Arizona Correctional Institute for Women to process telephone requests for room reservations. The company pays the women $4.50 to $8.53 per hour, the same wage it pays all its reservation agents. Convict staffing met the company's need for agents willing to work holidays and weekends and permitted easy expansion and contraction of the reservation force to meet seasonal increases in calls. (In summer, as many as forty prisoners may work the Best Western phones.) The company also used the project to train supervisors. Since 1981, Arizona inmates have earned more than $951,000 from Best Western and have paid $182,000 in taxes, $187,000 to the state's general fund, and $112,000 in family support.

However heartening the success of these projects, the thousand or so they employ makes only the tiniest dent in the idleness that remains routine for an estimated 90 percent of a state prison population exceeding half a million. Could the models be made to work on a larger scale?

There is no question that prisons are capable of putting thousands rather than dozens of inmates to work. Some penitentiaries in the South, most notably in Texas, are blessed with enough property to permit farming on a large scale. Much of an institution's inmates go out each day to till the soil or raise livestock. Others work in modern shop complexes. The produce, meat, and goods are consumed either by the prison itself or by other state agencies. In 1934 the federal prison system set up the Federal Prison Industries program to provide inmates with work manufacturing a wide variety of products for sale to federal agencies. In 1987, the program employed about 14,000— about 34 percent of the total federal prison population. In 1986, earnings were $16.6 million on sales of $237.5 million. Inmates are paid from 22 cents to $1.10 per hour, well below the minimum wage. Federal prison officials point out that the less-than-living wage is all gravy— nothing is deducted for room and board or restitution.

Unfortunately, few states can provide the large and varied government markets necessary to support prison industry on that scale, even though the prison populations of larger states approach or in some cases exceed that of the federal prison system. Yet prison-industry managers remain wary of the free market, with excellent reason. Fred Braun personally absorbed Zephyr's losses for six years—a total of about $500,000—until the company finally climbed out of the red in 1985. Minnesota's first big success story was a shop that at one time employed 160 inmates assembling disk drives and wiring harnesses for sale to a subsidiary of Control Data Corp., the giant computer company. The operation folded in 1986 when Control Data, battered by foreign competition, decided to shift production of the Stillwater products to Portugal. Howard Johnson's Inc., following Best Western, set up a telephone reservation service in an Oklahoma prison in 1984, but the program died a year later when Marriott Corporation purchased Howard Johnson's.

Labor unions are another source of worry. Especially with free-world unemployment remaining high even in a strong economy, the idea of prisoners underbidding other workers makes organized labor nervous, despite the apparent protections written into the Percy laws. In 1984, for example, John Zalusky, an economist for the AFL-CIO, complained to a Congressional committee that while the prisoners assembling disk drives for Control Data in Minnesota were earning $3.40 to $3.80 per hour, the prevailing wage for similar work nationally was $7.37 per hour. While he asserted that "the AFL-CIO shares" the "humanitarian concerns" of the prison labor movement, "prison labor must not displace free labor by entering into a labor market where there are free workers seeking similar jobs, or cause the loss of existing free labor job opportunities through the loss of existing contracts for goods or services."

In 1981, a competitor charged that Zephyr was in a position to gain unfair advantage in bidding on contracts in Kansas City because the minimum wage it paid inmates undercut the market. The matter was resolved when Arthur Young and Company conducted a detailed cost/benefit study of inmate labor at Zephyr. It concluded that inmate labor yielded no advantage since the prisoners' inexperience and lack of skills reduced productivity more than enough to compensate for the low pay.

Yet another line of resistance comes from prison administrators. Their first responsibility, they point out, is custody—many struggle to hold the line against total loss of control—and custody may conflict with smooth operation of a manufacturing plant. What happens, for example, when tensions inside the penitentiary require locking it down for a few days? They also resist the expanded clerical work involved in keeping track of inmates' earnings and payments. Some may fret over the wisdom of letting inmates earn all that money legitimately, given the problem of illicit earnings. And those struggling to maintain control of the worst prisons will dismiss the idea as unworkable.

Promoters of real work counter the misgivings such problems generate with plausible ideas. The prisons, they point out, in fact have something to sell when it comes to labor forces. Prison inmates are grateful just for the chance to work and earn some money; employers don't need to deal with the need to promote or lose workers who consider a first-rung job only the beginning of a career. The Minnesota disk-drive assemblers, for example, outperformed all other Control Data feeder plants and won an award from the company for productivity. Prisoners are willing to work nights and weekends without expecting extra pay, and can easily be organized into a work force that expands and contracts with seasonal needs. Such flexibility may be growing more valuable as the general labor force ages and more workers feel entitled to full job security and regular hours.

As for the anxieties of unions and competing businesses, they might be allayed by hiring out prison workers for the manufacture of products that long ago ceased to provide any work for free-world labor in the United States, products like transistor radios and pocket calculators. As long as prison workers are competing with Taiwan and South Korea, Americans could only applaud.

The worries of prison administrators are plausibly countered by the simple fact that their options are shrinking fast. In 1985, America spent a staggering $10.98 billion on correctional institutions, and that barely contained the swelling flood of convicts. Yet the public shows as little tolerance for such spending as it does for easing up on the sentencing policies that have created the flood. Prison administrators must either find more creative ways to manage and fund their institutions or resign themselves to the supervision of barbarity and chaos.

The worst maximum security penitentiaries may be too far given over to violence and gang rule to permit the introduction of so constructive a program. But plenty remain where it could work on some scale, and gaining the benefit of their inmate productivity can only help the broader struggle.

And should not the prospect of inmates having substantial earnings be seen as directly benefiting the public, beyond defraying prison and welfare costs? The longer an inmate served, the larger would be the savings available to him on the day of release—doled out in installments, perhaps, should paroling authorities consider it wise. For a few months, at least, he would have a fighting chance to avoid a return to crime, a chance few inmates now are granted.

The best arguments for real-pay prison work, however,

are somewhat more than practical. The rehabilitative ideal originally was based on putting prisoners to work, not just to keep them busy, but to make clear the moral value of self-discipline and honest, productive labor. The nineteenth-century experience with leasing of inmates insulted the idea that work might rehabilitate and generated the business and union pressure that would banish the concept from prisons for most of the twentieth century. Yet the quasi-slavery of the contract system reflected the cynicism of administrators rather than any innate corruption of prison industry. Its absence, meanwhile, forced rehabilitation into the more tenuous realm of psychotherapies. The most effective would have been intensive one-on-one counseling, but few prisons could afford such a service for any but the most disturbed inmates. Instead, rehabilitation in the modern era centered on programs of education, vocational training, and psychotherapy in groups.

In the 1970s, the pop therapies sweeping free America inevitably found their way into prisons. Transactional Analysis, Assertiveness Training, Transcendental Meditation, and Reality Therapy all enjoyed a period of vogue with wardens and inmates. Some even contracted with the authoritarian est movement. And thousands of convicts signed up for the courses in Positive Mental Attitude that a Chicago multimillionaire, W. Clement Stone, had developed to motivate insurance salesmen. For a time the movement even offered a career path for ambitious inmates. Promoters of the therapies liked nothing better than a successful graduate. The ideal instructor/role-model for inmates who aspired to self-control was the reformed sinner, the person whose weak personality and poor self-image had been to blame for his criminality, but who now had achieved inner peace. It was not uncommon to find inmates planning post-parole careers as counselors of other inmates, or perhaps of juvenile offenders, based on résumés that presented as credentials their years of felony convictions and drug addiction, followed by successful conversions through group therapy.

In effect the savvier inmates, sensing the element of hustle in the pop therapies, sought to pursue it for themselves. Here was sad evidence of the real point: Prisoners don't want or need better self-images or relationship skills nearly so much as they need a legitimate way to survive in the modern American economy. Not all will recognize that need during their time in prison, and for them the idea of "rehabilitation" remains problematic. But countless prisoners do recognize such a need, and more might be persuaded of it. The most sensible and realistic mission for a penitentiary is to respond to that need in those prisoners who express it and to try to arouse it in those who don't. What better vehicle for doing so than a job that approximates work in the real world as closely as the prison's custodial obligation will permit?

Prisons punish by separating criminals from the rest of society and drastically limiting their freedom. First and foremost, an expansion of real work for real pay, producing goods and services for sale in a real marketplace, would gain desperately needed relief for some prison administrators' problems of financing and discipline. But the process might also finally provide a way to realize the rehabilitative ideal.

9

CRIMES
of
JUSTICE

In the early chapters of *The Fatal Shore*, a compelling account of Australia's settlement by criminal exiles, Robert Hughes depicts a Georgian England fearful and fed up with crime. The second half of the eighteenth century saw rapid population growth and urbanization that severely strained English life—the population of London doubled between 1750 and 1770. A result was mass poverty and unemployment that overwhelmed the traditional workhouses and other institutions in place to address such problems. English cities were overrun with poor, idle young men. Meanwhile, distillers had learned how to produce a cheap, powerful alcoholic spirit from grain and flavor it with crushed juniper berries. This was gin; no more than a penny's worth could produce a roaring drunk. It was a historic innovation: Until then, drinking had been the pastime of an aristocracy that could afford port or brandy. Gin, Hughes writes, became a "common solace." It was "England's national stupefacient, the heroin of the eighteenth century (but worse, because its use was far wider)."

Thus was born a historic crime wave that aroused the fear and indignation of decent folk. Hughes quotes Jonas Hanway, in 1775: "I sup with my friend; I cannot return to my home, not even in my chariot, without danger of a pistol being clapt to my breast. I build an elegant villa, ten or twenty miles distant from the capital: I am obliged to provide an armed force to convey me thither, lest I should be attacked on the road with fire and ball."

The official apparatus in place to deal with crime seemed ineffective. The English resisted setting up a national police force that might become the tool of repressive government, as had happened on the continent of Europe. Robert Peel's bobbies would not patrol the streets until 1827. And English courts granted criminal defendants basic rights: They were innocent until proved guilty and could not be held indefinitely without trial.

Thus "to avenge their sense of a disturbed social order," Hughes writes, the English passed harsh laws. "If detection and arrest were feeble and trials tenderly fair, what punishment could keep men from crime? Only the extreme one: hanging without benefit of clergy." English law prescribed death for "what seemed a limitless variety of human deeds, from infanticide to 'impersonating a Egyptian' (posing as a Gypsy)." A person might also hang for forgery, "stealing an heiress," burning a hayrick, poaching wild game. Public hangings drew crowds of thousands—the gruesome spectacles were intended to convey a powerful message about the rule of law. Yet the growing volume of hangings eventually would inspire as much revulsion as respect for authority.

In these desperate circumstances, the English adopted a "humane" alternative to death: transportation to Australia. It was a wholly improbable idea. England had only sketchy knowledge of the distant continent based on reports of Captain James Cook, who had landed briefly in 1770. No one knew for sure how, or even if, the strange land would sustain a sizable penal colony. In the early years, thousands starved. That the result was modern Australia may give the lie to those who insist crime is bred in the genes, but it hardly vindicates what was done in those early years of inhumanity—beginnings that Australians to this day hesitate to acknowledge.

England's reliance on hangings and transportation were classic examples of state excesses committed in response to surging fear and outrage. They were crimes, if you will, of justice itself. Modern America isn't Georgian England, but it exhibits a similar syndrome: Social forces produce an underclass of idle youngsters prone to make trouble. Thriving traffic in drugs promotes misbehavior. The public's anxiety and indignation, combined with frustration at the apparent impotence of the police and the courts, warp any official humanity and common sense. After its de facto abolition, the death penalty returns, a grisly ritual that offers only symbolic gratification. And prison terms are carelessly extended, with scant regard for the penal system's ability to manage. As a direct result, and by tacit agreement, prisons become places of routine atrocity, where the only way to avoid being beaten and raped is to learn to beat and rape. Beyond the view of a public that promotes such a system, even as it averts its gaze, the crimes of justice grow wild.

Meanwhile, the police and courts become accustomed to a life of pretense. No one knows better the limits of patrol and of plea bargaining, the neglect of lower courts, the daunting arithmetic of the funnel. Yet rare is the police executive, prosecutor or judge who will discuss them frankly with the public.

History suggests that the social forces nurturing crime remain dynamic. In time the problem could correct itself, if only because all those troublemaking young men eventually will reach middle age, and not as many are taking their places. But such correction requires time, a quarter century or more. The challenge of criminal justice—the hard question to love—is to figure out what to do in the meantime.

Admitting that so far we know of nothing to do that would guarantee much reduction in crime rates may be to admit defeat. It is also to accept reality and thereby gain welcome freedom from a debate that has reached a dead and potentially destructive end. We have come a long way from Georgian England—far enough to know that much may be done to improve our responses to crime even in the absence of any sure way to control it. To what ends? To the very important ends of upholding our values and telling the truth.

Therein lies the strength of the ideas offered in this

book. Whether or not a greater social work and neighborhood problem-solving role for the police controls crime, it promotes greater public understanding of the police, greater police understanding of the public, and a greater sense of community for all. Whether or not tougher, more creative probation controls crime, it reduces the cynical dismissal of young first and second offenders without meaningful punishment. Probation-based programs of court-ordered employment and restitution send powerful messages about work and accountability. Whether or not real jobs for real pay rehabilitate prisoners, they reduce an appalling waste of human productivity and send more messages about the value and satisfaction of legitimate work.

These are constructive responses to fear and outrage. They make clear that we need not allow crime its ultimate triumph: the debasement of cherished ideals, the theft of ourselves.

NOTES

A HARD QUESTION TO LOVE

15 CHARLES GUICA: "Brooklyn Youth Is Shot to Death at a Schoolyard," *The New York Times*, Sept. 25, 1980.

16–17 BERNHARD GOETZ: The popular support for Goetz would be vindicated on June 16, 1987, when a jury acquitted him of attempted murder and other serious criminal charges. He was convicted only of illegal gun possession, for which his sentence included a six-month jail term, four and a half years of probation, a $5000 fine, and 280 hours of community service.

18 "WHAT EXACTLY WAS GOETZ SUPPOSED TO DO?": Patrick Buchanan's column, "Rights That Go Beyond the Law," appeared on the op-ed page of the *New York Post*, Jan. 4, 1985.

19 "THIS INCIDENT CANNOT BE UNDERSTOOD IN ISO-LATION": Kenneth Clark's article, "In Cities, Who Is the Real Mugger?" appeared on the op-ed page of *The New York Times*, Jan. 14, 1985.

20 "HE WAS HELL-BENT ON RETALIATION": Lea Evans Ash's article, "The Goetz Incident and Mine," appeared on the op-ed page of *The New York Times*, Dec. 16,

1985. The funeral that she and her priest believed had inspired the attack upon her was apparently that of Clifford Glover, a boy of nine who had been shot by a white police officer, Thomas Shea, early on the morning of April 28, 1973. Clifford had been walking with his stepfather, Add Armstead, when the police officers, patrolling in plainclothes, approached to question them about a crime in the area. Armstead said that the two did not identify themselves as police officers and that he and Clifford, fearing they were about to be robbed, began to run. Shea fired on Clifford, killing him.

Following the funeral on May 3, groups of young blacks acted out the community's anger and despair with sporadic street violence, much of it directed randomly against whites, that continued until nightfall.

Officer Shea would say that he fired on Clifford because the boy had pulled a gun during the encounter, but no gun was ever found. Nonetheless, a jury acquitted him of criminal charges in the case. Some weeks later, however, both Shea and his partner, Walter Scott, were dismissed from the force after a departmental inquiry found the shooting unjustified.

2

THE FACTS CRUMBLE

23–24 "SIU DETECTIVES DID NOT BOTHER . . .": Robert Daley, *Prince of the City* (New York: Berkley Books, 1978), pp. 3–16.

24 THEY EVENTUALLY "BEGAN TO DISPENSE THEIR OWN JUSTICE. . . .": *Ibid.*, p. 307.

25 "THERE CAME A TIME . . .": *Ibid.*, p. 322.

25 IVAN MENDOZA: For a discussion of his case, see David C. Anderson, "Bargaining Over Murder," *The New York Times*, Aug. 19, 1983.

28 JACK HENRY ABBOTT: Jack Henry Abbott, *In the Belly of the Beast: Letters from Prison* (New York: Random House, 1981).

28 THE FULLER STORY: Robert Sam Anson, "The Brief and Violent Freedom of Jack Abbott," *Life*, November 1981, pp. 118ff.

32–35 CRIME STATISTICS: National figures quoted on these pages for reported crimes and victimizations are from various charts included in Timothy J. Flanagan and Edmund F. McGarrell, eds., *Sourcebook of Criminal Justice Statistics—1985* (Washington, D.C.: U.S. Department of Justice, Bureau of Justice Statistics, 1986).

35 REPORTS OF AUTO THEFT DROPPED BY 20 PERCENT: Author's interview with New York City Police Department officials involved with the operation.

35–36 HISTORY OF CRIME RATES: Ted Robert Gurr, "Historical Trends in Violent Crimes: A Critical Review of the Evidence," in Michael Tonry and Norval Morris, eds., *Crime and Justice: An Annual Review of Research* (Chicago: University of Chicago Press, 1981), vol. 3, p. 295.

3

"AMERICA CAN CONTROL
CRIME IF IT WILL"

42 RACIAL DISTURBANCES: Thomas F. Parker, ed., *Violence in the U.S.* (New York: Facts on File, 1974), vol. 1, pp. 75ff, 104ff, 179ff.

42 ASSASSINATION OF MARTIN LUTHER KING: *Ibid.*, vol. 2, pp. 15ff.

42–43 KENT STATE: *Ibid.*, p. 163.

43 "RAPE WAS AN INSURRECTIONARY ACT": Eldridge Cleaver, *Soul on Ice* (New York: McGraw Hill, 1968), p. 14.

43 "ALL MY LIFE . . .": George Jackson, *Soledad Brother: The Prison Letters of George Jackson* (New York: Bantam, 1970), p. 19.

44 JACKSON'S IMPRISONMENT AND DEATH: Parker, vol. 2, pp. 223–25. For another account, see Blake McKelvey, *American Prisons: A History of Good Intentions* (Montclair, N. J.: Patterson Smith, 1977), pp. 353–54.

45 "SLUMS, RACISM, IGNORANCE AND VIOLENCE": Ramsey Clark, *Crime in America* (New York: Simon & Schuster, 1970), p. 17.

46 "THERE IS NO CONFLICT BETWEEN LIBERTY AND SAFETY": *Ibid.*, p. 274.

46 PRESIDENTIAL CAMPAIGN OF 1964: Good summaries of how crime became a national issue are included in Thomas E. Cronin, Tania Z. Cronin, and Michael E. Milakovich, *U.S. v. Crime in the Streets* (Bloomington: Indiana University Press, 1981), pp. 18–24; and in Gerald

Caplan, "Reflections on the Nationalization of Crime, 1964–68," *Law and Social Order*, vol. 1973, no. 3, pp. 583–90.

47 "PERHAPS WE ARE DESTINED TO SEE . . .": Cronin *et al.*, p. 20.

47 "IT WAS CLEAR . . .": Caplan, p. 589.

48 "THERE WAS NO PREEXISTING THEORY . . .": *Ibid.* p. 590.

49 "THE LAY READER MIGHT RESPOND . . .": James Q. Wilson, "A Reader's Guide to the Crime Commission Reports," *Public Interest*, Fall 1967, p. 65.

50 "WARRING ON POVERTY . . .": President's Commission on Law Enforcement and Administration of Justice, *The Challenge of Crime in a Free Society* (Washington, D.C.: U.S. Government Printing Office, 1967), p. 6.

50 "CONTROLLING CRIME IN AMERICA . . .": President's Commission, p. 291.

53 "CANDIDATES FAILED . . .": Cronin *et al.*, p. 76.

54 "I HAD BEEN GIVEN . . .": Edward Jay Epstein, *Agency of Fear* (New York: Putnam, 1977), p. 73.

55 THE RIVER OF LEAA MONEY: Cronin *et al.*, chart, p. 112.

55 PATROL CARS THAT POLICE FOUND TOO CRAMPED: *Ibid.*, p. 90.

56 "CRIME IN AMERICA WAS GROWING . . .": Quoted in Victor Navasky with Darrell Paster, "Background Paper," in Twentieth Century Task Force on the Law Enforcement Assistance Administration, *Law Enforcement: The Federal Role* (New York: McGraw-Hill, 1976), p. 45.

57 PROJECT SCHEHERAZADE: *Ibid.*, pp. 111–12.

59 "WE ARE NOT CONVINCED . . .": Attorney General's Task Force on Violent Crime, Final Report (Washington, D.C.: U.S. Department of Justice, 1981), p. 2.

59–60 "IT HAS OCCURRED TO ME . . .": Excerpts from President Reagan's crime speech were published in *The New York Times* on Sept. 29, 1981.

61 A "MAJOR INITIATIVE THAT I BELIEVE . . .": Dick Kirschten, "Reagan's Crime-Fighting Proposals—Shoot First and Then Load the Gun?" *National Journal*, Nov. 13, 1982, p. 1934.

61 THE BEST EFFORTS OF LAW ENFORCEMENT: "Agencies Seize Small Portion of Smuggled Drugs," *The New York Times*, May 18, 1984.

63–64 THE PRESIDENT'S TASK FORCE: President's Task Force on Victims of Crime, *Final Report* (Washington, D.C., 1982).

65 "WHEN THE COMMISSION'S *FINAL REPORT* WAS RELEASED . . .": Elliott Currie, "Crimes of Violence and Public Policy," in Lynn A. Curtis, ed., *American Violence and Public Policy* (New Haven: Yale University Press, 1985), pp. 41–42.

4

"WE HAVE MADE OUR SOCIETY AND WE MUST LIVE WITH IT"

68 RACE AND CRIME: Charles Silberman, *Criminal Violence, Criminal Justice* (New York: Random House, 1978) pp. 66ff.

68 "FOR MOST OF THEIR HISTORY . . .": *Ibid.*, p. 123.

68 "[BLACK] INVOLVEMENT IN STREET CRIME . . .": *Ibid.*, p. 164.

68 "IT WOULD BE DISINGENUOUS . . .": *Ibid.*, p. 165.

69 "[CAN] 'THE MORES' BE STRENGTHENED . . .": *Ibid.*, p. 429.

69 WHAT, THEN, IS POSSIBLE? *Ibid.*, pp. 429–46.

70 "WE ARE NOT LIKELY TO ENJOY . . .": *Ibid.*, p. 446.

70–71 "IN A WORLD OF DRAMATIC NATIONAL VARIATIONS . . .": Elliott Currie, *Confronting Crime: An American Challenge* (New York: Pantheon, 1985), p. 49.

71 FUTILITY OF IMPRISONMENT: *Ibid.*, pp. 89–90.

71 MENU OF SOCIAL PROGRAMS: *Ibid.*, pp. 275–76.

72 "TAKING THIS ROAD . . .": *Ibid.*, pp. 276–77.

73 "SOCIAL PROBLEMS . . .": James Q. Wilson, *Thinking About Crime* (New York: Basic Books, 1975), pp. 50–51.

73 "ONE MAY DETER . . .": *Ibid.*, p. 53.

73 "A SERIOUS POLICY-ORIENTED ANALYSIS . . .": *Ibid.*, pp. 55–56.

74 "WICKED PEOPLE EXIST . . .": *Ibid.*, p. 209.

74 "WE KNOW MORE IN 1983 . . .": James Q. Wilson, *Thinking About Crime*, rev. ed. (New York: Basic Books, 1983), p. 9.

74 "IT IS POSSIBLE . . .": *Ibid.*, p. 143.

75 "THE FACTORS THAT MOST DIRECTLY INFLUENCE CRIME . . .": *Ibid.*, p. 247.

75 "WE HAVE BECOME A NATION . . .": *Ibid.*, pp. 248–49.

75 "WE HAVE MADE OUR SOCIETY . . .": *Ibid.*, p. 249.

75 WILSON'S MOST RECENT BOOK: James Q. Wilson and Richard J. Herrnstein, *Crime and Human Nature* (New York: Simon & Schuster, 1985).

78 *NEWSWEEK* MAGAZINE POLL: "The Plague of Violent Crime," *Newsweek*, Mar. 23, 1981, p. 49.

78 LOUIS HARRIS SURVEY: Timothy J. Flanagan and Maureen McLeod, eds., *Sourcebook of Criminal Justice Statistics—1982* (Washington, D.C.: U.S. Department of Justice, Bureau of Justice Statistics, 1983), p. 244.

78 JOB BEING DONE BY LOCAL LAW ENFORCEMENT: *Ibid.*, p. 239.

78 CAUSES OF CRIME: *Ibid.*, p. 227.

5

THE FUNNEL

82 FRED CLARKE: David C. Anderson, "Footnote to a Subway Shooting," *The New York Times*, Jan. 14, 1985.

83–84 STATISTICS FOR NEW YORK CITY: Figures supplied by the New York City Criminal Justice Agency.

84 FELONIES . . . COMMITTED AMONG FRIENDS AND ACQUAINTANCES. Figures are for 1983 as reported in Flanagan and McGarrell, pp. 272–73.

85–86 A RECENT NATIONAL INSTITUTE OF JUSTICE STUDY: Caroline Wolf Harlow, "Reporting Crimes to the

Police," *Bureau of Justice Statistics Special Report*, December 1985.
86–87 "IN CALLING THE POLICE . . .": *Ibid.*, p. 2.

6

COPS AND COMMUNITIES

95 "THE POLICE CLEANED STREETS . . .": Robert M. Fogelson, *Big-City Police* (Cambridge: Harvard University Press, 1977), p. 16.
95 "THE PRECINCTS RATHER THAN HEADQUARTERS . . .": *Ibid.*, p. 37.
95–96 "SMALL WONDER . . .": *Ibid.*, p. 28.
96 CEALA URCHITTEL: *Ibid.*, p. 40.
100–101 "THE PATROLMAN IS NEITHER A BUREAUCRAT NOR A PROFESSIONAL . . .": James Q. Wilson, *Varieties of Police Behavior* (Cambridge: Harvard University Press, 1978), p. 283.
101 CHIEF O'NEILL'S QUOTE: Fogelson, p. 70.
102 THE KANSAS CITY PATROL STUDY: Discussion is based on Wilson, *Thinking About Crime*, rev. ed. pp. 66–68. See also Herman Goldstein, *Policing a Free Society* (Cambridge: Ballinger, 1977), p. 52.
103 VICTIMS TYPICALLY WAIT SEVERAL MINUTES: *Ibid.*, p. 71.
103 A 1975 RAND CORPORATION STUDY: Peter Greenwood, Jan M. Chaiken, and Joan Petersilia, "The Criminal Investigation Process."

105 NEW YORK CITY'S 90TH PRECINCT: Interviews with researchers for the Vera Institute of Justice familiar with the 90th Precinct projects.

107–8 "THE ROOKIE SHARES . . .": Jonathan Rubinstein, *City Police* (New York: Farrar, Straus & Giroux, 1973), p. 219.

108 "FOR THE POLICEMAN . . .": *Ibid.*, pp. 339–40.

108–9 "NEGROES ARE THOUGHT TO WANT . . .": Wilson, *Varieties of Police Behavior*, p. 141.

109 "A LEGALISTIC DEPARTMENT . . .": *Ibid.*, p. 172.

110 THEY "TAKE SERIOUSLY ALL REQUESTS . . .": *Ibid.*, p. 200.

110 "THE STUDIES REPORT . . .": Goldstein, p. 25.

111 THE POLICE OFFICER IS OFTEN "CALLED UPON TO SERVE . . .": *Ibid.*

111 "SHOPLIFTING IN BEVERLY HILLS . . .": David C. Couper, *How to Rate Your Local Police* (Washington, D.C.: Police Executive Research Forum, 1983), p. 8.

113 "IF BOTH LEGAL MANDATES . . .": Goldstein, p. 10.

113 "A FORMIDABLE FORCE . . .": *Ibid.*, p. 11.

113 "THE POLICE ORGANIZATION DEVELOPS . . .": Wilson, *Varieties of Police Behavior*, pp. 48–49.

115–16 NICOLAS LEMANN'S ARTICLE: Nicolas Lemann, "The Origins of the Underclass," *Atlantic Monthly*, June 1986, pp. 31–55, and July 1986, pp. 54–68.

117 "THE POLICE NOW GIVE HIGHEST PRIORITY . . .": James K. Stewart, "Public Safety and Private Police" (unpublished), p. 3.

117 LOS ANGELES CRIME AND ARREST FIGURES: *Ibid.*

118 THE GALLUP POLL: Flanagan and McLeod, p. 212.

120–22 WILSON AND KELLING ON COMMUNITY FEAR: James Q. Wilson and George L. Kelling, Jr., "Broken Windows: The Police and Neighborhood Safety," *Atlantic Monthly*, March 1982, pp. 29–38.

123 PEEL'S UNIFORMED "BOBBIES": Carl B. Klockars, "Order Maintenance, the Quality of Urban Life, and Police: A Different Line of Argument," in William A. Geller, ed., *Police Leadership in America* (Chicago: American Bar Foundation and Praeger, 1985), p. 310.

124 "UNIFORMED PATROL . . .": *Ibid.*, p. 311.

124–25 THE BROKEN-WINDOWS THEORY, WALKER ASSERTS: Samuel Walker, " 'Broken Windows' and Fractured History: The Use and Misuse of History in Recent Police Patrol Analysis," *Justice Quarterly*, March 1984, pp. 75–90.

125–26 "ONE GROUP HAS ATTEMPTED . . .": Kelling, "Neighborhoods and Police" (unpublished, 1985), p. 10.

126 THE SKILLS AND ACTIVITIES INVOLVED: *Ibid.*, p. 23.

128 THE LAPD'S EXPERIENCE WITH COMMUNITY POLICING: Description and quotes are from David M. Kennedy, "Neighborhood Policing in Los Angeles" (unpublished, 1986).

128–29 TEAM POLICING IN OTHER CITIES: David C. Anderson, "Getting Down with the People," *Police Magazine*, July 1978, p. 5.

129–30 ST. LOUIS TEAM POLICING: *Ibid.*

131–33 OPERATION PRESSURE POINT: Mark A. R. Kleiman, "Community Policing in Action: Street Level Heroin Enforcement" (unpublished, 1986).

133–34 WILSHIRE AREA: Kennedy, p. 15.

136 PROBLEM-ORIENTED POLICING: Herman Goldstein, "Improving Policing: A Problem-Oriented Approach," *Crime and Delinquency*, April 1979, pp. 236–58.

139 COMMUNITY PATROL IN NEW YORK'S 72D PRECINCT: Quotes and anecdotes are from Michael J. Farrell, "The Community Patrol Officer Program: Community Oriented Policing in the New York City Police Department," Interim Progress Report Number 2 (New York: Vera Institute of Justice, 1986). See also "The 'Blues' on Beat Street," *Newsweek*, Jan. 28, 1985, p. 49.

142–43 "POLICE OFFICER MARIA IRIZARRY . . .": Benjamin Ward, "The Community Patrol Officer Program," New York City Police Department report (undated), Appendix C.

143–47 BALTIMORE COUNTY COPE PROJECT: Discussion is based on Philip B. Taft, Jr., *Fighting Fear: The Baltimore County COPE Project* (Washington, D.C.: Police Executive Research Forum, 1986); and John E. Eck and William Spelman, "Who Ya Gonna Call? The Police as Problem-Busters," *Crime and Delinquency*, January 1987.

147–49 NEWPORT NEWS: The roller-rink incident is described in Eck and Spelman, "Who Ya Gonna Call?" The case of the Washington Avenue prostitutes is contained in Eck and Spelman with Diane Hill, Darrel W. Stephens, John R. Stedman, and Gerard R. Murphy, *Solving Problems: A Test of Problem-Oriented Policing in Newport News* (Washington, D.C.: Police Executive Research Forum, 1986).

149 SKEPTICISM REMAINS: The discussion of potential

problems with community policing owes much to Herman Goldstein, "Realizing the Full Potential in Community Policing: Some Essential Elements and Threshold Questions" (unpublished, 1986).

7

PUNISHMENT WITHOUT PRISON

165 THE HISTORICAL ROOTS OF PLEA BARGAINING: Albert W. Alschuler, "Plea Bargaining and Its History," *Columbia Law Review*, vol. 79, no. 1 (January 1979), pp. 1–43.

166 RAYMOND MOLEY'S STUDY: Raymond Moley, "The Vanishing Jury," quoted in Alschuler, p. 18.

166 FIFTY YEARS LATER: Vera Institute of Justice, *Felony Arrests: Their Prosecution and Disposition in New York City's Courts*, rev. ed. (New York: Longman, 1981), p. 143.

166 "IN URBAN JURISDICTIONS IN VIRGINIA . . .": *Ibid.*, p. 27.

166 SENTENCE PURCHASING: *Ibid.*, p. 24.

167 "I DON'T SEE ANY VALUE . . .": *Ibid.*, p. xxv.

167 "THE QUALITY OF JUSTICE . . .": *Challenge of Crime in a Free Society*, p. 134.

168 ALASKA'S BAN ON PLEA BARGAINING: David C. Anderson, "You Can't Cop a Plea in Alaska Anymore," *Police Magazine*, January 1979, p. 4.

169 EXAMINATION OF THE 1,888 CASES: *Felony Arrests*, pp. 1–2.

169 "PRIOR RELATIONSHIPS . . .": *Ibid.*, pp. 19–20.

170 "AN OBVIOUS BUT OVERLOOKED REALITY . . .": *Ibid.*, p. 135.

171 "WHERE CRIMES ARE SERIOUS . . .": *Ibid.*, p. 134.

171 35 PERCENT OF WASHINGTON ROBBERY ARRESTS: Brian Forst, Judith Lucianovic, and Sarah J. Cox, *What Happens After Arrest?* (Washington, D.C.: Institute for Law and Social Research, 1977), chart, p. 24.

171 UNWILLINGNESS OF COMPLAINANTS TO COOPERATE: *PROMIS Research Project*, quoted in Silberman, p. 266.

171–72 "BY AND LARGE . . .": Silberman, pp. 265–66.

172 JAIL TIME AND PRISON TIME: Silberman, p. 260.

173 "BECAUSE OUR SOCIETY . . ." *Felony Arrests*, p. xv.

174 "RARELY HAS ANY PUBLIC INSTITUTION . . ." "The Criminal Court: A System in Collapse," *The New York Times*, June 26, 1983.

174–75 THE COURTROOM "IS FAMOUS FOR BEING A DUMP . . .": Howard T. Senzel, *Cases* (New York: Viking, 1982), pp. 2–3.

175 "THE FAILURE OF THE CRIMINAL COURT . . .": Criminal Courts Committee of the Association of the Bar of the City of New York, "Saving the Criminal Court: A Report on the Caseload Crisis and Absence of Trial Capacity in the Criminal Court of the City of New York," June 7, 1983, p. 2.

175–76 A JUDGE'S AVERAGE DAILY CASELOAD: Figures and quote are from Sol Wachtler and Joseph Bellacosa, "A Report and Recommendations on the Need for Additional Judicial Resources," February 1986.

176 "A JUDICIAL SYSTEM IS LEGALLY DEAD . . .": Criminal Courts Committee, p. 3.

176–77 "JUDGES AND PROSECUTORS CONSIDER THESE CRIMES 'NUISANCES' . . .": *Felony Arrests*, p. 95.

177 "VIRTUALLY NO ONE WILL BE PROSECUTED . . .": *Ibid.*, p. 113.

177 A 1984 EXAMINATION OF OPERATION PRESSURE POINT CASES: New York City Criminal Justice Agency, "Operation Pressure Point 1/19/84–2/18/84 Final Report on Arrest Characteristics and Criminal Court Outcomes," June 1984.

177 A STATE STUDY OF FELONY DRUG CASES: New York State Division of Criminal Justice Services, Office of Policy Analysis, Research & Statistical Services, "Criminal Sale of Controlled Substances Analysis of Criminal Justice Processing," August 1986.

180 EARLY AMERICAN PRISONS: Good histories are provided by David Rothman, *The Discovery of the Asylum: Social Order and Disorder in the New Republic* (Boston and Toronto: Little, Brown, 1971); and McKelvey.

180–81 "YOU ASK ME FOR HOW LONG A TIME . . .": S. J. May quoted in Alan M. Dershowitz, *Fair and Certain Punishment: Report of the Twentieth Century Task Force on Criminal Sentencing* (New York: McGraw-Hill, 1976), p. 90.

181 "PREEMPTORY SENTENCES OUGHT TO BE RE-PLACED . . .": Quoted in Sandra Shane-DuBow, Alice P.

Brown, and Eric Olsen, *Sentencing Reform in the United States: History, Content, and Effect* (Washington, D.C.: National Institute of Justice, 1985), p. 5.

182 THE AMERICAN FRIENDS SERVICE COMMITTEE'S REPORT: *Struggle for Justice*, prepared for the American Friends Service Committee (New York: Hill and Wang, 1971).

182–83 "AN ASSAULT UPON A FEDERAL OFFICER . . .": Marvin E. Frankel, *Criminal Sentences* (New York: Hill and Wang, 1972), p. 5.

183 "THOSE WHO VIOLATE OTHERS' RIGHTS . . .": Andrew von Hirsch, *Doing Justice: The Choice of Punishments* (New York: Hill and Wang, 1976), p. 54.

183 "DEMOCRATIC THEORY WOULD SEEM TO INDICATE . . .": Dershowitz, pp. 123–24.

188 PUBLIC ATTITUDES ABOUT THE DEATH PENALTY: Flanagan and McGarrell, p. 175.

189 "DURING THE PAST 10 YEARS . . .": Shane-DuBow *et al.*, p. 279.

189–90 MARVIN WOLFGANG'S BIRTH COHORT RESEARCH: For a good discussion of the Wolfgang findings, see Currie, pp. 84–85, 146–48.

190 GREENWOOD'S "SELECTIVE INCAPACITATION" STUDY: Peter W. Greenwood with Alan Abrahamse, *Selective Incapacitation* (Santa Monica, Calif.: Rand Corporation, 1982).

194 "A NINE-STATE STUDY OF 1,293 FIRST-DEGREE MURDERERS . . .": Stephen H. Gettinger, *Sentenced to Die* (New York: Macmillan, 1979), p. 116.

195 "AN ADDITIONAL EXECUTION PER YEAR . . .": Quoted in Gettinger, p. 120.

196 "THE AVAILABLE SCHOLARLY WORK . . .": Wilson, quoted in Roger Thompson, "Emptying Death Row: More U.S. Executions," Editorial Research Reports, January 18, 1985, p. 58.

197 ALFRED BLUMSTEIN AND ELIZABETH GRADDY: See discussion in Currie, p. 86.

197 CRIME IN COLUMBUS: See Currie, p. 87.

199 "AMID A DECADE OF FOCUS ON SENTENCING . . .": Shane-DuBow, p. 280.

203 BENEFIT OF CLERGY: Harry E. Allen, Chris W. Eskridge, Edward J. Latessa, and Gennaro F. Vito, *Probation and Parole in America* (New York: Free Press, 1985), p. 38.

203 JOHN AUGUSTUS: *Ibid.*, p. 40.

204 MORE THAN 2 MILLION ON PROBATION: Lawrence A. Greenfeld, "Probation and Parole 1985," Bureau of Justice Statistics Bulletin, January 1987, records a total of 1,879,132 adults under federal or state probation supervision at the end of 1985, an increase of 7.4 percent over the previous year.

205 "CASELOADS OF INDIVIDUAL OFFICERS . . .": Kevin Krajick, "Probation: The Original Community Program," *Corrections Magazine*, December 1980, p. 8.

205 POSTCARD PROBATION: *Ibid.*

205 "PROBATION IS NOT A PENALTY . . .": Judge Forer is quoted in *ibid.*, p. 7.

205–6 A 1985 RAND CORPORATION STUDY: Joan Petersilia, Susan Turner, James Kahan, and Joyce Peterson, *Granting Felons Probation: Public Risks and Alternatives*, (Santa Monica, Calif.: Rand Corporation, 1985).

206 NEW YORK PROBATION IN 1986: New York State

Senate Committee on Investigations, Taxation, and Government Operations, "The Collapse of the New York City Probation System," January 1987.

207 "GUN-CARRYING PSYCHIATRIST . . .": Rothman is quoted in Krajick, "Probation," p. 11.

207–8 PROBATION WORKER BURNOUT: Walter Lide, "A Victim of Probation's Burnout Blues," *Corrections Magazine*, December 1980, pp. 16–18.

209–10 15 PERCENT OF ALL PROBATIONERS: James M. Byrne, "The Control Controversy: A Preliminary Examination of Intensive Probation Supervision Programs in the United States," *Federal Probation*, June 1986, p. 4.

212 HOUSE ARREST: Joan Petersilia, "Exploring the Option of House Arrest," *Ibid.*, p. 50.

213 HARRY BROCK: Stephen Gettinger, "Intensive Supervision: Can It Rehabilitate Probation?" *Corrections Magazine*, April 1983, p. 7.

215 INTENSIVE SUPERVISION IN GEORGIA: Billie S. Erwin, "Turning Up the Heat on Probationers in Georgia," *Federal Probation*, June 1986, p. 17.

216 ANGELA CANTRELL: Gettinger, "Intensive Supervision," p. 13.

217 ROOTS OF THE RESTITUTION IDEA: Joe Hudson and Burt Galway, "Restitution and the Justice Model," in David Fogel and Joe Hudson, eds., *Justice as Fairness: Perspectives on the Justice Model* (Cincinnati: Anderson, 1981), p. 52.

217 "IF A WOUND AN INCH LONG . . .": The laws of Alfred are quoted in Lois Forer, *Criminals and Victims* (New York: Norton, 1980), p. 147.

217–18 "COMPENSATION CANNOT UNDO THE WRONG
. . .": Quoted in *ibid.*, p. 289.

218 "FROM MY LIMITED EXPERIENCE . . .": *Ibid.*, p. 296.

218 A 1981 SURVEY OF RESTITUTION PROGRAMS: Jay Worrall, "Restitution Programming for Correctional Agencies: A Practical Guide" (College Park, Md: American Correctional Association, 1981).

219 "CHRIST'S EMPHASIS . . .": Quoted in David C. Anderson, "Earn-It, a Key to the Prison Dilemma," *Across the Board*, November 1983, pp. 34–42.

221 EARN IT: For accounts of Judge Kramer's program, see *ibid.*; see also Andrew Klein, *The Earn It Story* (Boston: Citizens for Better Community Courts, 1981); see also John Ciner, "If You Want a Second Chance, 'Earn It,' " *Corrections Magazine*, June 1979, p. 64.

223 "A FAIRLY SUBSTANTIAL BODY OF RESEARCH ON EQUITY THEORY . . .": Hudson and Galway, p. 60.

223 GILBERT GEIS ON "FISCAL ATONEMENT": *Ibid.*, p. 59.

8

THE CRISIS OF CONTROL

231 "THEY WOULD COMBAT THE EVIL . . .": Rothman, *Discovery*, p. 15.

231–32 "IN THIS FIRST BURST OF ENTHUSIASM . . .": *Ibid.*, p. 61.

232 THEY WOULD ATTEMPT TO "JOIN PRACTICALITY AND HUMANITARIANISM . . .": *Ibid.*, p. 79.

233–34 THE DEBATE OVER THE AUBURN AND PENNSYLVANIA APPROACHES: *Ibid.*, pp. 85–88.

235 "THE PRISON IN MAINE . . .": McKelvey, p. 57.

235 "BUT IF THE OBJECT . . .": Rothman, *Discovery*, p. 242.

235 SILENCE RULE USED TO HARASS INMATES: McKelvey, p. 110.

235–36 THE CINCINNATI CONVENTION: *Ibid.*, pp. 90–91.

237 "THE TRAINING INCLUDED . . .": *Ibid.*, p. 134.

237 "THE CRIMINAL WAS AN ERRING BROTHER . . .": *Ibid.*, pp. 113–14.

237 1894 HEARINGS ON ABUSES AT ELMIRA: David J. Rothman, *Conscience and Convenience: The Asylum and Its Alternatives in Progressive America* (Boston: Little, Brown, 1980), p. 36.

238 "BIZARRE PUNISHMENTS": *Ibid.*, pp. 18–21.

239–40 "SUCH DIVISIONS WERE OF LITTLE USE": Rothman, *Conscience*, p. 134.

240 NORFOLK "PRISON COLONY": *Ibid.*, pp. 379–421, gives an excellent account of the Norfolk experiment, based on Howard Gill's extraordinary diary.

242 "IN EFFECT, THE STATE AND THE PRISON . . .": *Ibid.*, p. 157.

243 "THE GOAL WAS ALWAYS . . .": James B. Jacobs, *Stateville: The Penitentiary in Mass Society* (Chicago: University of Chicago Press, 1977), p. 38.

243–44 "FAILURE TO BUTTON A SHIRT . . .": *Ibid.*, p. 42.

245 "LIFE IN MANY INSTITUTIONS . . .": *Challenge of Crime*, p. 159.

245 "A SPECIAL INMATE CULTURE . . .": *Ibid.*, p. 163.

247 CHICAGO STREET GANGS IN ILLINOIS PRISONS: Jacobs, pp. 138–74.

247–48 GANG RULES: Quoted in Jacobs, pp. 149–50.

248 PRISON GANGS IN THE WEST AND MIDWEST: Stanley Penn, "Brothers in Blood: Prison Gangs Formed by Racial Groups Pose Big Problems in West," *Wall Street Journal*, May 11, 1983.

250 DAVISON'S STUDY OF PRISON DRUG SMUGGLING: see David C. Anderson, "A Letter from America's Prisons," *Across the Board*, September 1981, pp.73–82.

250 "THE SUREST, EASIEST AND QUICKEST WAY . . .": McCoy is quoted in David C. Anderson's review of Ethan Hoffman and John McCoy, *Concrete Mama: Prison Profiles from Walla Walla*, in *Corrections Magazine*, April 1983, pp. 46–48.

251–52 THE INMATE ECONOMY AT JACKSON: For a summary of the Kalinich study, see Anderson, "A Letter from America's Prisons."

253 "WHEREAS AT ONE TIME PRISONERS . . .": Kathleen Engel and Stanley Rothman, "Prison Violence and the Paradox of Reform," *Public Interest*, no. 73 (Fall 1983), pp. 91–92.

254 "STATEVILLE HAD ACQUIRED A REPUTATION . . .": Kevin Krajick, "At Stateville, the Calm Is Tense," *Corrections Magazine*, June 1980, p. 10.

255 "IT WAS CONTROL FROM WITHIN . . .": Aric

Press, "Inside America's Toughest Prison," *Newsweek*, October 6, 1986, p. 49.

255–56 " 'ANYTIME WE WERE BEATING SOMEONE .. . .' ": *Ibid.*

256 JUDGE JUSTICE'S OPINION: *Ibid.*, p. 51.

256–57 RAPES IN THE PRINCE GEORGE'S COUNTY JAIL: Loretta Tofani's series began in the *Washington Post* on Sept. 26, 1982.

258 "THERE WAS NOT A SUFFICIENT CORE . . .": Brewer is quoted in Krajick, "At Stateville," p. 10.

258–59 "IN MOST PRISONS . . .": *Ibid.*

259 "THEY SPENT ONLY A FEW HOURS . . .": *Ibid.*, p. 16.

260 AN ASTONISHING INVENTORY OF WEAPONS: *Ibid.*

260–61 THE SANTA FE RIOT: For good accounts of the riot, see Roger Morris, *The Devil's Butcher Shop: The New Mexico Prison Uprising* (New York: Franklin Watts, 1983); and Michael S. Serrill and Peter Katel, "New Mexico: The Anatomy of a Riot," *Corrections Magazine*, April 1980, pp. 6–24.

262 "AS INDIVIDUALS, THE CORRECTION OFFICERS HAD LONG COMPLAINED . . .": Serrill and Katel, p. 24.

262 "A PRISON RULED BY A CRAVEN, UNSTABLE CO-ALITION . . .": Morris, p. 43.

262 "INADEQUATE PEOPLE WERE SURROUNDED BY IN-ADEQUATE PEOPLE": *Ibid.*, p. 52.

264 NATIONAL ACADEMY OF SCIENCES ON DETER-RENCE: Michael Sherman and Gordon Hawkins, *Imprisonment in America* (Chicago: University of Chicago Press, 1981), p. 96.

265 "ONLY A SEVERELY STRINGENT POLICY . . .":
Ibid., p. 119.

266–67 "IN ONE PLACE OR ANOTHER . . .": Francis
A. Allen, *The Decline of the Rehabilitative Ideal: Penal
Policy and Social Purpose* (New Haven: Yale University
Press, 1981), p. 51.

267 "I HAVE . . . SEEN GOOD, DECENT PEOPLE . . .":
Forer, p. 81.

267–68 MARTINSON'S "NOTHING WORKS" STUDY:
Robert Martinson, "What Works: Questions and Answers
About Prison Reform," *Public Interest*, no. 36 (June 1974),
pp. 22–54.

270–71 THE VIENNA CORRECTIONAL CENTER: Silberman, pp. 417–23.

274 A RIOT OF CAPITALISM: For an account of the
"novelties" phenomenon in the Thomaston penitentiary,
see Edgar May, "Maine: Was Inmate Capitalism Out of
Control?" *Corrections Magazine*, February 1981, pp. 17–
23.

277–78 ATTORNEY GENERAL'S SURVEY OF PRISONS:
Rothman, *Conscience*, p. 138.

278 NEIL SINGER ESTIMATES THE VALUE OF PRISON
MANPOWER: Singer's study is quoted in Gordon Hawkins,
The Prison: Policy and Practice (Chicago: University of
Chicago Press, 1976), p. 121.

279 CRIMINAL JUSTICE ASSOCIATES 1986 SURVEY: Bar-
bara J. Auerbach, George E. Sexton, Franklin C. Farrow,
and Robert H. Lawson, *Work in American Prisons: The
Private Sector Gets Involved* (Lafayette Hill, Pa: Criminal
Justice Associates, 1987), p. 3.

279–80 AN EARLIER SURVEY: Criminal Justice Associates, *Private Sector Involvement in Prison-Based Businesses: A National Assessment* (Washington, D.C.: National Institute of Justice, 1985).

280–81 ZEPHYR PRODUCTS: For a description of Zephyr's early development, see Michael Fedo, "Free Enterprise Goes to Prison," *Corrections Magazine*, April 1981, pp. 5–15.

283 "PRISON LABOR MUST NOT DISPLACE FREE LABOR . . .": Zalusky's statement was printed in the transcript of a hearing on the Prison Industries Improvement and Federal Correctional Assistance Act before the House Judiciary subcommittee on courts, civil liberties, and the administration of justice, August 2, 1984.

286 POP THERAPIES IN PRISON: Anderson, "A Letter."

9

CRIMES OF JUSTICE

288 A GEORGIAN ENGLAND FEARFUL AND FED UP WITH CRIME: Robert Hughes, *The Fatal Shore*, (New York: Alfred A. Knopf, 1987), p. 23.

289 "I SUP WITH MY FRIEND . . .": *Ibid.*, p. 25.

289 "TO AVENGE THEIR SENSE OF A DISTURBED SOCIAL ORDER . . .": *Ibid.*, p. 29.

INDEX

Index

assassinations, 42, 52
assaults, 5, 117, 190, 215
 in crime statistics, 33
 among friends and acquaintances, 84
 reporting of, 86
 during robberies, 5
 street, 12–13
 in subways, 19–20, 82
Attica, N.Y., penitentiary at, 245, 260, 263
attorneys, 174
 plea bargaining and, 163–65, 200–201
Augustus, John, 203
Australia, as penal colony, 290
authority:
 conservative view of, 42
 1960s rebellion against, 41, 44–45
automobiles, see cars

bail, 55, 81, 203
Bailey, Trevor, 160
Baltimore County, Md., community policing in, 139, 143–47
beatings, 82, 107, 255–56, 260
 in prisons, 28, 237, 238, 260
Beccaria, Cesare, 179–80, 231
Bell, Griffin, 57–58
Bell v. Wolfish, 272
Bentham, Jeremy, 217, 242, 243
Best Western International, 281
Bishop, Jesse, 188
Black Muslims, 246
blacks, 19, 186
 assaults on, 84
 in Goetz case, 17, 19–20
 homicides of, 36
 police views on, 108–9
 in prison, 43–44, 245–47
 riots of, 42, 97, 106–7, 162
 as robbery victims, 84
 Silberman's views on, 68
block associations, 125, 134, 139, 141–42, 150
block grants, 51
Blumstein, Alfred, 197
Boyle, Robert, 159
Bradford, Brandt, 144–45
Braun, Fred, 280, 282
break-ins, see burglaries
Breslin, Charles, 161
Breslin, Helen, 161
Brewer, Lou, 258

Brewster, Kingman, 48
Brierton, David, 258
Brock, Harry, 213–14
Brockway, Zebulon, 181, 235–37
broken-windows theory, 120–24, 131, 134, 136
Brooks, Charlie, 188
Buchanan, Patrick, 18
Buckley, William F., Jr., 193
building tenders, 255–56
Bureau of Prisons, U.S., 248
Burger, Warren, 279
burglaries, 113, 117, 133, 138, 143, 146, 187, 215
 in apartments, 4, 118
 in cars, 10–11
 in crime statistics, 34
 in houses, 39, 86, 118
 as nuisance crimes, 176–77
 prior relationships in, 169–70
 state vs. federal control of, 53–54
Bush, George, 61
business, restitution programs and, 221–23, 226
business districts, 65
Byrne, James, 209–10

Cabey, Darrel, 19, 20
California, 190–91, 198, 199, 271–72
 prison gangs in, 248
 probation in, 205–6, 208
 see also Los Angeles, Calif.; Los Angeles Police Department
Cantrell, Angela, 216
Caplan, Gerald, 47, 48
Carroway, Gay, 130
cars, 109, 132
 burglarizing of, 10–11
 insurance of, 118
 patrol, 98, 99, 102–3, 107, 120, 121, 127–28
 theft of, 34–35, 80–81, 86, 118, 128, 177
Carter, Jimmy, 57–58
Cary, Susan, 159
cases, caseload, 175–76, 205, 206
Census Bureau, U.S., 32
chain snatching, 5
Chicago, Ill., 115, 122
chop shops, 34–35
Cincinnati, Ohio, 129

Index

Index

Index

Index

May, S. J., 180–81
medical model of crime, 239–40
Mendoza, Ivan, 25–27, 29
Mennonites, 219–20
Merton, Robert K., 69
Mexican-American gangs, 248
Miami, Fla., 106–7
Michigan, 190, 199, 251–52
Middle Ages, 203, 217
middle class, 68, 110, 119
 antiwar movement and, 41–45, 53, 162
 black, 116
 drug use of, 41, 45
Milakovich, Michael, 53
Milk, Harvey, 198
Minnesota, 192, 280, 282–83, 284
Mitchell, John, 53, 54, 56
Moley, Raymond, 166
Monge, Luis Jose, 186
morality, 41–42, 45, 74–75, 108
More, Sir Thomas, 217
Morris, Norval, 268
Morris, Roger, 262
Moscone, George, 198
Moynihan, Daniel Patrick, 114
muggings, muggers, 15, 16, 113, 138
 chain snatching, 5
 police routine for, 104–5
 sources of, 19
 in subway, 17
 see also purse snatching
municipal government, economic crisis of,
 114, 116–19
murders, see assassinations; homicides

National Advisory Commission on Criminal
 Justice Standards and Goals, 168
National Association for the Advancement of
 Colored People, 114–15
 Legal Defense Fund of, 186, 187
National Council on Crime and Delin-
 quency, 269
National Crime Commission, 48–51
National Crime Survey, crime statistics of,
 32–35, 86
National Institute of Justice, 85–87
National Prison Association, 181
neglect, 37–38, 78
neighborhood groups, 123, 125–26, 134,
 139, 141–42, 145–46
 politics and, 150, 152–54
"Neighborhoods and Police" (Kelling), 125

Nevada, 188
New Haven, Conn., 166
New Jersey, 234
Newport News, Va., community policing
 in, 139, 147–49
Newsweek, 78, 255–56
New York, N.Y., 125, 166, 174–78
 crime statistics for, 83
 probation in, 206, 208–9
New York (state), 194, 199, 206, 211,
 220, 270, 271, 277
 Martinson research in, 267–68
 prisons in, 232–37, 245, 260, 263,
 267–68
New York Police Department, 106, 107,
 116–17, 150
 Operation Pressure Point of, 131–34,
 136, 177
 72nd Precinct of, 139–43, 151
 90th Precinct of, 105
 Special Investigating Unit of, 23–25
New York State Defenders Association, 194
New York Times, The, 174
Nixon, Richard M., 52–58
Norfolk, Mass., "Prison Colony" at, 240–
 42
North Carolina, 187
"Northeast City" (Kelling), 125–26

Office of Management and Budget (OMB),
 57
Oklahoma, 212
Olmsted, Frederick Law, 8
On Crimes and Punishments (Beccaria), 179–
 80
O'Neill, Francis, 101, 102
Operation Pressure Point, 131–34, 136,
 177
organized crime, 97, 106, 108

PACT Institute of Justice, 219–20, 222
parks, 8, 146–47
Park Slope, Brooklyn, 3–16, 69–70
 crime in, 3–7, 10–16
 cultural revolution in, 8
 gentrification of, 8–9
Park Slope Paper, "Police" column in, 3–6,
 14
parole, 28–29, 181, 183, 185, 189, 192,
 193–94, 198–200
Peace Corps, 90–93, 139, 153, 155
Peel, Sir Robert, 123, 289

Index

penitentiaries, *see* prisons; *specific prisons*
Pennsylvania, 232–34, 277
Percy, Charles, 278, 279, 283
Peter Principle, 31
Petersilia, Joan, 213, 265
photographs, police, 104–5
Pilsbury, Amos, 235–36
plea bargaining, 26, 27, 29, 163–78, 200–201, 270
  prior relationships and, 169–70
  roots of, 165–66
pocket picking, 86
police, 55, 77, 82, 291
  alienation of, 113, 114, 135
  antiwar movement and, 44–45
  brutality of, 106–7, 123, 124, 149–50
  communities and, 89–157
  corruption and, 23–25, 95–97, 105–6, 119–20, 149–50, 152
  as craftsmen, 100–101
  crime of, 23–25, 29
  crime evaluation by, 108
  crime reporting and, 33, 34
  education of, 99, 107
  ethnic politics and, 95
  foot patrol of, 123, 131
  funnel image and, 83, 84, 87, 88
  history of, 94–100, 123–25
  investigation procedures of, 104–5
  "means over ends" syndrome of, 136–37
  military analogy for, 97–102
  motorized patrol by, 98, 99, 102–3, 107, 120, 121, 127–28
  municipal economic crisis and, 114, 116–19
  in National Crime Commission report, 49, 50–51
  non-crime responsibilities of, 95, 110–11, 135–36
  Peace Corps and, 90–93, 139, 153, 155
  politics and, 95–96, 98, 105, 123–24, 150, 152–54
  press coverage of, 22–23, 150
  prison riots and, 245, 259–60
  professional model for, 98–102, 120, 149–50, 157
  public confidence in, 78
  rapes and, 34, 39–40, 63, 138
  rating of, 111–12
  Reagan's speech to, 59–60
  reform of, 53, 96–102, 105, 106, 119
  team policing by, 127–30
  triage policy of, 117–18

  underclass growth and, 114–16
  undercover, 119
  U.S. vs. European, 94
  victims of crime and, 34, 39–40, 63
  violent actions of, 20
  volunteer corps of, 155–56
  Wilson's views on patterns of, 108–10, 122, 123
  see also Los Angeles Police Department; New York Police Department
Police Administration (Wilson and McLaren), 98
Policing a Free Society (Goldstein), 110–11
politics, 118
  neighborhood, 150, 152–54
  police and, 95–96, 98, 105, 123–24, 150, 152–54
  probation and, 224–25
polls on crime, 78, 118
Ponce, P. R., 69, 70
poverty, 110, 288
  crime and, 38, 43, 45, 49, 50, 52, 71–72, 77, 239
  cultural revolution and, 41, 44
President's Task Force on Victims of Crime, 40, 62–64
press:
  crime coverage of, 22, 30–31
  drug issue and, 62
  police coverage and, 22–23, 150
  see also specific newspaperes and magazines
Prince of the City (Daley), 23–24, 106
Prisoner Review Board, 189
prisons, 43–44, 55, 77, 84, 179–85, 202, 225, 227–87, 290–91
  alternatives to, *see* probation
  control crisis in, 227–30, 245–64, 273
  cost of, 71, 194, 215, 225, 268, 271–72, 285
  Currie's criticism of, 71
  development of, 165–66, 179–80, 230–38
  drug use in, 249–52, 259, 261
  fear in, 227, 229
  funding of, 59, 85, 229–30
  funnel image and, 85, 88
  gangs in, 228, 247–50, 254, 255, 258–61, 264, 272
  guards of, 28, 44, 159–60, 184, 228, 230, 238, 241, 243–44, 246, 249, 250, 252–60, 262, 271
  homosexuality in, 210, 228, 245, 247–48, 256–58, 272

Index

ABOUT THE AUTHOR

David C. Anderson is assistant editor of *The New York Times* editorial page. He has also worked as an editor of *The New York Times Magazine* and as a reporter and editorial writer for *The Wall Street Journal*. From 1977 to 1981 he was editor and publisher of *Police Magazine* and *Corrections Magazine*.